Are Your Ancestors Gently Guiding You to Find Them?

In family histo... ...on. Some may also call it coincidence, hunch, synchronicity, fortuitous luck, paranormal, karma, ESP, providence, inspiration, psychic, sixth sense, inner voice, omen or just a 'miracle'. In any case, it happens to nearly everyone who is trying to build their family tree and connect to their ancestors over a long-time in one form or another. It's the process of accidentally or coincidentally making meaningful discoveries about one's ancestors while looking for something else entirely – as if your ancestors are pushing you in the right direction. It can be as simple as a thought or feeling. Many times it is manifest as extraordinary luck or fortuitous coincidence. People have experienced this *guidance* as simple as facts popping into their heads or as dramatically as an actual ancestral visitation from beyond the grave. *Here are a few examples and you can read more starting on page 9.*

It was Found on the Gravestone

"One of my cousins was trying to locate our great-grandmother's grave in the cemetery in Garden City, Kansas while on their way to Colorado for a vacation. After searching for quite a while, they were unable to locate it and decided to go on down the road. When they went to get into the car, they noticed their daughter had lost a shoe so they went back into the cemetery to find it. It was found – on the gravestone of our great-grandmother!" Mere coincidence?
Charles E. Templer, RootsWeb Review, Vol. 9, No. 43.

Something Kept Drawing Me Back

Dora Fisher had been searching all her life for more information about her father's youngest brother, believed by most to have been stillborn. An aunt told her she remembered her brother was born one evening about 1926 in Ontario, Canada. He died the following morning. But no one living knew his name. Dora relates that she was working with *FamilySearch Indexing*. "I would download a batch of 24 Ontario Death records, index them, and send them back. Then I would go do a load of laundry... but something kept drawing me back to the computer." After about 10 batches the names of her grandparents jumped off the page. They were listed as parents of a deceased boy:

John A. Taylor, Born: 20 Jan 1928, Died: 21 Jan 1928.

She said, "I scared the heck out of my husband. I threw my arms in the air and hollered, 'I found him!' Then I cried. ...It was one month to the day since his next oldest sister had passed away. I can just see the two of them up there, screaming: 'Get back to that computer!' If I had stopped earlier in the day, someone else would have gotten this batch, and I still wouldn't have the information."
Dora J. Fisher, http://archiver.rootsweb.com

The Last Remaining Evidence

After forty years, Edwin Cannon, Jr. decided to prune his old photographs from Germany. However, every time he planned to discard the photographs of a family – a mother and father and their small children – he was impressed to keep them, although he was at a loss as to why. He knew their surname was Berndt but could remember nothing more about them. He decided to give them to a friend, Thomas Monson, who was leaving shortly for Berlin. Amazingly, when Thomas Monson boarded the flight from Zurich, Switzerland to Berlin, one of his fellow passengers was Dieter Berndt who sat next to him. He told Dieter that he had some old photos of people named Berndt. He handed a photo to him and asked if he could identify those shown in the photographs. As he looked at them carefully, he began to weep. He said, "Our family lived in Stettin during the war. My father was killed [and] when...the Russians invaded...my mother took my sister and me and fled from the approaching enemy. Everything had to be left behind, including any photographs we had. I am the little boy pictured in these photographs and my sister is the little girl. The man and woman are our dear parents. Until today I've no photographs of our childhood...or of my father." They had miraculously come into possession of the last remaining visual evidence of a couple who seemed to be calling from beyond the grave, saying to their children, "Remember us!" Was their meeting mere coincidence?
Thomas S. Monson, CES Fireside, 11 January 2009
Courtesy of http://AncestryInsider.blogspot.com>Serendipity<

Your ancestors want to be found as much as you want to find them. This illustrated guidebook will help you learn how to trace your own family roots and stories and connect to your ancestors.

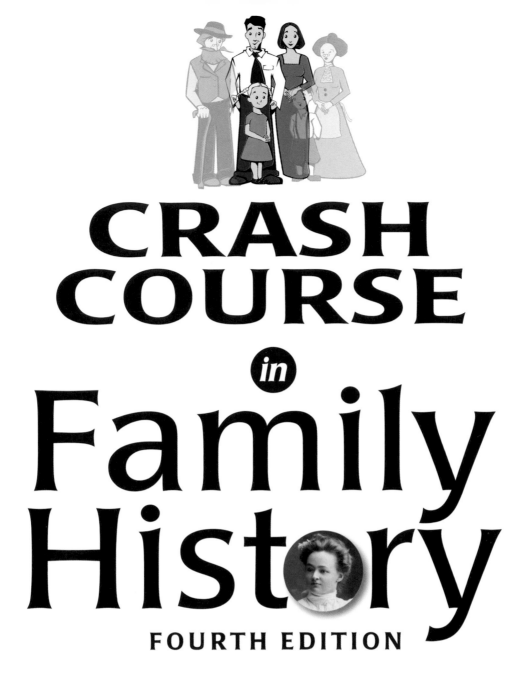

CRASH COURSE

in Family History

FOURTH EDITION

**An Easy Step-by-Step Illustrated Guidebook
and Comprehensive Resource Directory**

The Indispensable Guide to Tracing Your
Own Family Roots and Stories

Paul Larsen

**LIBRARY
VERSION**

Publisher's Cataloguing-In-Publication Data
(Prepared by the Donohue Group, Inc.)

Larsen, Paul.
  Crash course in family history : an easy step-by-step illustrated guidebook and comprehensive resource directory : the indispensable guide to tracing your own family roots and stories / Paul Larsen. -- fourth ed.

    p. : ill. (chiefly col.) ; cm.

    Includes bibliographical references and index.
    ISBN: 978-0-9742695-5-9

  1. Genealogy. 2. Genealogy--Handbooks, manuals, etc. I. Title. II. Title: Crash course in family history.

CS16 .L37 2010
929/.1   2010923539

Published by
EasyFamilyHistory.com
P.O. Box 1758, St George, UT 84771-1758

EasyFamily History.com
The Easiest Way to Your Family History™

To comment, or communicate with the author,
e-mail paul@easyfamilyhistory.com

Bulk Purchases / International Sales
To inquire about or arrange bulk purchase discounts for sales promotions, premiums, fund-raisers, or information on translations or book distributors outside the U.S.A., please contact the publisher at the above e-mail or mailing address.

 This symbol indicates a "Best of the Internet" website; a key website to make family history easier and save you valuable time.

ISBN 978-0-9742695-5-9
Library of Congress Catalog Card No. 2010923539

Printed in China

Contents

A Joy to Know Our Ancestors

"Unlock the knowledge of who you really are by learning more about your forebears....
We can have exciting experiences as we learn about our vibrant, dynamic ancestors.
They were very real, living people with problems, hopes, and dreams like we have
today.... It is a joy to become acquainted with our forebears...and can be one of the most
interesting puzzles you...can work on." – James E. Faust

To Peggy,

my sweetheart

and soulmate

forever.

From the bottom of my heart,
Thank you for
Your invaluable support,
Your unselfish patience,
Your true nobility, and
Your unquenchable love.
And thank you for being
My inspiration and
Devoted companion for a lifetime.

Preface

About this Fourth Edition

You are about to embark on a fascinating journey that will take you back into history and forward into the eternities. Never has there been a more exciting time to trace your roots and connect with your ancestors. Computers, technology, and the Internet have dramatically affected how we do family history today.

Technology and the Internet have continued to change rapidly and continues even at a faster rate today, hence the need to keep abreast of new exciting web sites, new resources, tools, and technology. We received many positive and gratifying responses from many people about the first three editions of this book (published 2003, 2005, and 2009).

This new edition is an updated version to help keep you abreast of the dynamic changes and progress in tracing your family roots and stories, empower you with these wonderful new resources, and make it easier and more fun for you. And by providing a traditional sewn binding – instead of the unique binding of the previous editions – it is more appropriate and acceptable for use in libraries.

In addition to this updated edition, we have developed a new companion  website, *EasyFamilyHistory.com,* to help keep you up-to-date and provide convenient hotlinks to all the web sites provided herein and beyond this printing. I believe that this new Web site and guidebook are *"the easiest way to your family history".*

Also, this illustrated guidebook is a comprehensive resource directory on family history. It provides thousands of extremely valuable, reviewed resources *not conveniently found elsewhere,* all in one location to help trace your family roots and stories, and make it easier to connect to your beloved ancestors. However, it is not a beginner's guide on using software or the computer. I anticipated that you already know something about computers and basic software. My intention is to try and make things simple and understandable for you; I want to help make the process of learning how to plant your family tree, nurture it, and help it grow *as easy as possible using today's technology.*

How This Book Came To Be

Have you ever had a moment where you were given a thought or an idea that could change your life? You know, one of those moments where you were prompted by an unseen but real force to do something that you never really thought about doing before.

My wife and I were out one evening, and we ended up at a bookstore just browsing and enjoying the evening together when out-of-the-blue a strong premonition or feeling hit me that I should write a book about family history.

I just about fell on the floor in the middle of the store because this was such an extremely foreign thought to me. I had absolutely no inclination whatsoever about doing any such thing as I was completely involved in a new business at the time – a new marketing company that I had recently started. I was essentially overwhelmed with this new business, and struggling to make it grow and become successful. Indeed, I was struggling to just survive, let alone make a living.

But this was a very strong feeling and I just couldn't shake it: *"You have the ability to write a book about family history, and there will be nothing like it in the marketplace."* I even had a great idea for the title, *A Crash Course in Family History.*

At first I was really taken back, but then I started thinking to myself. *Well, I am involved in teaching classes about how to do family history in today's tech world right now, and I have created lessons to teach these classes.* I reasoned, *these lessons could become the basis for the book, and there currently is no up-to-date book in the marketplace on how to do family history using today's technology.*

I was quite aware of family history books and other resources available in the marketplace at the

Some people differentiate between the terms *genealogy* and *family history;* genealogy meaning an account of kinship, and family history meaning the addition of details about lives and historical context.

time because I had been searching for resources to teach my class, and had come to the conclusion that there was no simple, convenient guidebook that really explained what helps were available for family history and how to use them. I had previously felt a great need and desire for people everywhere to easily learn how to do family history.

I reasoned with myself for a few moments, then I made an on-the-spot decision. *"OK I'll do it! I'll write a book on family history. I'll make it easy to follow, a simple step-by-step approach, and done in my own style with lots of colorful illustrations."* I don't know if I responded to myself out loud or just in my mind. In any case, I committed myself to do something I had never thought about before. I've written several small books before, but not on a subject that seemingly came "out-of-the-blue".

As we were driving home, I was going over in my mind how I could reorganize my time to be able to accomplish this. I decided that I would get up early each morning around 4 a.m. when my mind was fresh to try and fit it into my busy schedule. I did this and wrote until 8 or 9 a.m. then went to my day job.

It was an *amazing experience and blessing* to write the book. It was such a refreshing time; no sounds or distractions and nobody around at that early hour. I was able to focus with a totally open mind. It was magic. The words and thoughts just came

into my mind and I could type as fast as they came to me. It was a wonderful and thrilling experience! It took me about a year to write the first edition of this book even though it had taken some months previously to create the class lessons.

I readily confess that I learned a lot about family history from writing the book that I didn't know before about how we are to connect to our ancestors today. And I was *absolutely astounded* at the many new technological tools and resources that are available to help us trace our family roots and stories.

A Family History/ Computer Revolution

There is indeed a *revolutionary wave of interest* in family history around the entire world, including the availability of new exciting, advanced technology, resources and records. Dick Eastman, author of the premium *Eastman's Online Genealogy Newsletter*, a daily electronic publication with more than 50,000 readers located at ww.eogn.com recently wrote this about the computer revolution going on in family history today.

Dick Eastman

"We are in the midst of a computer revolution...in genealogy.... The "islands" of genealogy data on individual hard drives are merging into...very large online databases, accessible to thousands... simultaneously.... Online, web-based collaborative databases [are]... happening now.... This is a very exciting time to be a computer-using genealogist!"

Dick Eastman, January 17, 2010

http://blog.eogn.com/eastmans_online_geneal ogy/2010/01/a-new-computer-revolution-is-rising-around-us.html

Objectives of This Book

My main objectives for writing this book are to:

1. Describe and illustrate the new, easy, simplified process of how to do family history in an interesting step-by-step

Family history is enjoying a worldwide revolutionary wave.

method that can be understood and followed by everyone.

2. Help people readily identify and link their ancestors, and work together as they identify names, and reduce duplication of the work.

3. Broaden the number of people connecting with their ancestors, and gain insight and strength by learning how ancestors met life's challenges.

I hope that this new fourth edition and companion web site are valuable resources and guides to assist you in planting your family tree, connecting to your ancestors, discovering your family heritage, stories and photos, and blessing the lives of your family in the process.

How This Book is Organized

This is a fun "workbook" that tries to make it easier for you to connect to your ancestors, and hopefully fulfills a need in the genealogy community. It provides easily digestible bits of information throughout the book with guidelines, tips, and lots of resources that are visually appealing, easy to understand, and easy to follow. You can skip around in the book to areas that interest you most if you want...and not skip a beat.

For example, you can jump right into the *Best of the Internet* in chapter 5 and start surfing if you wish. It identifies Web sites that are **FREE** and those that require you to pay a fee. If some of the content on a Web site requires a fee, I've marked it with an **$**. Or you can start digging into *Organizing Your Information* in chapter 6. To begin with, you may want to at least get started on getting organized and archiving your precious photos because it makes you feel great to be organized, and staying organized is a continual work-in-process.

After getting your feet wet with the introduction, you should begin with the 3-Easy-Steps to begin building your family tree (chapters 1-3).

STEP 1: *Identify Your Ancestors Using Your Family* (chapter 1) is the easiest part because you're actually planting your family tree and interacting with your family in the process.

STEP 2: *Add New Branches to Your Family Tree Using the Internet* (chapter 2) will help you see if someone has already found information on your family roots. No sense re-plowing a field that has been plowed. It will also help you gather lots of information on your ancestors.

STEP 3: *Connect With the Lives and Stories of Your Ancestors* (chapter 3) helps you discover your family heritage, stories and photos; enumerates the many benefits of connecting with your ancestors; and aids you in appreciating your heritage and honoring your ancestors.

Thereafter, you'll surely want to *Share Your Family History* with family and friends (chapter 8) which provides many valuable resources to assist you. And chapter 7 offers many suggestions and resources for *Keeping Your Own History*, mostly leaving an enduring legacy you can pass on to your posterity, and building a bridge between generations.

Keep in mind that this step-by-step guidebook deals largely with tracing your family roots using *today's technology*, but is somewhat skimpy on other very valuable resources such as genealogical and historical societies, archives, public libraries, family history expos/conventions, institutes, etc. which can be among your very best resources and allows you to rub shoulders with others who have similar interests.

One more thing, it contains many valuable resources for UK, Canada, Mexico, and Europe, but there are more resources and guides for doing family history in America. Other editions are on the drawing board.

I hope that this new edition and companion Web site are valuable resources and guides to assist you in planting your family tree, connecting to your ancestors, and discovering your family heritage and stories while benefitting the lives of your family in the process.

Paul Larsen
Author and Publisher

Where Do I Start?

Our Unique Opportunity

Using today's technology – the Internet, exciting, new computer tools, and new, readily available, rapidly-expanding databases of records from all over the world – genealogy and family history work is possible with ease and in record-breaking time. No people in history have ever had the opportunity to connect with their beloved ancestors, learn about their lives and challenges, and grow to appreciate our heritage as easily and readily as we do today.

The Most Beautiful Family Tree

"Through family history we discover the most beautiful tree in the forest of creation – our family tree. Its numerous roots reach back through history, and its branches extend throughout eternity. Family history is the expansive expression of eternal love." J. Richard Clarke

J. Richard Clarke
© by Intellectual Reserve, Inc.

Suggested Activities

1. Begin to feel a "connection" to those who have gone before you.

2. Plant a seed in your heart for loving your ancestors that can sprout, and that you can nourish so it can grow and get root and bring forth fruit for you and your family for many generations.

3. Read, ponder and experiment upon the suggestions in this book; be persistent and patient.

4. Discuss ways your family can honor your ancestors.

5. Plan a special evening with your family to tell stories and enact a skit based upon your ancestors life.

Family History Insights - Introduction

Bruce C. Hafen
© by Intellectual Reserve, Inc.

A Bond that Ties Generations Together

"There really can be a bond and a sense of belonging that ties together generations. ... This bond gives us a sense of identity and purpose. Our ties with the eternal world suddenly become very real, sharpening our life's focus and lifting our expectations. ... We can discover within ourselves a reservoir of patience and endurance that we never will find without the deep commitment that grows from a sense of real belonging. Exerting such immovable loyalty to another person teaches us how to love.... Our sense of belonging to one another... foreshadows our belonging in the eternal family of God" Bruce C. Hafen

Abraham Lincoln

Man Was Made for Immortality

"Surely God would not have created such a being as man, with an ability to grasp the infinite, to exist only for a day! No, no, man was made for immortality."
Abraham Lincoln (1809-1865), *The Collected Works of Abraham Lincoln* edited by Roy P. Basler, p. 109.

Shakti Gawain

Guided by Intuition

"...we need to be willing to let our intuition guide us, and then be willing to follow that guidance directly and fearlessly."
Shakti Gawain, author

Alex Haley

A Hunger to Know Our Heritage

"In all of us there is a hunger, bone-marrow deep, to know our heritage—to know who we are and where we have come from. Without this enriching knowledge, there is a hollow yearning. No matter what our attainments in life, there is still a vacuum, an emptiness, and the most disquieting loneliness."
Alex Haley (1921-1992), Author of Roots

William Wordsworth

Where Do We Come From?

"Our birth is but a sleep
and a forgetting:
The Soul that rises with
us, our life's Star,
Hath had elsewhere its setting,
And cometh from afar:
Not in entire forgetfulness,
And not in utter nakedness,
But trailing clouds of glory do
we come From God,
who is our home."

William Wordsworth (1770-1850),
English Poet and Author.

Elaine S. Dalton
© by Intellectual Reserve, Inc.

We Did This For You

"...[As] my husband and I...walked through the Old Pioneer Cemetery searching for the grave of an ancestor... I was touched by the peaceful solitude and spirit I felt. I walked through the trees and read the names on the gravestones, many of them children and families. I wept as my heart was turned to our forefathers.... In my mind I asked many questions: Why did they leave their comfortable homes and families? Why did they suffer persecution, sickness, even death? Why did they sacrifice all that they had to come to this place? ... As I sat silently contemplating this scene, the answer came forcefully yet softly to my mind and heart: *'We did this for you.'* Those words...reminded me that our ancestors...sacrificed everything so that past and future generations would [receive] eternal blessings.... I know that if we [connect with our ancestors], the joyful day will come when we shall meet our ancestors once again and be able to say to them, *'We did this for you.'*"
—Elaine S. Dalton

Why Family History?

Unaware to some, *a quiet revolution* is sweeping the earth as millions of people worldwide are discovering new meaning in their lives. They are finding new meaning by simply connecting with their extended family and loved ones – whether it's a real life reunion or making a new connection with ancestors. Just the prospect of discovering one's family roots and heritage, and possibly reuniting with missing loved ones from long ago is absolutely *thrilling*. For many, it's a rewarding, deep-seated driving force. Family history is about families. And it's changing how some people see life, and helping them gain a sense of identify and purpose in life.

People all over the world, of all faiths, creeds and races, are inspired to search for their family roots and stories. Thus, they are increasingly enabled to more fully appreciate and value their precious and unique heritage, and rightfully honor their forefathers who have gone before them.

As generations pass, people and their lives may be forgotten, but researching your heritage gives you the opportunity to discover who your ancestors really are. And helps bring your family together. As you do this, your knowledge of your forebears will increase, you will gain strength by

learning how your ancestors met life's challenges, you will gain a sense of identify and purpose in life, you will feel a sense of belonging that ties generations together, and your family will grow closer.

Connecting the Generations

Most people have an inner desire for the deep sense of love they feel for their family and loved ones to continue beyond the grave. Don't all of us long to feel bound together in love with the assurance that it will last forever?

To illustrate this yearning, in the famous sonnet entitled "How do I love thee?" Elizabeth Barrett Browning ponders the profundity of her love for Robert, and then concludes: *"If God chooses, I shall but love thee better after death."*

Elizabeth Barrett Browning

Tracing your family roots and stories helps establish a sense of belonging that bonds generations together. This bond gives you a sense of identity and purpose in life.

"Till We Meet No More to Part"

One such person was Major Sullivan Ballou who wrote one of history's most beautiful and moving love letters to his wife Sarah during the American Civil War.

Sullivan Ballou had overcome his family's poverty to start a promising career as a lawyer in Providence, Rhode Island. Sullivan and Sarah hoped that they could build a better life than they had known growing up for their two sons, Edgar and Willie. In addition to being a successful lawyer, Sullivan also served twice as the Speaker of the Rhode Island House of Representatives.

Sullivan Ballou

At the age of thirty-two, being a strong opponent of slavery and devoted supporter of President Abraham Lincoln, Sullivan felt the need to serve the Union, leaving what would have been a very promising political career to enlist in the 2nd Rhode Island Volunteers in the spring of 1861.

On July 14, 1861, Major Ballou was stationed at Camp Clark, near Washington, D.C., while awaiting orders that led him to Manassas, Virginia. When he heard they were leaving, and that in the very near future they were to do battle with the Confederate Army, and not knowing if he would ever get another opportunity, he sat down and wrote a poignant letter to Sarah. A week later on 21st July, 1861, Major Sullivan Ballou was critically injured when a cannon ball shattered his leg and killed his horse during an attack by the Confederate Army at Bull Run, along with four thousand other Americans. He died July 29, 1861, eight days after the Battle of First Bull Run, Manassas, Virginia.

Though Sullivan had many noteworthy achievements to his credit, it was this letter to his wife for which he will always be remembered. His words professed his eternal love for Sarah, his unwavering belief in his cause, his heartfelt desire for the happiness of his sons, and his faith that they would be reunited after death. It is a truly moving and beautifully written piece which to this day, serves as a glowing testimonial to the love of a Father for his family. *Yankee* magazine published an article on the letter in which they stated "... his words of undying love brought millions to tears". His letter is on the next page.

When Sullivan died, his wife was age 24. She later moved to New Jersey to live out her life with her son, William, and never re-married. She died at age 80 in 1917. Sullivan and Sarah Ballou are buried next to each other at Swan Point Cemetery in Providence, RI. There are no known living descendants.

What Should We be Doing?

I believe that our family history opportunities may be to:

■ ***Develop a Desire.*** As we search out our ancestors, we grow to care more about those who have passed on, and feel a personal desire to connect with them. It all begins with a simple desire in our heart to connect with our ancestors.

We should allow a yearning for this marvelous blessing to take root in our hearts.

■ ***Determine What to Do.*** All of us can do something to search for our roots. It's not wise or necessary to attempt to do everything at once, but each of us can do something. Just what and how much we do depends on our own personal circumstances and abilities, and what our family may have already accomplished. We can, among other things:

• Complete family records as far as we can go

• Computerize our family history information and share with others

• Keep a personal journal and prepare personal and family histories, and

• Participate in family organizations.

■ ***Continue to Be Involved.*** We can be involved in some aspects of family history work throughout our lives. These are not necessarily activities we pursue for a brief time or put off until retirement.

Major Sullivan's Letter to His Wife Sarah

July 14th, 1861
Washington D.C.

My dear Sarah:

The indications are very strong that we shall move in a few days -- perhaps tomorrow. Lest I should not be able to write you again, I feel impelled to write lines that may fall under your eye when I shall be no more. ...

I have no misgivings about, or lack of confidence in, the cause in which I am engaged, and my courage does not halt or falter. ... I am willing -- perfectly willing -- to lay down all my joys in this life, to help maintain this Government....

Sarah, my love for you is deathless, it seems to bind me to you with mighty cables that nothing but Omnipotence could break; and yet my love of Country comes over me like a strong wind and bears me irresistibly on with all these chains to the battlefield.

The memories of the blissful moments I have spent with you come creeping over me, and I feel most gratified to God and to you that I have enjoyed them so long. And hard it is for me to give them up and burn to ashes the hopes of future years, when God willing, we might still have lived and loved together and seen our sons grow up to honorable manhood around us. I have, I know, but few and small claims upon Divine Providence, but something whispers to me -- perhaps it is the wafted prayer of my little Edgar -- that I shall return to my loved ones unharmed. If I do not, my dear Sarah, never forget how much I love you, and when my last breath escapes me on the battlefield, it will whisper your name.

Forgive my many faults, and the many pains I have caused you. How thoughtless and foolish I have oftentimes been! How gladly would I wash out with my tears every little spot upon your happiness, and struggle with all the misfortune of this world, to shield you and my children from harm. But I cannot. I must watch you from the spirit land and hover near you, while you buffet the storms with your precious little freight, and wait with sad patience till we meet to part no more.

But, O Sarah! If the dead can come back to this earth and flit unseen around those they loved, I shall always be near you; in the garish day and in the darkest night ...always, always; and if there be a soft breeze upon your cheek, it shall be my breath; or the cool air fans your throbbing temple, it shall be my spirit passing by.

Sarah, do not mourn me dead; think I am gone and wait for thee, for we shall meet again.

As for my little boys, they will grow as I have done, and never know a father's love and care. ... Sarah, I have unlimited confidence in your maternal care and your development of their characters. ... O Sarah, I wait for you there! Come to me, and lead thither my children.

      Sullivan

(The Book of Love: Writers and Their Love Letters, by Cathy N. Davidson, Pocket Books, 1992; Brown University Alumni Quarterly (Nov. 1990): 38-42; Geoffrey C. Ward, *The Civil War: An Illustrated History,* New York: Alfred A. Knopf, 1990, 82-83.)

Begin with a desire in your heart to connect your ancestors. Plant a seed in your heart that can sprout and grow and bring forth good fruit for you for many generations. Learning and writing about your ancestors can help you better understand them and yourself. Family history work not only helps connect generations together, it also strengthens bonds between living family members.

Loving Your Ancestors

No previous experience is required to begin planting your family tree today. You don't have to become an expert, but you can and need to be an expert in loving your ancestors. Connecting with your ancestors, learning more about their lives, and honoring them is an expression of your love for them.

A Family Activity

Because family history is done *for* families, it is best done most efficiently *by* families. The blessings of tracing your family roots increase

when families work together to identify your ancestors. Family members usually have information to share, or they may be willing to help you look for information. If you do not have immediate family members who are able and willing to assist you, then perhaps friends and extended family members can help.

The Importance of the Internet

One of my objectives for writing this book is to help portray the new, easy process and the sophisticated tools to help us. The Internet is one of these vital tools to help you connect with your ancestors.

The Internet has become the best and easiest way to publish and access vast resources of information available today for family history. The Internet is an excellent tool to get started searching for your family roots. One of the most amazing things about using the Internet is the ability to network with others. For example, *RootsWeb.com* hosts over 161,000 family history message boards devoted to surnames and other genealogy-related topics.

If you can't find what you're looking for, head to *Cyndi's List.com* which offers more than 265,000 links in over 180 categories. *See Chapter 5 for a directory of the Best of the Internet Family History Web Sites.*

People also talk about the vast amount of information on the *Web.* The Web is a bunch of searchable "pages" of information containing text, pictures, audio and video clips, animations, and *links* to other Web pages connected to each other around the world. And it's big! In 1998 there were about 26 million pages, and by 2000 it had reached the one billion mark. Today the Web has recently hit a new milestone: 1 trillion (as in 1,000,000,000,000) unique URLs (Web addresses), which can be compared to a map made up of one trillion intersections.

Essentially all of the Web sites described herein are free to access, however, I've added a $ symbol to each Web site listing or software that you need to pay a fee or a subscription to access a substantial part of the content.

Sharing Family History

The Internet also provides a simple and inexpensive way for you to publish your family history, thus adding to a rapidly expanding pool of shared family history information. The best way to share your family history information with others is by using the Internet. *(See Chapter 8 for details on Sharing Your Family History.)* By sharing your information, you can help others in their research, and reduce the duplication of effort.

We are blessed with computers and the Internet to help us communicate easily with people around the world. E-mail makes the sharing of family data almost instantaneous. By sending out your information, you will reap a rich harvest. As you trace your own family roots and connect with the lives of your ancestors, you help weld eternal family links, and draw yourself and your family closer together.

> Interest in discovering
> your roots is exploding.

Family History is Booming

In the early 1800s there were no organizations dedicated to gathering family history. Beginning in 1837, England and Wales began mandatory recording of births, deaths, and marriages for everyone in their countries. Many countries around the world thereafter started recording more information in their census records. For example, Great Britain's censuses began recording names and ages of individuals in 1841, and the United States added names of family members in 1850 (previously only heads of household were named). In 1844 the New England Historic Genealogical Society was organized in Boston. Today, there are thousands of family history societies around the world.

In addition, many people began to publish their family histories. The results have been dramatic. Between 1450 and 1836, fewer than 200 family histories were published. Between 1837 and 1935, almost 2,000 more were published. Today more than 2,000 family histories are published each week. Genealogy and family history has become immensely popular worldwide. If you search for the term *genealogy* on the Web, you get over 81 million hits on Google.com, 160 million on Yahoo.com, and 40 million on Live.com.

Popularity in America

A 2005 survey by Ancestry.com showed that 73% of the U.S. population was interested in or actively researching their family history. (Market Strategies, Inc. 2005) A more recent survey conducted in July 2009, showed that **87% of Americans have an interest in their family history.*** This means that approximately 199 million adults in the U.S. are interested (ranging from either very interested or somewhat interested) in learning about their family history. Compare that to the voter turnout for the 2009 American presidential election of 131.2 million, the highest in at least 40 years.

*Based on a survey commissioned by Ancestry.com conducted by Harris Interactive July 15-17, 2009 interviewing a nationwide sample of 2,066 US adults aged

18+. http://sec.gov/Archives/edgar/data/1469433/ 000095012309058478/d68252b4e424b4.htm

Web-based technologies, online data, and collaboration using the Internet greatly enhances opportunities for engaging in family history research by enabling new ways of searching and organizing your information, as well as significantly easier communicating and networking. The dynamic growth of social networks and online communities on the Internet has demonstrated the strong desire of people to connect and share information with each other. All of this makes family history research more accessible to a broader group of people.

Alex Haley

Link to Your Past

"In every conceivable manner, the family is our link to our past, and the bridge to our future." Alex Haley

Alex Haley, American biographer, scriptwriter, author (1921-1992). In 1965 Alex Haley stumbled upon the names of his maternal great-grandparents, when he was going through post-Civil War records in National Archives in Washington, D.C. He spent years tracing his own family back to a single African man, Kunta Kinte, who was captured in Gambia and taken to America as a slave around 1767. That discovery led to Haley's epic book *Roots,* published in 1976 to wide acclaim. The next year the television miniseries *Roots* ran for a week on network TV and became a national phenomenon. *Roots* won a Pulitzer Prize and the National Book Award, and Haley is often credited with inspiring interest in family history. www.kintehaley.org

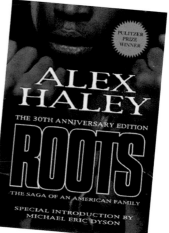

Do Your Ancestors Want to Be Found?

As you search for your family roots and stories, it's possible that you may make fortunate discoveries of significant information that you were not even looking for. This is called *serendipity or intuition* – the process of accidentally or coincidentally making meaningful family history discoveries while looking for entirely something else.

Most people that do family history have a healthy respect for serendipity and feel that the search for their family roots is often guided in mysterious, unexplainable, miraculous, coincidental ways. They usually have a similar story of an unlikely discovery falling into their lap, like a gift, which leaves them with a feeling of awe, as if their ancestors are helping with the search. It's almost as if your ancestors are standing behind you pushing you in the right direction. This prodding may come in the form of inspiration, intuition, a dream, a thought that enters your mind, or *just being in the right place at the right time.* But in the end it's a little help from above that can lead you to information you may never find otherwise.

I believe that our forebears are deeply interested in our welfare. Clearly, as we do this work there is unseen but definitive help from those who have passed on before us.

Examples of Serendipity

- Running into a previously unknown cousin at a far-away cemetery, even though neither person had been there before *as if the meeting had been planned.*

- Effortlessly discovering an ancestor's grave that you shouldn't have easily found.

- Family photos and heirlooms that are reunited with their families under unexplainable circumstances.

- Mysterious discoveries of books that seemingly magically open to exactly the right page for long sought-after information.

- Having a book fall off the shelf and land on the floor to the page containing information you want.

- Several unacquainted people showing up at a library in a city where none of them live, on the same day, at the same time *each seeking the same common ancestor.*

Megan Smolenyak

Ancestors Will Meet You Halfway

"We do indeed honor our ancestors when we search for them, and it seems, they return the favor. ... When one makes the effort to learn about the lives of ancestors, they will often meet you halfway." Megan Smolenyak, *In Search of Our Ancestors*, 2000, Adams Media Corp.

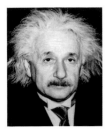
Albert Einstein

Valuable Intuition

"The only really valuable thing is intuition." Albert Einstein (1879-1955), physicist

Intuition and Inspiration

"I believe in intuition and inspiration; at times I feel certain I am right while not knowing the reason." Albert Einstein

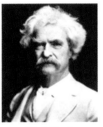
Mark Twain

Instinct is Worth More

"For all the talk you hear about knowledge being such a wonderful thing, instinct is worth forty of it for real unerringness." Mark Twain (1835-1910). author, humorist

Searching With an Open Heart

"I was amazed to find success in genealogy often comes from intuition, searching not with just the mind, but also an open heart, enjoying warm feelings with the deceased." George W. Fisk, author

RIchard Buckiminster Fuller

Cosmic Fishing

"I call intuition cosmic fishing. You feel a nibble, then you've got to hook the fish." Richard Buckminster Fuller (1895-1983), inventor

Looking for a Needle

"Serendipity is looking in a haystack for a needle and discovering a farmer's daughter." "Serendipity, the art of making an unsought finding." Pek van Andel

Jules Henri Poincaré

Intuition Discoveries

"It is through science that we prove, but through intuition that we discover." Jules Henri Poincaré (1854-1912), physicist, mathematician, philosopher

Inspirational Stories

Our forebears are anxious for us to connect with them. Here are some inspirational stories that will warm your heart and illustrate the point in tracing your family roots. Check out these books and Web sites for more stories.

Megan Smolenyak's Books -

www.honoringourancestors.com

You can enjoy many inspirational stories in Megan Smolenyak's books of how people have experienced amazing incidents in the search for their roots. She was struck by the number of stories about random acts of kindness, coincidence, intuition, and serendipity. She found herself inundated with stories of distant cousins "coincidentally" meeting while visiting the cemetery of their ancestors, and she learned of family photos, papers, and Bibles that were reunited with their original families under circumstances that boggle the mind. $12.95

Hank Jones

Hank Jones' Books -

www.hankjones.com $16.95

Henry (Hank) Z. Jones, Jr. has written two books concerning the positive influence of coincidence and serendipity in family history research. Over a hundred respected researchers discuss their experiences in light of synchronic-

ity, intuition, and genetic memory. *Psychic Roots: Serendipity & Intuition in Genealogy* and *More Psychic Roots* contains a collection of stories and experiences contributed by people the world over. As the author concludes: *"I do believe that our ancestors have no wish to be forgotten: they want to be found."*

Genealogy Today.com -

http://genealogytoday.com/family/ **FREE** stories/serendipity.html

Joanne Rabun relates stories about people being led to certain information in some mystical way.

Ancestry Insider.com - **FREE**

http://ancestryinsider.blogspot.com > *Serendipity*

The anonymous Ancestry Insider writes this popular blog that includes more stories about serendipity in genealogy for your enjoyment.

Ancestors at Her Fingertips

Kathleen had promptings at various times throughout her life. She sensed her Swedish ancestors were there, somewhere, waiting for her. She had searched for information for many years without success, but decided to try again. Before long she had the opportunity to go to Sweden, and found herself in the village church of her ancestors.

She followed the old, white-haired Swedish minister down a narrow flight of stairs into a small room where rows of brown leather-covered volumes lined the shelves from floor to ceiling. She told the minister her grandmother's birth date. He pulled a book from the shelf, opened it, and pointed to an entry. It was her grandmother's birth record. With excitement she watched as he pulled other books from the shelves showing the

records of her grand-mothers and great-grandparents families. In five minutes, she had in front of her information that she had not been able to find in ten years.

She quickly and happily copied all the records the minister had found for her, and wondered what she should do next. With only a short time to work in the church, she picked up the book for the next five-year period, but could not figure out the index in the front. She turned the page to where her family had been in the other book, but they were not there. She flipped through the book, trying to find some kind of pattern. With mounting panic and desperation, she gazed at the books lining the shelves. At her fingertips were the records she had been wanting for so long, but she didn't know how to use them! Each book was too thick to go through page by page.

She opened the book again and flipped a few pages. What could she do? She simply sat there, numb with disappointment. Gradually, she became aware of the book that she had just opened. The names on the page looked familiar. Despair gave way to joy as she recognized the names of her great-great-grandparents. There were 417 pages in the book, but completely at random, she had opened it to the one page that had the records of her family.

The Face on the Other Side

G.G. Vandagriff wanted to learn more about her great-grandmother. She had all the "data" about the dates and places, but wanted to really know her. She felt drawn to her in a way she couldn't explain, and the desire to know her grandmother consumed her. In a bold move, she knelt and prayed one night that she might become familiar with her in an intimate way. She wanted to know what she looked like, what her personality was, what her feelings were by following her husband to seven frontier settlements.

She knew that she was praying for a miracle, but the next morning she received a phone call that shocked her. The phone call was from her unknown third cousin, Joyce, also a descendent

of her grandmother. Her cousin had obtained her phone number by coincidence and stated that she was the granddaughter of the favorite granddaughter of their grandmother and that she had her pictures, her quilts, and story upon story about her.

Within 36 hours of her prayer, she sat looking at her grandmother's face for the first time, and in the months that followed, she got to know her. She now measures her character against her grandmothers, hoping that when they meet, that she will be worthy of her extraordinary heritage. www.meridian magazine.com/turninghearts/ 020919faceveil.html

One-Chance-in-a-Million

Cathy Corcoran was searching for information on her grandfather. She knew his birth date, but when faced with the daunting task of going through eleven thousand babies born in Boston in 1876 in someone's old handwriting, she was troubled. She randomly opened a dusty book and idly flipped to page 525. The name practically leaped off the page. What are the odds that she would open a book to that page and see that record? A million to one? It was amazing. It was a miracle. Read this story in

Megan Smolenyak's book, *In Search of Our Ancestors,* p. 7-9.

My Ancestor Helped Me

Cheryl Bean went to the courthouse to view court records on her ancestor only to discover that the records had been misplaced during a recent move. After digging through book after book for some time in a huge basement room, she bowed her head in prayer, and then walked to the most remote row of books. She picked up the last volume on the shelf, but the title didn't look promising. She opened it anyway and discovered that the apparently mislabeled book had been used to record early territorial court hearings. She tried not to get her hopes up too high, but after some frantic page turning, there was the information she was seeking. She got an overwhelming feeling that she wasn't alone, and prayed silently again to be led to any additional information about her ancestor. She found herself drawn to another row where she plucked out a book at random and found additional information. After that experience, she was convinced that she was not alone in the work of searching for her ancestors. Read this story in Megan Smolenyak's book, *In Search of Our Ancestors,* p. 10-11.

Their Families Finally Found Each Other with Help from the Other Side

Athena's Mother was suffering from terminal cancer, and she was near death. But her Mother said that she didn't want to go until she could find her family. Athena told her Mother that she would be with them soon, so why not send her back the information and she would see what she could do to help. Her father immigrated to the United States from Greece in 1915, and had changed his name, but they had never

met any of his family, nor did they know any information about them, including their names.

Soon after her Mother passed away, Athena had some interesting things happen. In searching on the internet, she found a name that she thought was her father's true surname, but had never been able to verify it for sure. She wrote a letter and before long received a reply that his father was her grandfather's brother, and that they were living in Canada. Soon after that, she received a phone call from another man who told her that his wife was her mother's first cousin and they had emigrated from Greece to Canada and also been looking for them for many years. She came on the phone and cried and cried. She told her how they had come to Salt Lake many times trying to locate them, but they were never able to find them, due to the name change.

Not only were they able to associate with living members of the family as well as learn about ancestors for the first time, but from the information she received, she went to the Family History Library and found over 100 names of relatives. When they had their very first family reunion, the love between them was immediate and it felt as though they had always been in their lives and there was an immediate bonding. They realized that their families had been looking for one another for 85 years. It seems there are times when family members can be more help to us in finding our roots from the other side. http://deseretbook.com

The Book Fell Open to the Right Place

Sherlene Hall Bartholome writes: "While living in New York...I had randomly chosen a book from among many about Ohio history. While thumbing through it, I remarked...that I sure would like to find the marriage of a certain couple from that state. No sooner did I name them than this book fell open to a page that had an entire paragraph about them, as their names practically jumped off the page to catch my attention! As the back of my neck went electric, and my eyes teared, I forgot any sense of reserve and demanded of the startled men: what names did I just mention to you? Look at this page – can you believe? Just look at this! This book fell right open to their names! Why, here's their marriage date! Do you know how long I've been looking for this? I tell you, there really are angels guiding this work! They inspected the open page, acknowledged that I spoke those same names before I opened it, and seemed to be almost as excited and caught up in the moment as I." www.meridian magazine.com/turninghearts/021122bookfell.html

I Hope You Remember Me

David Heyen awoke one morning with a strong feeling that he had left something undone in his family history and that *now* was the time to do it. The impression was so strong that he decided he should visit Rockport, Missouri, the place his father's family had lived. He hadn't visited there since he was young and was apprehensive about seeing long-lost family members, but the urgency he felt was strong so he decided to go anyway. His fears were soon put to rest as his relatives welcomed him with open arms. He became more and more astonished as piece after piece of his family's history fell into place. Family lines he had abandoned because of lack of information suddenly began to produce generous information. He found old photographs of grandparents four and five generations back whose information he had previously given up all hope of ever finding.

In reviewing the original documents his great-grandmother had given him, he happened upon a poem written in 1830 by John Brown, his fourth

great-grandfather. It read, in part:

My Christian friends, both old and young, I hope, in Christ, you'll all be strong. I hope you'll all remember me, If no more my face you'll see. And in trust, in prayers, I crave That we shall meet beyond the grave. Oh glorious day, Oh blessed hope. My heart leaps forward at the thought! When in that happy land we'll meet. We'll no more take the parting hand, But with our holy blessed Lord, We'll shout and sing with one accord.

His eyes filled with tears as he felt impressed that these words from 1830 were written for him. He felt that his family members who had passed on were determined not to be forgotten and were urging him to discover who they were. He knew that someday he would have the chance to meet them in that joyous reunion John Brown wrote of so very long ago. By following the prompting he received, he found that a way was opened to him in his search, and now he knew we are never really finished with discovering our family roots and stories.

Sheer Dumb Luck?

Beth Uyehara found her great grandfathers grave and decorated it with flowers. The next morning at the courthouse, while looking through deed indexes, she accidentally grabbed a book from the wrong shelf, and opened an index from the 1920s – decades after her family had left the area. Before noticing her mistake, she found two quit-claim deeds signed by her great grandfather's descendants and their spouses, showing their relationships and other valuable information. It was a bonanza of information. Was this just luck? In another city, while searching immigration and naturalization records for another great grandfather, she found his file and inside was not only his final certificate of citizenship, but also his personal copy of the Declaration of Intention. He must have left it behind at his swearing-in as a citizen. Since he died just twelve days after becoming a citizen, he had never returned to pick it up and there it sat for 120 years. As she and the clerk examined the file together, they discovered that the clerk's ancestor had been the character witness for Beth's ancestor when he applied for citizenship, so they had obviously been friends. Was their chance meeting just coincidence? Read this story in Megan Smolenyak's book, *In Search of Our Ancestors,* p. 3-5.

Our Ancestors are Close to Us

Reverend Billy Graham

The Soul of Man is Eternal

The Reverend Billy Graham delivered a message entitled *What Happens When You Die?* published in *Decision* magazine in June 2003. He was referring to the April 2003 death of NBC journalist David Bloom who died in Iraq of a blood clot.

In the article, he stated that it's not possible *"that a Creator would...allow His highest creation... to become extinct at death."* He went on to say that while our body is temporary, our spirit or soul is eternal and will live forever. You can read the full article at http://billygraham.com/ourMinistries/ decisionMagazine. Billy Graham, "The Reality of Eternity," Decision magazine, June 2003, Charlotte, N.C., BGEA

Boyd Packer
© by Intellectual Reserve, Inc.

Our Forebears are Close to Us

"It is a veil, not a wall, that separates us from the spirit world. ... Veils can become thin, even parted. We are not left to do this [family history] work alone. They who have preceded us...and our forebears there, on occasion, are very close to us. ..." Boyd Packer

John Taylor
© by Intellectual Reserve, Inc.

Forming an Alliance

"We are forming an alliance, a union, a connection, with those that are behind the veil, and they are forming a union and connection with us; and while we are living here, we are preparing to live hereafter, and laying a foundation for this." John Taylor, *Journal of Discourses,* 11:12/11/1864

Free Tutorials, Lessons and Charts

You can find FREE beginner lessons, references and tutorials about how to do family history and tips on research on the Internet. A few of which are:

FamilySearch.org - www.familysearch.org *Get Started* in the *Start Your Family History* box.

They briefly explain six basic steps to do research. In addition, there are many 'How To' articles under the *Research Helps* tab.

FamilySearch.org Video Classes -
www.familysearch.org *>Library tab >Education >Family History Library Research Series Online*

Free video classes online; you can learn the basic methods and key resources to start your family history, including: England, Germany, Ireland, Italy, Mexico, Russia and U.S. research.

FamilySearch.org Guides -
www.familysearch.org *>Get Started*

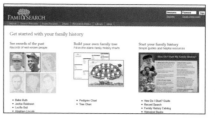

Get started with your family history with their free tools to help: Build your own family tree charts, and simple guides and helpful resources. You can also click on *>Library >Education >Publications* to access *Research Outlines* (publications that describe the records and strategies that can be used to pursue family history research in a specific geographic location or particular type of record), *Research Guides* (how to use a particular family history source), and *Step-by-step Guides* (specific instructions and tips about how to search the record type you have chosen).

FamilySearch.org Research Helps -
www.familysearch.org *>Research Helps tab*

You can click on Articles to select from an alphabetical list of hundreds of research helps (sorted by place, title, subject or type). Be sure and check out the valuable different types of charts, worksheets and forms. Or you can click on *Guidance* to have the online "research assistant" help you locate records in specific geographical locations that may contain information about your ancestors.

BYU Independent Study -
http://ce.byu.edu/is *>Courses >Free Courses*
http://ce.byu.edu/is/site/ courses/free.cfm

Free family history tutorials online, including Finding Your Ancestors; vital, family, and military records; and German, French, Scandinavian and Huguenot sources.

Genealogy.com - www.genealogy.com >
Learning Center > Free Genealogy Classes **FREE**

There are
many different
lessons
under the
following
categories:

- Getting Started
- Getting Organized
- Developing your Research Skills

DearMYRTLE -
www.dearmyrtle.com *Lessons* **FREE**

There are
dozens of
excellent
lessons
under the
following
categories:

Beginning Genealogy Lessons
Finally Get Organized
Kid's Genealogy
Step By Step
Using Family History Centers
Writing Your Personal History

Ancestry.com -
www.ancestry.com > *Learning Center* **FREE**

They offer
videos by
experts
and a Quick-
Step Guide
providing
all the key
components for beginning your family
history. Their learning center helps you
reach into the past and make meaningful
connections with your forbears.

Here's some Things You Can
Do Today to Get Started

10 Things You Can Do Today to Get Started

1. **Plant a seed in your heart**
for a desire to connect to your
ancestors; nourish the seed so it
can grow; learn about the sacrifices they made
to make your life better, prepare to receive help
from your ancestors. (Pages 4-6)

2. **Take a free online "How To" lesson**
(or tutorial). (Page 14)

3. **Subscribe to** a free e-newsletter or magazine;
register for a free blog. (Pages 16-20)

4. **Review and purchase** a family history
software program and get acquainted with
the basics. (Chapter 4)

5. **Write down everything you know** about your
ancestors; contact your family's "keeper of the
flame" (your family's historian), and ask him/her
to share their information. (Page 27)

6. **Search existing online family tree Web sites**
and published family histories for information
on your ancestor. (Page 43-50)

7. **Scan your precious photos** and documents
to a digital format to protect them and be able
to easily share with others. (Page 204-210)

8. **Begin to write your family history;** gather
your family stories; record the life stories of
your parents/grandparents before its too late;
record your own story while you can still
remember; interview a relative; get grandkids
involved to help establish a bond between
generations. (Page 215)

9. **Collaborate with others** to add branches to
your family tree using a social networking Web
site; connect with your family, swap stories,
and share photos, recipes and information.
(Page 93)

10. **Hold a family reunion;** organize your family;
reach out to your extended family members;
start a family blog or online photo album;
volunteer to help index public records at home.
(Page 239)

RootsWeb Guides -

http://rwguide.rootsweb.ancestry.com **FREE**

CAUTION: GUIDES ARE GRAPHICS-INTENSIVE

RootsWeb Guides to Tracing Family Trees contain illustrated articles and valuable tips written by professional genealogists about: where to begin, types of records with links, and ethnic groups.

e-Newsletters / Magazines / TV Programs

The Latest How-to Info for Tracing Your Family Tree

Eastman's Online Genealogy Newsletter -

www.eogn.com **FREE** $

A popular, daily newsletter summary of events, tips, reviews, and topics of interest from genealogist Dick Eastman, available in a *free Standard Edition* and a *Plus Edition* for $19.95/year.

Family Tree Magazine -

www.familytreemagazine.com **FREE** $

A leading how-to publication for those who want to discover, preserve and celebrate their roots. It covers all areas of potential interest to family history enthusiasts, reaching beyond strict genealogy research to include ethnic heritage, family reunions, memoirs, oral history, scrapbooking, historical travel and other ways that families connect with their pasts. Provides engaging, easy-to-understand instruction that empowers you to take the next steps in the quest for your past—with a beginner-friendly approach that makes family history a

hobby anyone can do. The website has some free content, but the emphasis is on getting you to subscribe to the print edition of the magazine. $24.00/year

Family Chronicle Magazine -

www.familychronicle.com **FREE** $

Bi-monthly magazine written for family researchers by people who share your interest in genealogy and family history. This "how-to" genealogy magazine has gained a reputation for solid editorial, presented in a highly attractive, all-color format. The website has some free content, but the emphasis is on getting you to subscribe to the print edition of the magazine. $25.00/year

GenealogyInTime.com -

www.genealogyintime.com **FREE**

An online genealogy magazine containing articles, how-to guides, listings of the latest online genealogy records as they become available on the internet, unique news stories, and the popular weekly column *Genealogy This Week*, a compilation of the best and most interesting new genealogy tools, resources and stories to help you get the most out of your family history research..

Global Gazette -

http://globalgenealogy.com/ globalgazette/index.htm **FREE** $

An online family history magazine from Canada with helpful tips on researching family history. Includes "how-to" articles and genealogy news as well as general genealogy information. There is some free content and a considerable amount of content that you can buy through their store at http://globalgenealogy.com.

GenealogyMagazine.com -
www.genealogymagazine.com

A free online magazine with databases, photographs, articles and books for sell for tracing your ancestors. Free content just pay for the books you order.

Internet Genealogy -
http://internet-genealogy.com

A bi-monthly magazine from the publishers of *Family Chronicle* and *History Magazine*. It deals primarily with doing genealogy research using the resources of the Internet. The rate at which new databases are coming online is staggering and many of these new records are linked to the original images, making them effectively original sources. $25/year

Family Research –
www.lineages.co.uk **FREE**

A free specialty online UK magazine for tracing your English, Scottish and Irish roots.

FamilyHistoryPlace.net -
www.familyhistoryplace.net

Their mission is to make genealogy research fun and easy by providing a simple to use,

fun, and informative website that helps you to do your research and get results quickly. Contains articles, links to over 1000 genealogy societies and associations, book reviews, and a newsletter.

Topix.net -
www.topix.net/hobbies/genealogy **FREE**

News from thousands of sources, sorted geographically for US cities, as well as a wide variety of subjects.

RootsWeb Review -
http://newsletters.rootsweb.ancestry.com **FREE**

This free monthly e-zine provides news about RootsWeb.com, its new databases, mailing lists, home pages, and Web sites. It also includes stories and research tips from its readers around the globe.

WorldVitalRecords Newsletter -
www.worldvitalrecords.com >*Newsletter* **FREE**

A free weekly e-newsletter that provides how to articles and tips by industry experts, tutorials to help you make the most of technology, information about the newest collections on WorldVitalRecords and upcoming events.

GenealogyToday.com -
http://news.genealogytoday.com **FREE**

Articles and news releases from various resources around the Web.

Journal of Genetic Genealogy – FREE

www.jogg.info

This is a technical scientific magazine that covers DNA testing for genealogy.

Forum - www.fgs.org >forum $

The Federation of Gencalogical Societies (FGS), consisting of more than 550 member societies and over 500,000 individual genealogists, publishes this quarterly magazine providing current information essential to the informed genealogist. $18.00/year (non-member)

Who Do You Think You Are? TV Series - FREE

www.nbc.com/who-do-you-think-you-are

This new 7-episode NBC TV program leads celebrities on a journey of self-discovery as they unearth their family trees – the quest to discover the genealogical roots of who they are – that reveals surprising, inspiring and even tragic stories that are often linked to crucial events in American history. Each episode exposes surprising facts and emotional encounters that will unlock your emotions – showing just how connected everyone is not only to the past, but to one another.

Book - Who Do You Think You Are?: The Essential Guide to Tracing Your Family History $

www.honoringourancestors.com

There is no such thing as an ordinary family. Each one has its own stories. No matter how plain you think your background is, chances are there is a saga just waiting to be discovered. This is the companion guide to the

ground-breaking NBC TV series. You will learn how to chart your own journey into your past and discover the treasures hidden in your family tree. Features step-by-step instructions from one of America's top genealogical researchers, Megan Smolenyak. $24.95

Faces of America TV Series - FREE

www.pbs.org/wnet/facesofamerica

What made America? What makes us? These two questions are at the heart of the new PBS TV series Faces of America with Henry Louis Gates, Jr. The Harvard scholar turns to the latest tools of genealogy and genetics to explore the family histories of 12 renowned Americans. Watch the fascinating episodes on their website anytime. They explore the making of America, becoming American, and American stories. A big part of the attraction, of course, is the celebrities and those irresistibly dramatic moments when we watch them learn of untold family histories.

The Generations Project TV Series - FREE

http://byutv.org/thegenerationsproject

A new BYU TV reality series about discovering your roots. The show will help you solve unsolved mysteries about your family's history. This new series helps you investigate your own identity by walking in the shoes of your ancestors. You often uncover the hidden identities in family pasts, and come to see that in many cases the best way to know who you are is to know who you came from. Other family history series can be found at www.byub.org/new/genealogy.

Blogs

Free-style, Interactive Web Sites with News and Commentary on Family History

A blog (or web log) is a website consisting of entries appearing in reverse chronological order with the most recent entry appearing first. Blogs typically include comments, photos, and web links. You may want to consider creating your own family blog because it's a great way to connect with your extended family and others who share your interests. *See Chapter 8 for information on creating your own family blog.*

Ancestry Insider -

http://ancestryinsider.blogspot.com **FREE**

The unofficial blog of two big genealogy websites: Ancestry.com and FamilySearch.org.

Dear MYRTLE.com -

http://blog.dearmyrtle.com **FREE**

Pat Richley's website is a fun, helpful family history site with a regular blog column of free news and tips.

Genealogy Insider - **FREE**

http://blog.familytreemagazine.com/insider

Diane Haddad's genealogy blog at FamilyTree Magazine.

Genealogy Blog -

www.genealogyblog.com **FREE**

Leland Meitzler's popular genealogy blog.

The Genealogue -

http://genealogue.blogspot.com **FREE**

Genealogical notes, notions, and meanderings.

The Chart Chick -

www.thechartchick.blogspot.com **FREE**

The brainchild of Janet Hovorka, Development Director at Generation Maps – a genealogy chart printing service. Content includes research and general genealogy how-to's, information on involving your family, genealogy charting ideas, genealogy industry insights and news, and other musings.

Think Genealogy -

www.thinkgenealogy.com **FREE**

A popular blog by Mark Tucker about genealogy, software, ideas, and innovation.

Genealogy Roots -

http://genrootsblog.blogspot.com **FREE**

A newsletter and blog to help find online genealogy databases, records and resources. Major topics include death indexes, military, census, and immigration records. It is usually distributed about 1-3 times a month.

FamilyTree: Best Genealogy Blogs -

www.familytreemagazine.com/article/fab-forty

Here are FamilyTree Magazine's top 40 best genealogy blogs as published in the May 2010 issue.

GeneaBloggers.com -

www.geneabloggers.com

The genealogy community's resource for blogging by Thomas MacEntee. He keeps things humming with tech tips and advice for bloggers, industry news, geneablogger profiles, and blogging event calendars.

Genea-Musings -

www.geneamusings.com

Genealogy research tips, genealogy news items, genealogy humor, and some family history stories by Randy Seaver.

RootDig.com -

www.rootdig.com

Michael John Neill's genealogy blog website with news and information.

Olive Tree -

http://olivetreegenealogy.blogspot.com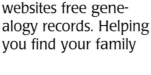

Updates and news about Olive Tree Genealogy and other websites free genealogy records. Helping you find your family tree and ancestry.

Kimberly's Genealogy Blog -

http://genealogy.about.com/b/

A popular blog by Kimberly Powell, the host of About.com's Guide to Genealogy, a professional genealogist, Web developer, and author of *Everything Family Tree.*

Creative Gene -

www.creativegene.blogspot.com

A popular blog about genealogy and more by Jasia.

AnceStories Blog -

http://ancestories1.blogspot.com

Miriam Robbins Midkiff writes about genealogy from Spokane, Washington as well as teaches courses in Online Genealogy through her local community college.

The Footnote Maven Blog -

www.footnotemaven.com

Another widely viewed blog on genealogy happenings.

Genetic Genealogy -

www.thegeneticgenealogist.com

A blog by Blaine Bettinger featuring the use of modern genetic research to study genealogy, the relatedness between individuals. It also explores the latest news and developments in the related field of personal genomics.

Tracing the Tribe - **FREE**
http://tracingthetribe.blogspot.com

A blog by Schelly Talalay Dardashti about Jewish genealogy; all the developments, tools and resources you'll need to peer more closely into your family tree.

Transylvanian Dutch Blog - **FREE**
http://transylvaniandutch.blogspot.com

Everything about those of Germanic ancestry who immigrated to the state of Pennsylvania and vicinity prior to 1800 by John Newmark.

GenDisasters -
http://www3.gendisasters.com **FREE**

Focusing on events that touched our ancestors lives by Stu Beitler with over 12,000 disaster articles and message boards.

What is a PodCast?

Genealogy News, Views and Interviews at Your Leisure

PodCasts are downloadable radio or TV-style shows that you can listen to or watch on your computer or MP3 player anytime you want. If you're not familiar with podcasting, you're missing a great source of information and inspiration. Podcasts have grown tremendously in popularity in the last few years with over 41,000 shows available online. You're in control to fast forward, rewind, stop, and start at your convenience. You don't need an iPod to listen, but with the companion software *iTunes* (www.apple.com/itunes) you can set up an account, listen, and organize any podcasts for free on your computer. Then you can download a podcast to your personal music device or burn onto a CD to listen to in your car if you wish. Anyway, it's a great way to keep up with the latest genealogy news or Web sites, or to pick up new techniques, tips and research skills. Learn more about PodCasts at http://video.about.com/ipod/itunes_podcasts-mov.htm. You don't have to subscribe to podcasts if you don't want, just visit the Web site of your favorite podcast whenever you wish to see what's new.

DearMyrtle Podcasts - **FREE**
http://podcasts.dearmyrtle.com

Catch DearMyrtle's interesting *Family History Hour* podcasts at this site with hotlinks to the mentioned Web sites online.

GenealogyGuys.com - **FREE**
www.genealogyguys.com

George Morgan and Drew Smith discuss genealogy news, new technology, and provide tips to help you with your research.

GenealogyGems.tv - **FREE**
http://genealogygems.tv

Host Lisa Cooke shares research strategies and inspiration to help you get the most out of your family history research time. New podcasts are about 25 minutes long, and generally published on a weekly basis.

Books, Forms, Supplies, Marketplace

FamilyHistoryExpos - FREE
www.fhexpos.com

This website and service helps you understand the new tools, techniques and technology to trace your roots in today's ever-changing technological environment. They manage the premier *Family History Expos* held each year around the country which teach beginners true methods of research and help experienced researchers improve their results by introducing them to new tools. Podcasts and TV/Videos feature interviews with family history professionals, software developers, and product/service providers, including expert advice from some of the country's most successful genealogists. Click the TV tab at the top of the page. Their store offers books, forms, handmade rubber stamps, software, CDs, etc. Founded by Holly Hansen, author, lecturer, former editor of *Everton's Genealogical Helper* magazine and the *Handybook for Genealogists*.

FamilyRoots Publishing.com - $
www.FamilyRootsPublishing.com

They publish how-to titles by Kevan Hansen, William Dollarhide, and others, and distribute selected genealogy guidebooks, periodicals, and supplies to the community via the Internet, mail and phone order. Owned by Leland and Patty Meitzler, best-known for having started Heritage Quest in 1985. A popular speaker, Leland has given over 2000 genealogy lectures, with audiences always coming away enthused and ready to take on more genealogy research. 801-992-3705

EasyFamilyHistory.com - FREE
www.easyfamilyhistory.com/store

Your convenient online store for the most popular family history books, software and CDs to guide beginners and empower experts using today's technology. All the resources you need at your fingertips to make your family history easy. They published this guidebook, one of the best-selling step-by-step guides and resource directories in the market, and an assortment of 'how-to' CDs. The website also provides a free Learning Center with how-to articles, guides, and tips; free Teaching Aids (power-point presentations); and an LDS Center. Owned by Paul and Peggy Larsen. 801-358-6692

HeritageQuestOnline.com -
www.heritagequestonline.com

Heritage Quest is a large comprehensive genealogical data provider in the United States and a leading purveyor of data, products, supplies and equipment to consumers and institutions with over 250,000 titles. The company is dedicated to producing high-use data, landmark publications, general reference books and timely, informative periodicals for genealogy enthusiasts. Available free by using your local library card, and at some Family History Centers.

Genealogy Charts and Forms - FREE
http://genealogy.about.com/cs/freecharts

Free downloadable family tree charts, pedigree charts research logs and other free forms to help you in your genealogy research and keep your family tree organized.

Global Genealogy.com -
www.globalgenealogy.com

Shop online for family history supplies, maps, forms, software, books, etc.

Genealogical.com - $
www.genealogical.com

A publisher and distributor of 2000 genealogy books, CDs, and supplies.

Generation Maps.com - $
www.generationmaps.com

An easy to use, very affordable, genealogy chart design and printing service. They offer personalized working charts, beautiful decorative charts, custom heirloom charts, and a printing service for charts you've created. Now you don't have to fill in a chart yourself — just send your genealogy computer file and/or your digital photos, tell them how you want it to look, and it arrives on your doorstep for a very reasonable price. They can help you get your research out where you can see it and surround your family with a sense of their heritage. It's also a wonderful, easy way to explain to your family members the research that has been accomplished.

Family Chartist -
www.generationmaps.com/familychartist **FREE**

A new web application that makes creating and designing beautiful genealogy charts easier and faster than ever before. With beautiful graphics and embellishments it is easy to create something personalized for your family. You choose the layout, information to be included, size, paper, color, pictures, borders, backgrounds and artistic design. You can create an 8.5 x 11 chart free and save it to your computer to print whenever you choose. If you decide you want to print a larger size for your home, just order from the same menu and your chart will be printed and shipped to you promptly for a small fee. Whether you are decorating your home, creating a familybook, looking for a special gift for someone you love, or bringing your heritage to life for a family gathering, they will help you fashion a beautiful expression of your family's history for your surroundings.

Alibris.com -
www.alibris.com > *genealogy* $

Alibris connects people who love books, music and movies to thousands of independent sellers around the world. Their proprietary technology and advanced logistics allow them to offer over 40 million used, new and hard-to-find books to consumers, libraries and retailers.

Heritage Books.com -
www.heritagebooks.com

Has over 12,000 genealogy books, maps and CDs.

Picton Press.com - www.pictonpress.com

Specializes in publishing genealogical and historical manuscripts.

Ancestry Store.com - www.theancestrystore.com

Family history and genealogy books, software, photos, and maps.

Family History Store -
www.thefamilyhistorystore.com

An international online retailer of a growing line of genealogy and history related products & gifts since 2003.

RootsBooks.com -
www.rootsbooks.com and www.rootsbooks.co.uk

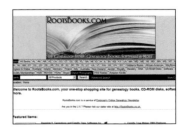

A one-stop online genealogy bookstore for books, computers, software and more.

Getting Started

Most people do not know how to start to trace their own family roots and stories, or what has already been done by others. This book was written because we need help to learn *how* to do the work. And we need it *simple, easy* and *quick*. We need to know the exciting, easy way today to connect with our ancestor's lives and stories, and learn about our heritage. This illustrated guidebook was written for this express purpose.

Maybe you're curious about the idea of learning about your family history, but don't know where to start. Maybe you've listened to amazing stories from your grandfather, scoured old family photo albums, and attended family reunions. Now what? What records should you look for? What can they tell you about your ancestors and heritage? And what has already been done by others?

We hope this family history guidebook/ resource directory offers a convenient, easy step-by-step approach to answering these questions, and learning how to trace your family roots. We hope you find this expanded, updated Fourth Edition helpful, inspiring, and to your liking. And we hope it offers a convenient, easy step-by-step approach to learning and doing the work. Get started today tracing your own family roots and stories and discover new meaning in your life and the thrill of uncovering new-found treasures.

Paul Larsen

CHAPTER 1

3-Easy Steps
Follow These 3-Easy Steps to Begin Building Your Family Tree and Connect to Your Ancestors

STEP 1 - Identify Your Ancestors Using Your Family

The success of tracing your family roots and stories increases when families work together. Family members will often have information to share, or they may be willing to help you look for information. Your relatives may remember important events and dates that have not been recorded. They may have family heirlooms, records, mementos, photographs, and other valuable items. They may have interesting family stories to tell, and they can sometimes direct you to others who knew your ancestors or to other relatives you may not know.

1 Use Your **Family**

Suggested Activities

- Purchase family history software to help you if you haven't already and learn the basics *(see Chapter 4: Family History Software)*.

- Start writing down what you know about your family.

- Print out a blank *pedigree form* and *family group sheet* from the Internet to make it easier.

- Call relatives to find out if someone has already compiled a family history or other records that might contain the information you're looking for. Ask them to e-mail a GEDCOM file of their information. This is a great head start.

- Look around your house for documents that might provide new information or verify the information you already have. Keep copies of everything you find in your search. It may not seem important now, but it will in the future.

Family History Insights - 1

Boyd K. Packer
© by Intellectual Reserve, Inc.

Collect Everything About Your Life

"Get a cardboard box. Any kind of box will do. Put it someplace where it is in the way, . . . anywhere where it cannot go unnoticed. Then, over a period of a few weeks, collect and put into the box every record of your life..... Collect diplomas, all of the photographs, honors, or awards, a diary if you have kept one, everything that you can find pertaining to your life; anything that is written, or registered, or recorded that testifies that you are alive and what you have done." Boyd K. Packer,

A Light From Our Ancestors

Gaius Sallustius Crispus

"Distinguished ancestors shed a powerful light on their descendants, and forbid the concealment either of their merits or of their demerits." Gaius Sallustius Crispus (86-34 BC), Roman historian

An Inheritance From Our Ancestors

Samuel Adams

"The liberties of our country, the freedom of our civil constitution, are worth defending at all hazards... We have received them as a fair inheritance from our worthy ancestors... [they] transmitted them to us with care and diligence." Samuel Adams (1722-1803), Founding Father

Benefits From Ancestors

"What task could be more agreeable than to tell of the benefits conferred on us by our ancestors, so that you may get to know the achievements of those from whom you have received both the basis of your beliefs and the inspiration to conduct your life properly?" – William Malmesbury, 1125 A.D.

Traits from Ancestors

Ralph Waldo Emerson

"A man finds room in the few square inches of the face for the traits of all his ancestors; for the expression of all his history, and his wants." Ralph Waldo Emerson (1803-1882), Poet and author

A Quotation from Ancestors

"Every book is a quotation; and every house is a quotation out of all forests, and mines, and stone quarries; and every man is a quotation from all his ancestors." Ralph Waldo Emerson

Made from Our Ancestors

"...a man represents each of several of his ancestors, as if there were seven or eight [ancestors] rolled up in each man's skin ... and they constitute the variety of notes for that new piece of music which his life is." Ralph Waldo Emerson

Feel A Special Connection

Gordon B. Hinckley
© by Intellectual Reserve, Inc.

"As you look into the [computer] you may be surprised to find names of your parents, of your grandparents, of your great-grandparents, and your great-great-grandparents, who have bequeathed to you all you are of body and mind. You will feel a special connection to those who have gone before you and an increased responsibility to those who will follow." Gordon Hinckley, National Press Club Speech, March 8, 2000

STEP 1 – Identify Your Ancestors Using Your Family

BEGIN BUILDING YOUR FAMILY TREE WITH WHAT YOU ALREADY KNOW

The information you gather about your ancestors gives you a greater appreciation of your heritage, the sacrifices your ancestors made for you, and a better understanding of what their life was like. Your knowledge of your forebears will increase, your family will grow closer, families will be strengthened, and the opportunity to learn more about your kindred dead will bless lives.

As you gather information about your ancestors, you are welding family links, and drawing yourself and your family closer to God. Your ancestors want to be found as much as you want to find them.

> Follow the 3-Easy-Steps to begin building your family tree and connect to your ancestors.

QUICK TIPS ON GETTING STARTED

1. Begin with a pedigree chart. It will be a road map for your Family history search. Create your own four generation pedigree chart. From memory, begin to fill in information on the lines indicating your father, your mother, your grandparents, and so on.

2. Start with yourself and what you already know about your parents and grandparents.

3. Work back one generation at a time, from the known to the unknown.

4. Be as complete as possible when you record information.

5. Don't be overwhelmed by the process.

6. Choose one of the commercially available family history software programs (See Chapter 4)

Write Everything You Know About Your Ancestors

Identifying your ancestors is fun and so much easier today. You can begin right now by picking up a pencil and writing down information on a piece of paper.

Begin with what you already know by writing information on yourself and work back one generation at a time. The most important family history information you already posses – your memories and the memories of your loved ones. Gather information about yourself, your siblings, your parents, your grandparents, and

1 Use Your Family

your great grandparents. Make a list of each member in your family that can help you identify your ancestors. Typically, information about your close relatives is readily available simply by talking to them, and searching through information in your home.

Write down specific information, such as: names, dates and places of important events such as birth, marriage, and death, ancestral village, occupation, etc. Try to gather 3-4 generations (or more) of information on your ancestors. Don't be concerned if you're missing information because you can go back and fill it in later.

A *research log* is a comprehensive list of what you have already searched and what you plan to search next for an ancestor.

Why Keep a Research Log?

A research log is like a treasure map outlining your progress and documenting your search for your own family roots and stories. It can tell you what you have searched, what you found or didn't find, and save you time because you don't need to search the same source again. You can also tell your family or others what you have already searched, and help you decide on the next steps. Your family or others may want to look at the same sources as you did, so it's a quick way to provide confidence to others, and your records will be more complete. You can easily photocopy or print out a copy of your log. Don't go hunting for family history treasures without your map.

Forms and Computers Make It Easier

You can start just by writing information on paper. However, it's best to obtain a family history software program to help you keep things organized and print forms you can use to record your family information. These programs make the task of recording and organizing your information much easier. *Refer to Chapters 4 and 6 for more help.*

There are many useful forms, but the first forms of most value to you are a *Pedigree Chart, Family Group Record,* and *Research Log*.

Pedigree Chart

(Family Tree Chart) Lets you list your pedigree – your parents, grandparents, great grandparents, and so on.

Family Group Record

A tool to help you organize your research by families. Because information about an individual ancestor is most often found with information about your ancestor's siblings or parents, this form is a helpful organizational

Free Charts and Forms

You can also download family tree charts, pedigree charts, research logs, internet research logs, and other genealogy charts and forms for free on various web sites to help you record and track your research and keep your family history organized. Once you have installed a family history software program on your computer, you can print some forms using your computer program.

FamilySearch.org - www.familysearch.com. *FREE*

On the front page, in the box titled *Start Your Family History*, click on *Forms*, then scroll down to each form and click on PDF.

About.com -

http://genealogy.about.com/cs/freecharts *FREE*

Another excellent directory of free forms.

PBS Ancestors Series - www.byub.org/ancestors

You'll find fun PDF files for research questions, *FREE* source notes, and charts. Scroll down the menu at the left of the screen and click *Free Charts*.

Family Tree Magazine - *FREE*

www.familytreemagazine.com/forms/download.html

This magazine has created interesting forms that can help you access and organize your family history information.

tool. It includes room to write information found about a husband, his wife and their children.

Research Log

Helps keep track of the information you find. Include the name of the ancestor you are researching, the information you find, and the sources. This will help you remember what records you have searched and what information you found.

Look for More Information in Your Home

Look for sources in your home that might contain the missing or incomplete family

Suggested Activities

- Look at your pedigree chart and make a list of the records you need to verify the information you have gathered. You probably have some blank spots on your chart; think about what kinds of records you need to help you fill in those blanks.

- Look around your house for photographs, documents, old letters, journals, newspaper clippings, family Bibles—anything that might provide new information for your pedigree chart or verify the information you already have. Document your own life first by gathering records and information about your birth, marriage, graduation, military service, and so on. It is the same process you will eventually use to document the lives of your ancestors.

- Make copies of your original documents and organize your materials in labeled file folders. Enter any new information on your pedigree chart.

To Locate Living Relatives

Write to people with the same surname. Search the free "white page" Internet directories:

www.att.com/directory
www.switchboard.com
www.whitepages.com
www.peoplesearch.com

See also "Find Living People" on page 36.

information you're seeking. Useful sources include: birth, marriage, and death certificates, family bibles, journals, letters, photo albums, funeral programs, obituaries, wedding announcements, family registers, church records, military records, legal

> Remember that records are created because of important life events.

Research Tip

Look for two kinds of records:

■ Original (primary) records created by eyewitnesses at the time an event occurs.

■ Compiled (secondary) records created by genealogists and historians, sometimes many years after an event has occurred.

First, check compiled records because someone may have already done much of the research you are trying to do. However, when using compiled records, try to verify the information you find there by then obtaining the original records and documenting the information.

papers, newspaper clippings, etc.

Add this information to your pedigree charts and family group records. It's important to record the sources of the information. This helps you and others know where the information came from. To do this, it's easier to use the *Notes / Sources* (or citations) function on your family history software program.

Choose a Family or Ancestor You Want to Learn More About

After gathering names, dates and perhaps some stories about your family, the next step is to choose a specific ancestor, couple, or family line on which to focus your search. Look for missing or incomplete information on your pedigree chart and family records. You could choose to learn more about your grandparents, or an ancestor you were named

after. Start with the generations closest to you, and work your way back. The key here isn't who you may choose to study; just that it is a small enough project to be manageable. This is especially important if you're just starting out building your family tree. People who try to do too much all at once tend to get bogged down in details. Identify questions you want to answer about your ancestor, such as: "When and where did he die?" Select one question at a time as the objective.

> Family history is like putting together pieces of one big jigsaw puzzle with no boundary edges and an unpredictable number of pieces.

> Call relatives to find out if anyone has already compiled a partial or complete family history that might contain the record(s) you are looking for.

You can also check with local libraries, historical societies and genealogical societies to see if family histories are on file there.

Ask Relatives for Information

Make a list of relatives and the information they may have. Contact them – visit, call, write, or e-mail them. Be sure to ask specifically for the information you would like. Add the information to your pedigree charts and family group records. Record your relatives names, addresses, phone numbers, email addresses, relationship, and the date of your interview(s) in the *Notes* or *Sources* function of your family history software program.

Documenting Your Information

Citations and Sources

Information technology has been a great boon to tracing your own family roots and

The Family History Jigsaw Puzzle

People like solving puzzles. But with the family history puzzle, you have to show that new pieces actually belong to your puzzle. It's fun! The first pieces you start with are *yourself* and *your spouse*. Then, hopefully, you will have both sets of your parents (4 pieces) and grandparents (8 pieces) that have at least some records of their birth and marriage dates and places. Then find the next 16 pieces – your great grandparents – to fit next to them. If you don't put the pieces together in just the right way, then you'll never get to see the final picture. To make sure your puzzle pieces end up in the proper positions you should use pedigree charts and family group sheets to record your research data and keep track of your progress.

Is Your Family Tree Naked?

Noted genealogist Helen Leary, CG, CGL, says, publishing or sharing your genealogy without citing sources is like sending it into the world naked. You should tell others where you obtained your information. The hundreds of hours you spent putting your family history together won't be respected unless you document your sources. Sources establish credibility. Citing and documenting sources is no longer important, it is *essential*.

Citing Sources

The six elements of a good source citation include:

- Author (who provided the information)
- Title
- Publisher (including location)
- Date of the information (usually the year)
- Location of the source you used (page number, library or archive) and the call number
- Annotations: These are optional comments by you about the source. [Place your comments in square brackets.]

Consistent formatting is useful, helpful, and even required in some cases, but for now, don't get hung up on the commas and colons. Just begin citing your sources, and cite them well enough that others can understand what you searched. *(See web sites below on where to find standardized formatting styles.)*

stories today. When tracing your family it is very important that you keep track of every piece of information. Taking time to document where you got your information will save you time later in your research and help prevent duplicating the research that you or others have already done.

This is important not only as a way to verify your data, but also as a way for you and others to go back to that source when future research conflicts with your original assumption. It helps you to easily go back to your previous source to see if you may have missed information or you want more details. It's also a way to let others know on which records you based your facts, i.e. did the birth date you have for your great-grandmother come from a published family history, a tombstone, someone's memory, or a birth certificate. With your sources documented, you and others can retrieve the same data bringing credibility and traceability to your

family history.

Whether the source is a probate court record, a tombstone, an email, a website, a yellowed newspaper clipping, grandfather's diary, or a conversation with your grandmother, cite your sources. It doesn't matter if you take notes by hand, use a computer, make copies on a copier or dictate them into a recorder; you need to carefully cite your sources.

You should provide quality citations for your sources so you can remember where you found the information. This will also guide you to where to look for more information, and provide a trail for others to follow. Besides your own posterity, others with whom you share your information have the same desire and need to verify the facts which you have researched.

Here's an important point you should know about citing sources.

Citing Online Sources

When citing websites, emails, scanned image files, CD files, or other electronic media sources, the basics still apply but you must include instructions to help others find the work. Consider an annotation from you to help understand the source, i.e. [This website <www.myfamilyhistory.com> contains numerous hyper-links to other websites. On March 31, 2009, these were checked and found to be active and additional data on Jack Austin's will was found]. Whenever material in a citation is not obvious, an explanation in the annotation is appropriate. For examples of how to document these technology sources, see the referenced websites below.

Use Your Family 1

Any statement of fact, whether it is a birth date or an ancestor's surname, needs to have its own individual documented source. You should consider documentation of an information source just as important as finding and recording the information itself. Record enough information about the source, and tie it to the information in your history so someone else can retrieve it. Today's family history software will do this for you.

Cite Your Own Source

A citation must cite the source *you* used, not the one that someone told you existed in their citation. Another person's research, even cited, is hearsay until you can verify the source for yourself. For example, if a cousin tells you that she extracted your grandfather's birth information from his birth certificate, then your cousin is your source for the information, unless he/she provided you a photocopy, a scanned copy, or you actually verified his/her copy of the certificate.

EasyBib.com - www.easybib.com **FREE**

A free web tool that automatically formats citations and bibliography based on your input.

> Organizing and documenting as you go is smart because it keeps the best information at your fingertips and saves time.

Organize and Document As You Go

One of the most fundamental and important principles of family history research is to organize and document AS YOU GO! Good documentation lays the groundwork for easier correlation and evaluation of sources. If you put off documentation until later, you may never do it.

> Here's a book that is the best single source of information for documenting your family history.

Evidence Explained

This must-have book for every genealogist conveys the principles behind source citation, the formats in which citation should be cast, and the fundamentals of evidentiary analysis itself. Whatever the source of information – courthouse land records, family Bibles, cemetery markers, microfilmed census registers, unpublished manuscripts, electronic e-mail, or a videotaped family reunion – you will find multiple examples of each in this book. It offers13 concisely explained points of genealogical analysis,

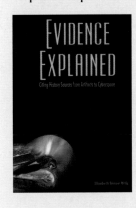

including: the distinction between direct and indirect evidence, and between quality and quantity, and the importance of custodial history. Elizabeth Shown Mills, published by Genealogical Publishing Company $49.95. www.genealogical.com

This results in information clog-ups. Failure to document starts a chain of confusion, redundant searches, missing or overlooked evidence, and uninformed linkage decisions.

Source citations should become a habitual part of all of your research. Include notes, sources, facts and complete information in the original file so that the information posted is complete and adequately documented. Not only do you want to document all of your evidence and sources, but others reading your family history may want to retrace your path as well. They may want to visit the same places, access the same web sites, documents, books or microfilm, and experience the thrill of the trail that you enjoyed.

Where do you put your notes and source citations? If you're writing a family history, citations may be embedded in parentheses within the text, shown as footnotes (at the bottom of each page) or as endnotes (at the end of a chapter or the work). If you're keeping your genealogy in a computer software program, it allows for recording your notes and sources under each individual and event. Good documentation includes:

Research Logs –

Fill in the purpose of each search, and source data on logs *before* looking at the source because repository catalogs often describe the source better than the source itself which makes your trail easier to follow. It also helps to keep track of unsuccessful searches (negative evidence). After success, list where you file the copy. Good research logs serve as a guide to all the sources on a family researched successfully or unsuccessfully. They help avoid repeated searches of the same unproductive sources. Good logs help you pick up research after a pause. They assist in evaluation by starting your thinking about a source as you describe it on the log. Research logs are also the best place to document your thinking and research strategies. Write lots of comments to yourself about your search strategies, suggestions, questions, and discrepancies you have noticed.

Family Group Records –

Compile a good family group record right at the start. Keep up-to-date with source footnotes for every event. Cite ALL the known sources for that family in footnotes tied to the events they document. Add more than just birth, marriage, and death events on the family group record. Add all events like census, military service, and migrations to the family group record. Well-documented and up-to-date family group records are the best source of ideas about where to search next. They show all the clues and background information needed to guess name variations, guess dates and places of events, and guess the most likely sources to document those events.

Photocopy Source Documents –

If the repository will allow it, *always* make a photocopy. Photocopies are better than handwritten copies because photocopies show ALL the clues, including things you would ignore if you copied by hand. Cite the footnote information in the margin on the front of the copy. This starts your thinking about and evaluation of the source. On the back of the copy write the name of the file and file number where you will store this copy.

Well-Organized Files –

Stay organized by completing paperwork and filing before starting another search. Start research on a family by preparing a new research log for the family and a well-footnoted family group record. Start each individual search by filling in part of your research log BEFORE the search. Give the date of the search, repository, purpose of the search (person and event you seek), and the source you will search. If the source does not have useful information put nil on the research log. Keep everything up-to-date. Don't start more research before doing all the paperwork and filing from the previous search.

Online Source Citations –

www.dianehacker.com/resdoc

An excellent booklet about creating source citations particularly electronic media. $9.95

About.com Citing Sources -
http://genealogy.about.com/cs/citing **FREE**

Tips on documenting your research and formats for citations, including citations for electronic genealogy sources and maps.

Why We Cite - www.ancestry.com/
learn/library/ article.aspx?article=782 **FREE**

An article on quality citations for electronic sources such as web pages, email, mailing lists, and CD-ROMs by Mark Howells.

Creating Worthwhile Genealogies - **FREE**
www.rootsweb.ancestry.com/~rwguide/lesson12.htm

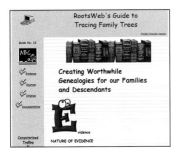

An interesting lesson on evidence, sources, documentation, and citation from RootsWeb's *Guide to Tracing Family Trees.*

Evaluate the Evidence

Family historians must also learn to weigh and evaluate evidence, especially conflicting evidence. Don't assume that if several pieces of information agree, the data must be correct. Such assumptions may lead to erroneous pedigrees which may create a dead-end to your family tree.

What is a GEDCOM?

A GEDCOM (**GE**nealogical **D**ata **COM**munications) is a type of file that takes family history information from one computer program and compresses it into a standard format which can be transferred into any other program. Importing and exporting a GEDCOM file is usually the best way to receive or send your information anywhere in the world via e-mail. You can receive from (import) or share (export) your information with other people, even if they use a different family history program. It was created by FamilySearch and The Family History Library in the mid-1980s to make it possible for people with different brands of software and computers to share their information.

To Create and Export a GEDCOM File

In most software programs, go to *File > Export to GEDCOM* and create a new file with a ".ged" file extension after the name. GEDCOM files can be uploaded to genealogy sites on the Internet, and can be adjusted for privacy and copyright concerns.

Steps to Import GEDCOM Files

When you import a GEDCOM file, all of the information from the GEDCOM file is added into your database file. To preview the data, you could import the GEDCOM file into an empty file. From there, you can correct or change information or select specific individuals and family lines to import into your actual database file. If you change information in the new file, you need to create a new GEDCOM file to import the information into your actual database.

■ From the *File* menu, select *Import.*

■ Select the drive and folder where the file is located.

■ Select the file.

■ Click *Import.*

■ Choose the import options that you want.

■ To import the file, click *OK.*

When receiving a new GEDCOM file, rather than merging the data back into your actual database file directly; always transfer it to a new, empty database file which you create.

After examining the new data, you can then import the records you wish into your primary family history database file. Even then, before you merge the new GEDCOM data, make a backup of your original database first.

GEDCOM (FamilyTree) Web Sites

There are many GEDCOM database web sites you can search for matches on names, dates, and locations; download the information; and share (or upload) your information. *Also see pages 43-45, 232.*

FamilySearch.org -
www.familysearch.org **FREE**

Ancestry.com -
www.ancestry.com **FREE** **$**

RootsWeb.com -
www.rootsweb.com **FREE**

GenServ.com -
www.genserv.com **$**

GenCircles.com -
www.gencircles.com **FREE**

One Great Family.com -
www.onegreatfamily.com **$**

MyTrees.com -
www.mytrees.com **$**

GeneaNet.org -
www.geneanet.org **FREE**

Remember to cite the specific sources *you actually used* in compiling your family history. "Source notes have two purposes: to record the specific location of each piece of data and to record details that affect the use or evaluation of that data." *(Evidence! Citation & Analysis for the Family Historian).*

If you have conflicting information, carefully examine it and sort it into either primary or secondary evidence. Primary sources are usually written records created at or near to the time of the event. Secondary sources are second-hand information that has come from some other person or record. Get as close to the original documents as you can as they are more likely to be correct. And don't blindly accept information you find in a book, CD, on the Internet, or from someone's memory.

One of the most important skills you can acquire will be learning to evaluate the accuracy of primary records and the relative reliability of secondary sources. Remember that most of the family history information you discover online is from a secondary source. You should consider it a *clue* to check out.

Find Living People

DirectoryAssistance Plus - **FREE**
www.daplus.us

Offers white and yellow pages, phone, area code, zip code and address searches for U.S. and Canada.

411 Info - www.411.info **FREE**

America's local search engine and reverse phone lookup service.

People Finder - **FREE**
www.yourfamily.com/people_finder.html

They have a Genealogy Message Board, a Lost Family Bulletin Board, Tips to Finding Missing People, plus links to other people-finder websites.

Infobel International -
http://infobel.com/world/default.asp **FREE**

The portal for international directories. Find individuals and companies worldwide in just a few clicks.

Infospace.com -
http://search.infospace.com **FREE**

Powered by metasearch technology, this web site gives you the best results from leading search engines including Google, Yahoo!, Bing, and Ask, so you find what you're looking for faster.

Numberway.com -
www.numberway.com **FREE**

Helps you find phone numbers all around the world.

20 Tips to Help Keep You on the Right Track

Some practical Do's and Don'ts

 The following suggestions may be helpful to keep you on the right track, and hopefully prevent misfortune when planting and growing your family tree. You need to be aware of some potential pitfalls (unforeseen or unexpected difficulties) when researching your family roots and stories. Here's some practical Do's and Don'ts for pulling everything together, saving you valuable time, and making your journey fun.

- **Begin with yourself** and your parents and work backwards on your pedigree, building on the supporting evidence you find, one generation at a time. Research is usually not difficult, but it does require understanding the basics. Basics are easily learned, and, with experience, productive and efficient research will become easier. Don't overwhelm yourself by taking on too much all at once. Take

Family history is a fun, exciting and rewarding hobby that will bring you great happiness! But it may also bring many sighs of disappointment. Here are some guidelines to help keep you on the right track.

baby steps. Focus on one small step at a time, like one single family, or a single surname in a particular place.

- **It is important for you to understand the difference** between building your family tree through actual research in appropriate records vs. that of merely collecting names without supporting evidence to verify that your family tree is correct. Don't assume something is correct just because someone says so, or it's in print, or on the Internet. Verify it with documented research from multiple sources (when possible) for every name, date, and place in your records.

- **Research is finding clues to lead you to records that prove relationships.** You build your case one or two facts at a time, and base continuing research on those proven facts. If the information you are working with is incorrect, then you are wasting your time. Do your research thoroughly as you go so that you can recognize your family among errors, misspellings, and various other imperfections.

Don't get sidetracked with multiple goals. Organize your overall search strategy and focus your efforts. Plan where you are going and keep track of where you have been.

1 Use YOur Family

Do NOT enter surnames (last names) in all uppercase letters into your database. Enter women using their maiden name. If you don't know their maiden name, just use their first given names, i.e. "Grandma" is not a first name. Do not use titles (Dr., Mrs., Mr., Colonel, Rev., etc.) in name fields, but you can enter suffixes like Jr., Sr., III, etc.

■ **Create a time line** of your ancestor's life listing all events in chronological order to view the whole picture. Then, log your progress. Write down supporting evidence for each event in the time line and the source of the evidence to keep you from duplicating the research. Make a *To Do* list of information you are seeking and the records that are available for the Surname or location you are searching. Start with www.familysearch.org and click on *Research Guidance* to help you locate records that may contain information about your ancestors.

■ **Realize that you will encounter spelling variations of names.** Assuming that there is only one way to spell your family name can cause you to bypass good information. Consider anything remotely close to the name you are looking for. And be alert for the use of initials and nicknames. The older the time period in which you are researching, the less consistent your ancestors were about the spelling of their surnames. Some of them may have been illiterate, and could not tell the record keeper how their names were spelled.

■ **Don't assume that "Jr" and "Sr" are father and son.** Usually they are, but sometimes they are not. They may be

uncle and nephew, grandfather and grandson, cousins, or even no relation. These are merely titles to distinguish an older man from a younger one with the same name. To add to the confusion, these titles shift as "Sr" dies and "Jr" becomes "Sr", and a younger person often becomes "Jr". Without sufficient research in official records, one can not detect these changes and identities. It only takes one misidentification to cause you to spend years researching the wrong people.

■ **Beware of compiled family data that does not support** documented names, dates, and places. Without evidence, one has nothing more than possible clues with which to try and find proof. However, even if existing Internet family trees contain likely errors, they may provide valuable clues – such as a date or place you had not known about – that can give you new ideas for searching.

■ **Always note the source of any material you copy.** Obtain copies of your proof documents as you find them. Finding information from multiple sources strengthens your case if it agrees, or indicates the need for deeper research if it disagrees. Studying the documents periodically often reveals clues previously missed.

■ You may often encounter **conflicting information** that you will have to weigh against other evidence. Try to

At times, if you feel like you're on your own in putting together your family history puzzle, remember that you're not alone. Your ancestors really are there pushing you in the right direction and cheering for you.

determine which is the most likely to be true. Periodically review and verify the conclusions you have reached concerning each of your ancestor's lives; this will help to prevent wasting time following blind alleys.

Make frequent backups of your computer disks. Consider long-term storage of all your computer information with a secure online, automatic-backup company, such as www.mozy.com or www.carbonite.com.

■ **Try not to let your organizing get behind.** Establish a filing system for your papers from the start (using file folders, 3-ring binders, and your computer) and file each page of notes, photocopy, etc. as you acquire it. It's disheartening to rummage through a high stack of unfiled papers to find that copy of a birth certificate you desperately need.

■ **Don't assume modern meanings** for terms used to describe relationships. For example, in the 17th century a step-child was often called a "son-in-law" or "daughter-in-law", and a "cousin" could refer to almost any relative except a sibling or child.

■ **Remember that indexes** to books rarely include the names of all persons mentioned in the book and, moreover, occasionally contain errors. If it appears that a book is likely to have valuable information, spend some time skimming its contents rather than returning it immediately to the shelf after a quick look at the index.

Genealogy Research Map -
www.thinkgenealogy.com/map **FREE**

A popular research map which you can download for free from Mark Tucker's blog.

■ **Collaborate with others searching the same names.** Advertise the surnames you are researching by submitting them to genealogical directories and surname lists on the Internet, such as RootsWeb Surname List at http://rsl.rootsweb.com. This will put you in touch with others who are researching the same surnames.

■ **Learn who the siblings of your ancestor were** because it can often lead to the desired information you need. Example: Perhaps a death record is not available for your grandmother, but if you have documents that prove who her siblings were, then maybe their death records might give parent information, etc. There might also be a biography about some of them that would give family background information. Knowing who the siblings and in-laws were can help sort out individuals with the same name.

■ **Pay attention to your ancestor's neighbors,** witnesses to their legal transactions (marriages, deeds, etc.), guardians or godparents of their children, and other close associates. All persons in these categories may be potential relatives of your ancestor, and investigating them can provide clues for you to work with in developing your family tree. Your ancestors were part of networks of social acquaintances, business contacts, military comrades-in-arms, extended family, in-laws, neighbors, and, of course, family members. Use those people to help you find your ancestors.

■ *Death records* usually contain parent information and various other important data. Death records usually are found in the county in which death occurred.

Examples would include death while traveling, visiting, hospitalized, in prison, etc. outside his or her county of residence. ***Probate records*** can prove family relationships that may be found nowhere else. If there was property to be distributed, probate records would be found in the person's county of residence. It's also possible that additional probate records might be found in other counties/ states where the deceased owned property.

■ **Wills don't always mention all children** of a deceased person. Often a child has already been given property and it simply does not specify that in the Will. If the gift was real estate or other personal property, then there likely would be a deed. Wills are only a small part of probate records. Much, much more can be revealed in *estate records, inventories, bills of sale, administrator bonds, order books, etc.;* all heirs are likely to be named in estate settlements. Law suits among family members often occurred and these can be a goldmine of factual information on which to build. Knowing the names of siblings and in-laws helps you to recognize key people in the indexes. Develop your family group sheets so the information will be handy.

■ **Don't assume that family stories are completely true;** often there is partial truth in them but details have become distorted through the years. A common one might be "great-great grandma was an Indian". Someone may have said "she looked like an Indian", or, "she might have been an Indian", or "she lived near Indians". Always seek out official records that can prove or disprove components of the story.

When you trace your ancestors back to a foreign country, the records will be different but the process is the same.

■ **Don't assume that children** in a pre-1880 census household (when relationships were stated) are children of the head of the household: They may or may not be. They may be nieces, nephews, step-children, grandchildren, or no relation. Study the ages and birthplaces of all household members. Other year's census records, probate, guardianships, deeds, etc. may help identify relationships and reveal the true children of the head of household. Understanding these relationships can be crucial to building your family tree and can unlock pieces of the puzzle. Census records through 1840 can be very helpful when analyzed with other records, but they can also be misleading if you insist on "accounting" for everyone; various circumstances affected household members.

The Greatest Happiness

Gordon B. Hinckley
© by Intellectual Reserve, Inc.

"God is the designer of the family. He intended that the greatest of happiness, the most satisfying aspects of life, the deepest joys should come in our associations together and our concerns one for another as fathers and mothers and children". Gordon B. Hinckley (1910-2008), American religious leader

Footprints On the Sands of Time

Henry David Thoreau

"The lives of great men all remind us we can make our lives sublime and departing leave behind us footprints on the sands of time." Henry David Thoreau, (1817-1862) American writer, philosopher and naturalist

CHAPTER 2

3-Easy Steps
Follow These 3-Easy Steps to Begin Building Your Family Tree and Connect to Your Ancestors

STEP 2 – Add New Branches to Your Family Tree Using the Internet

Computers, technology, and the Internet have revolutionized the way we do family history and genealogy today. We can search farther and faster than ever before, and we can record everything we find with just a few keystrokes. Computers allow us to discover, store, access, and share family history information with speed and convenience.

The Internet is an excellent and powerful tool for you to gather your family history information and share it with others. It's made up of millions of sites which are just files stored on computers around the world. Each site can contain any number of associated pages – each of which has an unique electronic address, i.e. *about.com.* It's estimated that more than two million separate web sites are devoted to genealogy / family history.

INSIDE THIS CHAPTER:

2 Add New Branches

Suggested Activities

1. Enter all of the family information you've gathered–including info from your relatives–into your family history program; learn the basics of your software program.

2. Search for your ancestors using existing family tree web sites described herein, and discover the wealth of information available.

3. Import any new information into your family history database.

Family History Insights - 2

Richard G. Scott
© by Intellectual Reserve, Inc.

Decide to Do Something Significant

"Set aside those things that don't really matter in your life. Decide to do something that will have eternal consequences. Perhaps you have been prompted to look for ancestors but feel that you are not a genealogist. Can you see that you don't have to be anymore? It all begins with love and a sincere desire. ... This is...a monumental effort of cooperation on both sides of the veil where help is given in both directions. It begins with love. Anywhere you are in the world, with prayer, faith, determination, diligence, and some sacrifice, you can make a powerful contribution. Begin now. I promise you that the Lord will help you find a way. And it will make you feel wonderful." Richard Scott

Barack Obama, President

Our Journey Continued

"... greatness is never a given. It must be earned. Our journey has never been one of short-cuts or settling for less.... Rather, it has been...men and women... who have carried us up the long, rugged path towards prosperity and freedom. For us, they packed up their few worldly possessions and traveled across oceans in search of a new life. For us, they toiled in sweatshops and settled the West; endured the lash of the whip and plowed the hard earth. For us, they fought and died.... Time and again these men and women struggled and sacrificed and worked till their hands were raw so that we might live a better life. ... This is the journey we continue today." Barack Obama, Presidential Inaugural Address, Jan. 20, 2009

Creating Memories

"Each day of our lives we make deposits in the memory banks of our children." Charles R. Swindol, pastor of the First Evangelical Free Church of Fullerton, California (1971-1994); radio host for *Insight for Living;* www.oneplace.com

George Santayana

Nature's Masterpiece

"The family is one of nature's masterpieces." "Those who cannot remember the past are condemned to repeat it." George Santayana (1863-1952), Philosopher & poet.

Tend Your Roots

A family tree can wither if nobody tends it's roots. Unknown

J. Fielding Smith
© by Intellectual Reserve, Inc.

Become Acquainted with Ancestors

"It doesn't matter whether your computer is able to compile all the family group sheets for everyone that every lived on the earth, it remains the responsibility of each individual to know his kindred dead…[it is] each person's responsibility to study and become acquainted with his ancestors." J. Fielding Smith

Lemons and Bad Apples

Any family tree produces lemons, nuts, and a few bad apples. Unknown

A Tree Without Roots

"To forget one's ancestors is to be a brook without a source, a tree without a root."   – Chinese Proverb

Digging in Dirt/Facts

The difference between a geologist and a genealogist is that one digs in the dirt and sometimes finds artifacts, while the other digs in facts and sometimes finds dirt. – Unknown

STEP 2 - Add New Branches to Your Family Tree Using the Internet

SEE IF SOMEONE HAS ALREADY FOUND INFO ON YOUR ANCESTORS

When you're tracing your family roots and stories, why re-plow a field that has already been plowed? You are most likely not the only—or the first—person searching for and building your family tree. So see if someone has already found information on your ancestors. You can save yourself hours of work, verify information that you already know, make connections between generations, and help you determine which ancestors to search for. Most web sites allow free searches, but some may require a fee or just registration. If you don't have a computer or an Internet connection at home, you can use one at a Family History Center, or your local library or university.

Some of the most useful websites offer invaluable databases of existing family trees, vital information and transcribed census records, such as *FamilySearch.org* and *Ancestry.com;* others are collections of links to other sites, such as *Cyndi'sList.com* and *Linkpendium.com;* some are more specific with genealogies from people or about a specific group of people, such as *GenServ.com* and *AfriGeneas.com;* others offer useful data such as land records, like *The Bureau of Land Management (BLM.gov),* and some specifically help you to learn how to do family history, such as *DearMYRTLE.com* and *Genealogy.About.com.*

We are living in exciting times because old records are being indexed to electronic formats at an ever increasing rate. This is changing family history dramatically. An enormous number of old records still exist which are very difficult to research right now because they have not been digitized, but sometime in the future essentially all old records will be converted to electronic formats. This means that we will most likely be able to connect with ancestors and solve family history problems in the near future that may still be very difficult today.

First, Search Existing Family Trees Online

There are many wonderful web sites with existing family tree databases to help you determine if someone has already found information on your ancestor. Here's the best of the Internet; they may also serve as web links to the entire Internet to help you find other family history web sites. *See also page 232 for more details.*

FamilySearch.org - www.familysearch.org

Free family history, family tree, genealogy records and resources from around the world. A web site that provides access to the world's largest collection of free family history information all in one place—from U.S. census data to the parish records of tiny European villages. It's a powerful computer software system to help you learn about your ancestors. You can do significant research online and also discover what records you need to search to

This symbol indicates a "Best of the Internet" website; a key website to make family history easier and save you valuable time.

find your ancestors in record-breaking time. It provides easy access for the gathering and sharing of family history information. *FamilySearch* provides access to these family tree databases: Pedigree Resource File, Ancestral File, International Genealogical Index, and Record Search (pilot). In addition, it offers a free copy of PAF *(Personal Ancestral File)*, a family history software program that allows you to record and publish your family history. *See information on "New FamilySearch" in Chapter 4.*

See information on "New FamilySearch" in Chapter 4.

2 Add New Branches

Ancestry World Tree -
www.ancestry.com/trees/awt **FREE**

Rootsweb WorldConnect - **FREE**
http://wc.rootsweb.ancestry.com

Ancestry World Tree and Rootsweb WorldConnect are free collections of user-submitted GEDCOMs (family trees). You can access World Tree and World Connect from two different websites, but either way, it is the same program and the same set of trees. The database contains more than 480 million names in family trees submitted by users. This is a leading provider of private Web sites for connecting families, with over 1.25 million paid subscriptions and more than 10 million people using its Web resources every month. The Ancestry.com network includes *MyFamily.com, Ancestry.com, Genealogy.com,* and RootsWeb.com providing both free and paid subscription.

Ancestry has thousands of family trees in different databases. They can help you identify how ancestors are related and give you clues about birth, marriage, and death information. You can expect to find names, ages, places, dates, family relationships, and more. You can also often find contact information for someone researching the same name. Family trees are an excellent resource for filling in gaps in your research or are great starting points for beginning your research. It is always good to find out what others have already learned and compiled about your ancestors.

Many who have built family trees on the Ancestry.com Web site have been frustrated about not being able to export or download their family tree (including images, documents, historical records, etc.) to their computer.

How to Export Your Family Tree from Ancestry.com

To download a family tree from Ancestry.com online family trees, you must be the owner of that tree. Open the Family Tree Pedigree View of your tree on Ancestry.com. Just above the dark green header, on the right side, click on the link for "Tree Settings" and you see your "Tree Info". On the right side is a section for "Export your tree"; click on the light green button for "Export tree", and Ancestry will prepare your GEDCOM file for downloading to your computer. If you want to save your file to your desktop or a file folder on your computer, click "Save". You can import the GEDCOM file into your own database later using your family history software.

OneWorldTree - 192 million, last updated Apr 2004

It takes family trees submitted by Ancestry members and "stitches" them together with family trees and historical records from other sources. It identifies probable name matches between these sources and displays consolidated results in a worldwide family tree that can help you with your family history research.

Private Member Trees - 162 million, updated Regularly

This database contains family trees submitted to Ancestry by users who have indicated that their tree can only be viewed by Ancestry members to whom they have granted permission to see their tree. These trees can change over time as users edit, remove, or otherwise modify the data in their trees. If you would like to view one of these trees in its entirety, you can contact the owner of the tree to request permission to see the tree.

To use these comprehensive Web sites and indexes, think about what you know about a specific ancestor or surname and then look in the appropriate categories.

Research Tip

If you are trying to find information on a Quaker couple married in Virginia in 1766, you could look in categories for marriages, Virginia, Quakers, or Colonial records. They can also help locate information about an ancestor's culture, traditions, homeland, and history.

Public Member Trees - 586 million, updated regularly

This database contains family trees submitted to Ancestry by users who have indicated that their tree can be viewed by all Ancestry members. These trees can change over time as users edit, remove, or otherwise modify the data in their trees. You can contact the owner of the tree to get more information.

Millennium File - 880k, last updated Apr 2005

A database created by the Institute of Family Research that contains linked family records with lineages from throughout the world, including colonial America, the British Isles, Switzerland, and Germany. Many of these lineages extend back to nobility and renowned historical figures. A good way to have success in using this database is identify at least one Gateway Ancestor, an early American immigrant who has been identified as having roots in British or European nobility. In this database there are about 300 individuals who have proven ties to nobility or royalty. Source information is also provided making it easier to verify the accuracy of the research done.

GenCircles Global Tree - FREE
www.gencircles.com/globaltree

A popular place for searching and submitting family trees. Surnames from over 90 million ancestors can be searched for free, and if you've submitted your own GEDCOM

file you can use their "matching technology" to pair the people in your pedigree with those already on file. They allow you to interact with your data and with other researchers in new ways, such as, posting messages on your file and on individuals i n your file. The integrity of your data will not be compromised in any way and you can delete these messages at any time. By doing this, you can have others immediately interacting with you.

One Great Family.com - $
www.onegreatfamily.com

A family history program that allows everyone to combine their knowledge and data to build one huge, shared database. Using sophisticated, patented technology, OneGreatFamily is linking all of the family trees together into one shared, worldwide database with shared multimedia, notes, research, biographies and citations. The idea is to leverage the effort and research of all users rather than duplicating research that others have already done. They have about 200 million ancestors worldwide. 7-day free trial. $9.95/month.

MyTrees.com - www.mytrees.com $

Contains a pedigree-linked database with over 370 million names, share your family tree worldwide, build your own family tree on-line, and store family history pictures online for display with your family tree. $7/10 days.

Family Tree Searcher.com - FREE
www.familytreesearcher.com

Enter your ancestor information just once to search existing family trees at nine online family tree databases. This free service creates the best family tree searches based on your ancestry. They also include hints for searching your family tree.

See more info on family trees on page 232.

See more info on family trees on page 232.

Search for a Family History That has Been Published

Family histories are books that give genealogical information about one or more generations of a particular family. Libraries and genealogical societies have been collecting published family histories for years. You can often find family histories in libraries in the area where your ancestors lived. Your family's stories might be among them. Compiled stories and histories can be an amazing source of information about the lives of your ancestors. They provide stories and interesting information that help you really connect with your ancestors. They are usually very well-researched for tracing your family roots; however, you still need to verify that the information is accurate and documented.

FamilySearch Published Histories - **FREE**

www.familysearch.org > *Search Records* > *Historical Books*
www.familysearch.org > *Library* > *Library Catalog* > *Surname Search*

The Family History Library has an extensive collection of published family histories and is digitizing more everyday—even faster. The effort targets published family, society, county, and town histories, as well as numerous other historical publications that are digitally preserved and made accessible for free online. FamilySearch has nearly a million publications in its famous library, and there are millions of similar publications elsewhere in the United States. Working with volunteers and select affiliate libraries, it plans to create the largest digital collection of published histories on the Web. It is helping to digitize and publish collections from the Allen County Public Library, Houston Public Library, and Mid-Continent Public Library Midwest Genealogy Center in Independence, Missouri. When all is said and done, there will be over a

> Another way to find out about your family tree and connect with others who may be doing the same research as you is to visit free *message boards and forums.*

Message Boards

You can post surname queries, ask questions, or just network with fellow genealogists. They allow people with common interests to "meet" and share their information. They cover a wide range of topics—surnames, localities, adoptions, occupations, etc. You may find a group devoted to your family name or a particular locale where one of your ancestors lived. If you find someone that you would like to contact, send them an e-mail. Go to these web sites:

Ancestry / Rootsweb - **FREE**
http://boards.ancestry.com
(Over 161,000 different boards)

GenForum - http://genforum.genealogy.com
(Over 14,000 online forums) **FREE**

About Genealogy -
http://genealogy.about.com/cs/surnamequery
(One of the most active) **FREE**

Cyndi's List Queries -
www.cyndislist.com/queries.htm **FREE**
(Links to web sites)

BBC - www.bbc.co.uk/messageboards
(Popular collection of UK-based
message boards) **FREE**

GenSource Common Threads - **FREE**
www.gensource.com (To find others
researching your family name)

Where to Search Chart (Types of Records)

OBJECTIVE	RECORD TYPES	
To obtain information about the following...	Look in the Family History Library Catalog, Locality and Subject sections for these type of records...	
	First look for:	**Then look for:**
Age	Census, Vital Records, Cemeteries	Military Records, Taxation, Obituaries
Birth date	Vital Records, Church Records, Bible Records	Cemeteries, Obituaries, Census, Newspapers, Military Records
Birthplace	Vital Records, Church Records, Census	Newspapers, Obituaries, Military Records
City or parish of foreign birth	Church Records, Genealogy, Biography, Obituaries, Naturalization & Citizenship	Emigration and Immigration, Vital Records*, History
Country of foreign birth	Census, Emigration and Immigration, Naturalization and Citizenship, Vital Records*	Military Records, Church Records, Newspapers, Obituaries
County origins & boundaries	History, Maps	Gazetteers
Death	Vital Records, Cemeteries, Probate Records, Church Records, Obituaries	Newspapers, Military Records, Court Records, Land and Property
Divorce	Court Records, Divorce Records	Newspapers, Vital Records*
Ethnicity	Minorities, Native Races, Societies	Church Records, Emigration and Immigration, Naturalization and Citizenship
Historical background	History, Periodicals, Genealogy	Church History, Minorities
Immigration	Emigration & Immigration, Naturalization & Citizenship, Genealogy	Census, Biography, Newspapers, Church Records
Maiden	Vital Records, Church Records, Newspapers, Bible Records	Military Records, Cemeteries, Probate Records, Obituaries
Marriage	Vital Records, Church Records, Census, Newspapers, Bible Records	Biography, Genealogy, Military Records, Probate Records, Land and Property, Nobility
Occupation	Census, Directories, Emigration and Immigration, Civil Registration, Occupations, Probate Records	Newspapers, Court Records, Obituaries, Officials and Employees
Parents, children, & other family members	Vital Records, Church Records, Census, Probate Records, Obituaries	Bible Records, Newspapers, Emigration and Immigration, Land and Property
Physical description	Military Records, Biography, Court Records	Naturalization, Civil Registration, Church Records, Emigration & Immigration, Genealogy, Newspapers
Place-finding aids	Gazetteers, Maps	Directories, History, Periodicals, Land & Property, Taxation
Place of residence when you know only the state	Census, Genealogy, Military Records, Vital Records, Church Records, Directories	Biography, Probate Records, History, Land and Property, Taxation
Places family has lived	Census, Land and Property, History	Military Records, Taxation, Obituaries
Previous research	Genealogy, Periodicals, History	Biography, Societies, Nobility
Record-finding aids	Archives and Libraries, Societies, Genealogy	Periodicals
Religion	Church Records, History, Biography, Civil Reg.	Bible Records, Cemeteries, Obituaries, Genealogy

2 Add New Branches

What is a Family History Center?

Typical Family History Center

Family History Centers (FHC) are local branches of the Family History Library located in Salt Lake City, Utah, and there are some 4,600 centers worldwide. The library houses a collection of genealogical records that includes the names of more than 3 billion deceased people. It is the largest collection of its kind in the world, including: vital records (birth, marriage, and death records from both government and church sources); census returns; court, property, and probate records; cemetery records; emigration and immigration lists; printed genealogies; and family and county histories.

Since many people are not able to travel to Salt Lake City to use the library, local Family History Centers make the library's resources accessible to those interested in finding their family roots. They enable you to research the vast holdings of the library including its computerized indexes. Family History Centers provide FREE access to top important websites, such as:

Footnote.com

Godfrey Memorial Library (Godfrey.org)

FamilySearch.org

WorldVitalRecords.com

KindredKonnections.com (My Trees.com)

HeritageQuestOnline.com (available in 1400 FHC in No. America)

Ancestry.com (Regional centers only)

Family History Centers also provide access to the vast family history records via the Internet, and most of the *microfilms* (a roll of film that contains reduced photographic images of various records) and *microfiche* (rectangular sheets of microfilm on which information is arranged in rows and columns) in the library to help you identify your ancestors.

Millions of records are stored on microfilms and microfiche. You can order microfilms and microfiche to view at your local Family History Center. The vast records available on microfilm and microfiche are currently being scanned and indexed and you can search the records online that are completed so far at www.family-search.org > Search Records > Record Search. Join thousands of volunteers around the world who are helping to make more free records available online through www.FamilySearchIndexing.org.

Everyone is welcome at a Family History Center at no cost to use their resources. Most of them are maintained in meetinghouses of The Church of Jesus Christ of Latter-day Saints (Mormon). When you want to look at actual records of the people you are researching, you can visit the Family History Center nearest you and order copies of the records from the main library in Salt Lake City. They provide friendly, knowledgeable volunteers at the centers to assist you without cost or obligation. To locate the nearest family history center, click on: www.familysearch.org, then click on: *Find a Family*

million publications in the digital collection online. It will be the largest free resource of its kind. You can also search the library catalog for histories by clicking on *Library > Library Catalog.* First, do a *Surname Search* in the catalog, then search for records from the place where your ancestor lived.

When you find existing family trees online, published family histories, or information on message boards, you need to evaluate the information to determine if it is reliable and accurate.

Suggested Activities

- Search for an ancestor using existing family trees on a comprehensive web site.
- Download the information you've found to your computer, import into your database, and synchronize the new information with your existing database records.
- Then, print a new pedigree chart for your review

Do I Need An E-Mail Address?

Q. I do not have e-mail or Internet access at home, but I would like to register on the Internet with various family history websites. They tell me I have to have an e-mail address to register. What can I do?

A. You must have an e-mail address in order to register with family history websites. There are several providers who offer free e-mail addresses that you can set up and access from a computer at a Family History Center, your library, or a university. These providers can be found by searching the phrase "free e-mail" in an online search engine (see *Search Engines* below).

Research Tip

Just because the information is printed in a book or available on the Web doesn't necessarily mean that it is factual. Work to organize, document, and verify your information as you go.

Ancestry.com - www.ancestry.com > *Search > Stories, Memories, Histories* **FREE**

Selected histories that profile families from all fifty U.S. states, Canada, and the British Isles going back to the 1700s.

Library of Congress - www.loc.gov/rr/genealogy

One of the world's premier collections of U.S. and foreign genealogical and local historical publications. **FREE**

WorldCat - www.oclc.org > *WorldCat* **FREE**

Online Computer Library Center (OCLC) hosts WorldCat, the window to the world's libraries. WorldCat is a global network of library content and services that uses the Web to let you be more connected.

Cyndi's List.com - **FREE**
www.cyndislist.com/lib-state.htm

Extensive Web links to state libraries, archives, genealogical and historical societies.

HeritageQuestOnline.com - **FREE**
www.heritagequestonline.com > *Search Books*

Find information on people and places in over 23,000 family and local histories. You can't access this website yourself, but you can through your local library. If your library subscribes, you can use your library card at home to access the Web site.

BYU Published Family Histories - **FREE**
www.lib.byu.edu/fslab

The BYU Family History Archive is a collection of published genealogy and family history books. The archive includes histories of families, county and local histories, how-to books on genealogy, genealogy magazines and periodicals (including some international), medieval books (including histories and pedigrees), and gazetteers. It also includes some specialized collections.

Google.com Books - **FREE**
www.books.google.com

Right now, you can search the *full text of some 7 million books,* including genealogy and family history books, through Google Book Search. The books come from two sources. *The Library Project:* they've partnered with renowned libraries around the world to include their collections. For books that are out of copyright, you can read and download the entire book.

Research Tip
Use the Family History Library's free Research Guidance for the state/county where your ancestors came from. It gets you quickly oriented to what's available to help you.

For books that are still in copyright, however, the results are like a card catalog; they show you info about the book and, generally, a few snippets of text showing your search term in context. *The Partner Program:* they've partnered with over 20,000 publishers and authors to make their books discoverable on Google. Right now, you can flip through a few preview pages of these books, just like you'd browse them at a bookstore or library. You'll also see links to libraries and bookstores where you can borrow or buy the book.

1000 Years of Family History - **FREE**
www.broughfamily.org/family_history_video.html

The Richard Brough Family Organization (one of the largest and oldest ancestral family organizations in the world) freely released worldwide a 37-minute high-quality video documentary which details the Brough ancestry of England and their descendants in Europe, America and Australia. It describes nearly a thousand years of history related to a well-known family surname in England. It also describes how genealogical research and recent DNA tests have been used to clarify family relationships and better understand family traditions.

How to Use the Online Family History Library Catalog

The Family History Library Catalog™ describes the books, microfilms, and microfiche in the Family History Library in Salt Lake City. The library houses a collection of genealogical records that includes the names of more than 3 billion deceased people from throughout the world. It is the largest collection of its kind in the world, including: vital records (birth, marriage, and death records from both government and church sources); census returns; court, property, and probate records; cemetery records; emigration and immigration lists; printed genealogies; and family and county histories.

When you want to look at actual records of the people you are researching, you can visit the Family History Center nearest you and order copies of the records from the main library in Salt Lake City. To locate the nearest family history center, click on *familysearch.org,* then *Find a Family History Center,* or you may call 800-346-6044 in the United States and Canada.

SEARCH OTHER RECORDS FOR MISSING INFORMATION

Search Engines

Use "search engines" to see if someone has posted information on the Internet about your ancestors and descendants of your ancestors. You may find family Web sites, pedigree charts, personal histories, cemetery records, etc. The good thing about using a search engine to find missing information is that they will typically search millions of Web pages within seconds. The bad thing is that they will search millions of Web pages. The sheer number of results can be overwhelming.

Generally, searching information on the Internet using a search engine requires a little finesse. For example, searching the term *'genealogy'* using Google.com or Yahoo.com will result in about

Using the Family History Library Catalog

Go to www.FamilySearch.org

- Click the *Library* tab > *Library Catalog.*
- Search in the catalog for your surname and various places that your ancestors lived, looking for information that might be relevant to your research. Choose from the various searches including:

Place - To locate records for a certain place such as city, county, state, etc. Search either by town/city, county, state/country. Each jurisdiction has different records available, so it is important to search all jurisdictions for your area (i.e. both the city and county records). Click *Film Notes* to see the microfilm number.

Surname - To locate family histories which include that surname. A list of family histories with that surname will be shown. Click on a title to see the detailed information. Review the

notes to decide if this history is one that would include your ancestor. Click View Film Notes to see the microfilm number for this record.

Keyword Search - To find catalog entries about records that contain a certain word or phrase. You can use this to search for keywords in titles, authors, places, series and subjects.

Title Search - To find catalog entries about records that contain a certain word or combination of words in the title.

Film/Fiche Search - To find the titles of items on a specific microfilm or microfiche in the Catalog.

Author Search - To find the author details record for a person, church, society, government agency, and so forth identified as an author of a specific reference. It lists titles linked to the author and may include notes and references.

Call Number Search - To find an item by its call number (the number used to locate items on the shelves in the Library).

Search Engines

A Web search engine is designed to search for information on the World Wide Web. Information may consist of web pages, images and other types of files. Some search engines also mine data available in newsbooks, databases, or open directories. You can use a search engine to find many helpful sites. Some of the major search engines include:

Google.com - This is currently the most popular and the one to beat: bigger, deeper, faster, more relevant and richer in features than all the other search engines. It enables users to search the Web, Usenet, and images. Features include PageRank, caching and translation of results, and an option to find similar pages.

Yahoo.com - The first Web directory and still one of the most popular search sites on the Internet. Features: personalized content and search options, chatrooms, free e-mail, clubs, and pager. It has become a true portal and content site.

Dogpile.com - Puts the power of all the leading search engines together in one search box to deliver combined results. The process is more efficient and may yield more relevant results.

Live.com - The fourth most used search engine offers some innovative features, such as the ability to view additional search results on the same web page and the ability to dynamically adjust the amount of information displayed for each search-result.

Ask.com - Provides relevant search results by identifying the most authoritative sites on the Web. It goes beyond mere link popularity (based on the sheer volume of links pointing to a particular page) to determine popularity among pages considered to be experts on the topic of your search.

Bing.com - A new search engine from Microsoft that finds and organizes the answers you need so you can make faster, more informed decisions. They took a new approach and added a powerful set of intuitive tools on top of a world class search service. They included features that deliver the best results, presented in an organized way to simplify key tasks and help you make important decisions faster. www.Bing-Vs-Google.com is a web page that allows you to conduct two searches at once: one on Google and another on Bing with a split screen.

160 million hits. Obviously, this is overwhelming and far too many to handle, so before you begin searching for information you need to be very specific about what information you are searching for. Also, understanding that some web sites are *databases* of information, while others are *directories* that will lead you to other useful web sites will help you to find the information you seek.

Using search engines and finding information and resources need not be complicated—all you need is to unleash the simplest math you know

Family History Library, Salt Lake City, UT

of to help you get the results you want. How do you do that? You *add, subtract* and *multiply* to do better searches. One of the best ways to focus your search is to use the add or plus symbol (+) and/or the subtract or minus symbol (-) to let the search engine find only the pertinent pages relating to your search. You multiply by using the quotation symbols (" ").

Beginning each keyword with a plus (+) symbol tells the search engine to find pages

How To use Free Research Guidance

© by Intellectual Reserve, Inc.

- Go to www.familysearch.org
- Click Research Helps > Guidance on the top bar
- Notice the Research Assistant on the left side bar. She will tell you what to do for each step. Read what she has to say and then select a place.
- Follow the Research Assistant's instructions and select an event and date range.
- You will then be given your "Search Strategy." Again, follow the instructions of the Research Assistant and choose a record.
- Continue through this site, reading and following the instructions from the Research Assistant. Use your Search Strategy as your "homepage" for this site, and make use of the many links available.

Free Research Guides and Outlines

The Family History Library has developed many comprehensive brochures and guides about researching ancestors around the world. The **Research Guides** describe how to use a particular source of family history information, and **Research Outlines** describe the records and strategies that can be used to pursue family history research in a specific geographic location or particular type of record. They are invaluable to help find your family roots, and you can access them online and download for FREE at *FamilySearch.org > Research Helps > Guidance > Document Type.* Click on PDF under each desired title to view or print the document.

Consider starting with the one titled, ***Tracing Immigrant Origins,*** a 49-page outline of tips, procedures, and strategies. Using the above described navigation, click on *Research Outline* and scroll down to *Tracing Immigrant Origins.* You can review the *Table of Contents* and click on the subject you want.

that include all of the words that you enter, not just some of them. For example, if you are looking for the surname GATES, Google brings up over 92 million pages which match your search request. But if you were really looking for information on Bill Gates, typing in +bill +gates narrows the results considerably (by 60 million pages) because you only want pages that contain both names.

Moreover, including the minus (-) symbol allows you to search for pages that exclude specific words or phrases. For example, typing (-fences -BBQ -robert -scholarship) excludes all pages with information on "gates and fences, Gates BBQ equipment, Robert Gates, and Gates scholarships". Another example, if you're searching the surname RICE, but want to exclude all the pages relating to food and cooking you type *rice -food -cook -recipe.*

Using the quotation symbols (" ") allows you to find results containing the exact phrase you specify, i.e. "hans larsen quaker" +1776.

Google Your Family Tree -
www.GoogleYourFamilyTree.com

Dan Lynch

This new book by Dan Lynch is written in a friendly, informative, and non-technical way, but still conveys the depth of power contained within each major part of the Google service. If you have ever used Google (or any Internet search engine) and experienced frustration with millions of listings resulting from your query, you are about to discover a true breakthrough. He dissects more than one hundred powerful commands and features of Google, but maintains a focus on how they can be used specifically to conduct family history research. It teaches you about many of the other capabilities of Google including: Language Tools, Google Books, Google News Archives, Google Images and Videos, Google Alerts and Google Maps. It includes special tips for finding people, places, and even filters for searching through different time periods. $34.95

Using Free Research Guidance, Research **FREE** Outlines, & Research Guides

When you're online in *FamilySearch.org,* click on *Research Helps > Guidance* on the top bar on the front page. This unique feature guides you in finding copies of original records, such as censuses

and birth records, based on where the person lived and the time of his or her birth, marriage, or death. You select the place and time, and Research Guidance provides a list of recommended things to do and records to search in priority order.

Research Guidance is designed to help you develop a "search strategy" for your research. Once you have provided a place, event and time period, you will be given a list of records to search, in a recommended searching order. Each record will give step-by-step instructions, tips, descriptions and addresses or web links to lead you directly to that record. There are many links on this site so do not get frustrated if you get lost. Always go back to your search strategy.

Many forms and guides are available in *Research Helps > Articles* which help you plan, record, and analyze your research. You can download and print these free forms and guides.

Census Records

A Snapshot of History
Building Blocks of Your Research

The census has proven to be a great resource for family historians. There are few other records that help you track your ancestors throughout their lifetime. Census records can place entire families at a specific point in time, help establish family relationships, and are one of the best sources to explore. You may want to consider starting with the Federal Census records—especially those since 1850—because they provide the best information. There is a 72-year privacy cap on census and military records so the records that are now available for research span the years 1790-1930; the census is taken every ten years.

From 1790 to 1840, the census takers asked few questions, thus limiting the value these records have for us today. Starting in 1850, however, more information was gathered by the census takers. For example, enumerators listed the names, ages, and gender for all persons living in the house, whereas prior censuses only listed the heads of household.

One of the basics of family history research is to start with yourself and work backward in time, moving from the known to the unknown. So start your search with the most current 1930 census. *See the comparison charts on page 58-59 for more information.*

Census Tutorial - http://census.byu.edu **FREE**

Designed to help individuals with little or no previous census research experience to learn how to effectively search and utilize the U.S. Federal Census schedules.

Key Tips for Census Success -
www.lostcousins.com > Help & Advice **FREE**
(in left column)

Here's a web site with an excellent article on census tips.

AccessGenealogy - www.accessgenealogy.com

A free search center that offers links for searching many different types of records, such as census reports, newspapers, periodicals, emigration and immigration forms, vital records, voting records, military records, Native American genealogy, library archives, cemeteries, churches, and courts; plus Native American and African American essentials. It includes tons of links to other web sites. **FREE**

Top 10 Search Tips for Census -
http://genealogy.about.com/od/census/a/census_search.htm

Kimberly Powell has compiled some good census search tips that you need to read.

One of the most well-known uses of Soundex indexes is for some of the federal censuses of the US.

Searching Census Records

Not all of our ancestors appear in Soundex indexes because they could have been overlooked or misread by the Soundex indexer, or the enumerator may have misspelled the person's name so badly that the Soundex was thrown off. These old microfilm indexes have been largely replaced today by online search engines. Although census records exist in Europe, Africa, Asia, and Latin America, they generally do not have indexes as do US census records.

Add New **2** Branches

Census Web Sites

Ancestry.com - www.ancestry.com >
U.S. Census Collection (scroll down)

This site offers the most census information available online – a Herculean effort that took a team of experts and workers a combined 6.6 million hours of labor. The information details more than just names or population numbers. It includes people's moves across the country, their race, marital status, assets, residence, schooling and other personal information. U.S. census records available at this time include: 1790, 1800, 1810, 1820, 1830, 1840, 1850 (including slave schedules), 1860 (including slave schedules), 1870, 1880, 1890 (fragment, census substitute, and veteran's schedules), 1900, 1910, 1920, 1930. Canadian census records are available at www.ancestry.ca and include the schedules for 1851, 1871, 1891, 1901, 1906, 1911 and 1916. Preview available for free, but you must subscribe to see any details. $19.95/month. Free at some Family History Centers.

FamilySearch Record Search -
www.familysearch.org > *Search Records* >
Record Search pilot

FamilySearch provides free family history, family tree, and genealogy records and resources from around the world, including census records. Many new and updated census records are becoming available regularly with increasing frequency with many on-going indexing projects by 170,000 volunteers, and are now currently available to search on the new Record Search pilot. In addition to census records, you can also search other worldwide record collections (birth, death, marriage, pension, church, tax, military, baptism, christening, burial, funeral, and civil registration records) currently in process of being indexed. Millions of new records are being added every month. You can join thousands of volunteers around the world who are helping to make more free records available online. Find out more at www.familysearchindexing.org.

HeritageQuestOnline.com -
www.heritagequestonline.com

Contains U.S. Census indexes and images, but only indexes "Head of Household". It is available free through your local library if they subscribe (you can log-on at home) with your library card, free at some Family History Centers.

World Vital Records.com -
www.worldvitalrecords.com

Various census images and transcriptions from 1790-1930. Free at Family History Centers. $5.95/month

Find My Past.com - www.findmypast.com

1841, 1851, 1861, 1871, 1881, 1891, 1901 and 1911 UK Censuses. It's free to search but to view the original images requires you to be a paying member. 1841 and 1861 Censuses are free at www.FamilySearch.org > *Search Records* > *Record Search pilot.* £14.95/month (about $23)

Footnote.com - www.footnote.com

Explore and search the new interactive 1860 and 1930 US Federal Censuses, and leave a

comment, photograph, story, or a document on a person's record. Free at Family History Centers. $11.95/month

Census Online.com - www.census-online.com

Guide to online census records with over 45,000 web links. **FREE**

Genealogy.com - www.genealogy.com/genealogy/uscensustxt_popup.html **FREE**

Detailed introductory summary of each U.S. Census

U.S. Census Bureau.gov - www.census.gov **FREE**

Census dates for countries and areas of the world: 1946 to 2004. Shows the dates of census enumerations over the past half century, as well as projected or scheduled enumerations in the near future for countries around the world.

Census Links.com - www.censuslinks.com **FREE**

Non-commercial directory of international census transcriptions published on the Internet.

2 Add New Branches

Many new and updated census records are becoming available regularly with increasing frequency due to on-going indexing projects, and are now available mostly on FamilySearch.org and Ancestry.com.

Census research is usually very rewarding and provides a snapshot of an individual or a household at a specific time and place in history.

Census Tutorial

It can also be frustrating if you don't understand how to effectively search the census. Learn how to search the census with the census tutorial on page 55, and acquire valuable tips for census success using these resources to ensure your success.

U.S. CENSUS COMPARISON CHART

Year	Ancestry.com* $ Soundex search Advanced Search Ranked Search (best results first) $19.95/month	Genealogy.com* $ No soundex search 19.99/month	HeritageQuestOnline.com FREE Only available through your local library; No Soundex search, Advanced Search	FamilySearch.org FREE Soundex search Advanced Search
1930	Every-name + Merchant Seamen	No Index	Head-of-Household*** 5 states (CT, DE, MD, TX, and VA)	
1920	Every-name	Head-of-Household	Head-of-Household (partially completed)	Every-name
1910	Every-name	Head-of-Household	Head-of-Household	
1900	Every-name	Head-of-Household	Head-of-Household	Every-name
1890	Every-name (Only 6,160 names) Substitutes**	Head-of-Household	Every name	
1880	Every-name		Every name	Every-name (index only)
1870	Every-name	Head-of-Household	Head-of-Household	Every-name
1860	Every-name + Slave schedules	Head-of-Household	Head-of-Household	Every-name
1850	Every-name Head-of-Household + Slave schedules	No Index	No Index	Every-name +Mortality schedule +Slave schedule
1840	Head-of-Household	No Index	No Index	
1830	Head-of-Household	No Index	No Index	
1820	Head-of-Household	Head-of-Household	Head-of-Household	
1810	Head-of-Household	Head-of-Household	Head-of-Household	
1800	Head-of-Household	Head-of-Household	Head-of-Household	
1790	Head-of-Household	Head-of-Household	Head-of-Household	
STATES	Individual states			Individual states

* Browse the census indexes for free, but you must subscribe to see details. Free at some Family History Centers.
** The Ancestry 1890 Census Substitute is a collection of replacement data for the 1890 census information that was destroyed in a fire in Washington D.C.; less than 1% of the schedules survived enumerating only 6,160 individuals. It includes fragments of the original 1890 census that survived the fire, special veteran's schedules, several Native American tribe censuses for years surrounding 1890, state censuses (1885 or 1895), city and county directories, alumni directories, and voter registration documents.
*** Head-of-Household: all men over 60, all women over 70, persons with different surname, all inter-racial marriages.

UK / BRITISH ISLES CENSUS COMPARISON CHART

Year	FamilySearch.org Soundex search **FREE**	FindMyPast.com 14-Day Free trial £54.95/6 months (about $86) $	TheGenealogist.co.uk and **Roots.UK.com** £4.66/month (12 months) (about $7.30) $	Ancestry.co.uk* Soundex search Advanced Search Ranked Search (best results first) $
1911		England and Wales Every name & address		
1901		Every name & address	Every name & address	Every name
1891		Every name & address	Every name & address	Every name
1881	Every name (Index only)	Every name & address	Every name & address	Every name
1871		Every name & address	Every name & address	Every name
1861	Every name	Every name & address	Every name & address	Every name
1851		Every name & address	Every name & address	Every name
1841	Every name	Every name & address	Every name & address	Every name

CANADA CENSUS COMPARISON CHART

Year	Canadian Genealogy Centre **FREE** www.CollectionsCanada.gc.ca/ genealogy/index-e.html	FamilySearch.org Soundex search **FREE**	Ancestry.ca* $ Soundex search Advanced Search Ranked Search (best results first) $11.95/month
1916	Every name		Every name: Manitoba, Saskatchewan and Alberta
1911	Every name		Every name
1906	Every name Northwest provinces		Every name: Manitoba, Saskatchewan and Alberta
1901	Every name		Every name
1891	Every name	Every name (no images)	Every name
1881	Every name	Every name	
1871	Ontario Index	Every name (no images)	Ontario Index, Head-of-Household **FREE**
1861	Every Name	Every name (in process)	
1851	Every name	Every name (no images)	Every name

* Browse the census indexes for free, but you must subscribe to see details. Free at some Family History Centers.

The Soundex Indexing System

Soundex is a phonetic index that groups together names (last name) that sound alike but are spelled differently, *for example*, **Smith** and **Smyth**, as pronounced in English. This helps searchers find names that are spelled differently than originally expected, a relatively common family history research problem. In the Soundex code, all surnames are reduced to a letter followed by three digits.

The easiest way to obtain the Soundex code for a name is to use one of several online Soundex converter programs as listed below. Simply type a name, and at the click of a button, the converter will divulge the corresponding Soundex code. There may be subtle differences between programs.

The most well-known genealogical use of Soundex is on parts of the 1880, 1900, 1910, 1920, and 1930 United States Federal Censuses. It is also used by the federal government for selected ship passenger arrival lists, certain Canadian border crossings, and some naturalization records.

The Soundex was a boon to many researchers in earlier days, but it does not work well with non-European surnames and is not as useful in today's technology. For more information you can go to:

National Archives -
www.archives.gov/publications/
general-info-leaflets-55.html

Immigration / Emigration

Tracking Your Ancestors Voyage

Where did your ancestors originate from? As our ancestors emigrated from one country to another, information about their lives were recorded on passenger lists and government documents. These documents can help you learn where your ancestors originated from, when they left, where they went, and who

The small passenger list manifest page showing your ancestor's name in the Ellis Island Archives can be enlarged by clicking on the small magnifying glass icon to the side of the photo.

When you click on the button, *Add to Your Ellis Island File,* you are given the opportunity to save any searches you have done on this website, saving you valuable time for future searches.

they traveled with. You can often find the age, occupation, place of residence, town of destination and the names of family members.

Ellis Island Records -
www.ellisislandrecords.org

The Ellis Island site contains the immigrant arrival records stored in the Ellis Island Archives containing some 22 million immigration records from 1892-1924 available for free searching. There are an estimated 100 million Americans who have

Here are some websites that will automatically convert any name you type into the Soundex code for that name.

Soundex Converter

www.searchforancestors.com/soundex.html
www.jewishgen.org/JOS/jossound.htm **FREE**
http://resources.rootsweb.ancestry.com/
cgi-bin/soundexconverter

at least one ancestor who entered the U.S. through Ellis Island. Information about each person was written down in ships' passenger lists, known as "manifests." Manifests were used to examine immigrants upon arrival in the United States. Searching the archives can help you write your own family's story. On this site you'll find: *Passenger records* (giving passenger name, date of arrival, ship of travel, age on arrival, and more); *original manifests* showing passenger names and other information; and *ship information,* often with a picture, giving the history and background of each ship that brought the immigrants.

One-Step Search Tools - FREE
http://stevemorse.org

Some people have been frustrated at not being able to locate a particular ancestor in the Ellis Island Archives or other passenger lists. Transcribing millions of foreign-sounding names and places written in often difficult-to-decipher handwriting on pages that were frequently faded, smeared, or otherwise damaged was difficult. And many of the names were perhaps faithful replications of mis-spellings in the original records. Dr. Stephen Morse developed his own specialized search form that enables us to search the immigration databases in more ways that are faster and in some cases more useful: by passenger, "sounds-like" using the last name, town search, Jewish passengers, ancestor's village, date, and damaged images which are not indexed. If at first you don't succeed, try using different names (or spellings) your ancestor may have used, last-name only searches, switching the first and last names in your search, and by approximating their arrival date.

CastleGarden.org - www.castlegarden.org FREE

Free access to an extraordinary database of information on 10 million immigrants from 1830 through 1892, the year Ellis Island opened. Over 73 million Americans can trace their ancestors to this early immigration period.

U.S. Citizenship and Immigration Services -
www.uscis.gov FREE

This website has a page for guiding us to records. Click on the *Site Map* on the top bar. There are lots of good tips, guides and information. It explains ports of entry, their records and has links to each state with a port, as well as U.S. cities with ports of entry from Canada. The *Immigration Arrival Records* page has links to passenger ship lists including Ellis Island and other ports.

Awesome Genealogy.com Directory - FREE
www.awesomegenealogy.com/Genealogy/immigration.shtml

A directory of immigration links, including naturalization, oaths of allegiance, passenger lists, ports, ships and ethnic immigration.

> Not all immigrants came to America through Ellis Island. It was the busiest port of entry, but there were many other entry points in the U.S., including Baltimore, Detroit, New Orleans, Philadelphia, San Francisco, etc.

Research Tip

Don't get discouraged if you don't find your ancestors in the Ellis Island database.

2 Add New Branches

Ancestor Roots Directory - FREE
www.academic-genealogy.com/
ancestorrootsinformationdatabases.htm

A directory of links to Immigration databases (scroll down to Immigration).

Tracing Immigrant Origins -
www.family search.org > *Research Helps >* FREE
Articles > Sorted by Title > T

A Research Outline that introduces the principles, search strategies, and various record types you can use to identify an immigrant ancestor's original hometown. These principles can be applied to almost any country.

Article About Immigration - FREE
www.genealogy.com/00000388.html

Links and information about the immigrant experience and finding records related to immigration.

AncestorsOnBoard.com – $
www.ancestorsonboard.com

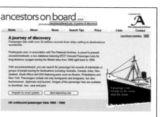

This site offers a complete collection (24 million records) of all UK outbound passenger lists 1890-1960 for all voyages made from any British port. You can search for free but there is a fee to view the full records.

Ancestry's U.S. Immigrant Collection – $
www.ancestry.com

Ship passenger lists, naturalization records, ship photos and much more.

Passenger & Immigration Lists Index – FREE $
www.ancestry.com > *Search > Card Catalog*

If you are seeking ancestors prior to the 1820s, this important work is the only place to go for tracing relatives to early colonial America and beyond. Prior to 1820, most ships did not keep documentation of who was on board. This work contains listings of over 4.7 million individuals who arrived in US and Canadian ports from the 1500s through the 1900s, and is updated annually, and makes finding your immigrant ancestors easier than ever. Thousands of different records have been used to compile this index, from original passenger lists to personal diaries. You may find the following information: Name and age, year and place of arrival, naturalization, source of record, names of all accompanying family members with their age and relationship to the primary individual. *Free to search and preview. Must subscribe to Ancestry to view details.* $19.95/month, $12.95/month (annual membership). Free at Family History Centers.

We want to know where our ancestors came from, when they arrived in North America, and when they became citizens. Naturalization and immigration records are the answer. Sometimes naturalization records for an ancestor are the only way to discover your family origins.

The typical naturalization process involved three steps.

U. S. Naturalization Process

1. Declaration. The immigrant filed a *declaration of intention* (first papers) to renounce allegiance to foreign governments and to later prove he or she had resided in the country long enough to apply for citizenship. Some were filed in a court at the port of arrival, some en route to a new home, and some in the immigrant's new home. The immigrant could use the court's record of his declaration to apply for homestead land, to enroll in the military, or to use as proof of residency if he went to another court to complete the naturalization process. The immigrant was also required to pledge his allegiance to the United States and sign a written oath which is often found with the petition, and generally gives his name, the date, and the country of origin.

2. Petition. After 2-7 years the immigrant filed a *petition for citizenship* (second or final papers).

Certificate of Citizenship

Most often the petition was filed in a court (any of 5,000 federal, state, or local courts) nearest to the town where the immigrant settled. After accepting the immigrant's petition and witnessing his oath, a court granted citizenship which was recorded in the court's official records. In some cases this is the only naturalization record that you will be able to find. Since 1929 most (but not all) naturalizations have been handled by federal circuit or district courts. You may need to search the records of each place where your immigrant ancestor lived.

3. Certificate. After all requirements were completed, the immigrant was sworn in as a citizen and issued a *certificate of citizenship* for his personal use. The certificates were printed in books with attached stubs.

Immigrant Ships.net – www.immigrantships.net

A free searchable **FREE** directory by volunteers who have transcribed over 9,000 passenger lists. It also offers a directory of sites to research emigration, immigration and naturalization, 100+ passenger list sites, ethnic research, libraries and archives, passenger ship types, descriptions and images, and additional worldwide maritime information.

Canadian Genealogy Centre -
www.collectionscanada.gc.ca/genealogy **FREE**

Canada's documentary web site offers immigration and naturalization databases in both official languages, as well as vital, census, military, and land record databases.

Suggested Activities

■ Review the information you already have on your pedigree chart to help you decide what new information to look for.

■ Use your computer to network with others who may be working on the same family line you're working on.

■ Verify the information you find online because it may not always be correct.

2 Add New **Branches**

Finding Your Ancestors' Naturalization Records

US Naturalization and Citizenship

Naturalization is the process of granting citizenship privileges to foreign-born residents. Naturalization papers are an important source of information about an immigrant's origin, his foreign and "Americanized" names, residence, and date of arrival, but are often overlooked. Before 1906 they are not likely to give town of origin or names of parents, but post-1906 records are more detailed and can help you find the date of immigration, ship's passenger list, spouse's name, port of arrival, and the place of birth for your ancestor. Some naturalization records include occupations, names and ages of minor children and more.

The 1900-1930 Census Records tell whether a person was naturalized.

Tip

Abbreviations used in the Citizenship column of census records: AL=Alien; NA=Naturalized; NR=Not Reported; PA=First Papers Filed (declaration of intention).

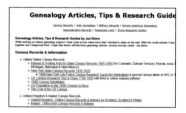

Find Declarations of Intent, First Papers, Alien Registrations, Passport Applications, Naturalization Petitions and Citizenship Certificates. Search substitute naturalization records - ships passenger lists, census records, oaths of allegiance, voters registration lists and more.

Many immigrants who applied for citizenship did not complete the requirements. You can find completed citizenship requirements in censuses, court minutes, homestead records, passports, voting registers, and military papers. Even if an immigrant ancestor did not complete the process, he may have begun the process and filed a *declaration of intention* which contains valuable information.

Family Search Wiki -

https://wiki.familysearch.org >*Naturalization*

More information about the naturalization process and records.

NaturalizationRecords.com –

www.naturalizationrecords.com

Search for your ancestors in free Naturalization Records in U.S.A. and Canada.

GenealogyBranches.com –
www.genealogybranches.com/naturalization.html

Types of U.S. Naturalization Records with links.

GermanRoots.com –
www.germanroots.com/naturalizationrecords.html

A guide to finding US Naturalization Records. Online Searchable Naturalization Indexes & Records.

Finding Naturalization Records

Naturalization Records	What to Look For	Location
Colonial Records	**Ancestry.com** Free to search and preview. Must subscribe to Ancestry to view details. $ FREE	www.ancestry.com > *Search* > *Card Catalog* *Passenger and Immigration Lists Index* * *Selected U.S. Naturalization Records 1790-1974* includes digitized naturalization records for some Federal courts in Calif., NY, and Penn. * *U.S. Naturalization Records Indexes, 1794-1995* includes indexes for some Federal courts in Alaska, Calif., Delaware, Wash. D.C., Maryland, Massachusetts, Michigan, New York, Ohio, Oregon, and Pennsylvania.
Before September 1906	**FamilySearch.org** FREE Look first for the petition (second papers) in courts of the county or city where your immigrant lived.	www.familysearch.org > *Library* > *Library Catalog* > *Place Search* [STATE], [COUNTY], [TOWN] - then look under "Naturalization and Citizenship".
	Courts	Contact the county clerk to determine where the records are presently located
	National Archives FREE	www.archives.gov/genealogy/naturalization - Introduction & web site links
After September 1906	**US Citizenship and Immigration Services (CIS).** $ FREE The federal government standardized the naturalization process (including the paperwork) requiring specific forms. Since 1929, most new citizens naturalized at federal courts.	www.uscis.gov > *Topics* > *Genealogy* Records available thru the mail (fee required): Naturalization Certificate Files and Alien Registration Forms. You can also use the Freedom of Information Act (FOIA) to obtain copies of these records.
	Footnote.com $ FREE Online records (indexed) for So. Calif. (1887-1940); Maryland (1906-1930); Mass. (1906-1929); Cleveland, Ohio (1907-1946); and Pennsylvania (1795-1930); plus some indexes for NY.	http://go.footnote.com/naturalizations Searches are free; downloading requires payment. Also search the *Naturalization Index for WWI Soldiers* (over 18,000 records).

2 Add New/Branches

Helpful Books

Guide to Naturalization Records of the US – www.amazon.com $

A key reference book (1997) about naturalizations by Christina Schaefer helps locate Naturalization records (especially prior to 1906). It contains a directory showing the available records for each place, and where to find them. $19.99

They Became Americans: Finding Naturalization Records – http://store.ancestry.com $

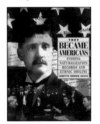

A book by Loretto Dennis Szucs (1998) suggests ways of finding naturalization records and discusses the weaknesses and strengths of the different types of records. 260 pages. $17.95

Military Records

Track Your Ancestors Footsteps Through History

History of battles and wars, and military records–service or pension records, bounty land records, muster rolls, discharge lists, fatalities, and prisoner of war records–are some of the most interesting and helpful records available to assist you in tracing your own family roots and stories. Military records contain large amounts of biographical inform-ation, from the color of a person's eyes to the day-by-day muster rolls that track your

ancestor's footsteps through history. There are numerous oppor-tunities to learn the stories of your ancestor's courage and sacrifice with hundreds of military record databases.

> Every war in American history has military records that are very valuable in family history research. All servicemen have records (regardless of rank) from private to general.

Revolutionary War Pension Files - www.heritagequestonline.com *FREE*

Index and supporting file images to participation in Revolutionary War. It is available free through your local library with your library card, and at some Family History Centers.

Daughters of the American Revolution.org - www.dar.org *FREE*

A volunteer women's service organization dedicated to promoting patriotism, preserving American history, and securing America's future through better education for children.

Sons of the American Revolution.org - www.sar.org *FREE*

A historical, educational, and patriotic non-profit corporation that seeks to maintain and extend the institutions of American freedom, an appreciation for true patriotism, a respect for our national symbols, the value of American citizenship, and the unifying force of one nation and one people.

American Civil War -
http://sunsite.utk.edu/civil-war and
www.cwc.lsu.edu

Directory of web links to hundreds of civil war
web sites and databases.

Civil War Soldiers and Sailors -
www.itd.nps.gov/cwss

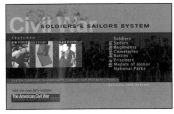

Index of Civil War
service records by
the National Park
Service. Searches
6.3 million names—
both Union and
Confederate—from 44 states and territories.

CivilWar.com – www.civilwar.com

Provides the
published Official
Record of the war,
battle maps, the
largest online
collection of Civil
War photos, and
hundreds of thousands of pages of information.
Reports from each battle provide insight into
what each commander witnessed and his own
perspective on the battle. Contains numerous
personal accounts which provide insight into
not only the Civil War, plus the life and times of
the 1860s from California to the Indian Wars of
the Great Plains.

WWI Draft Cards - www.ancestry.com >
Search > Military Records

Index and images
of draft registration
cards. Free at some
Family History
Centers.

WWII Army Enlistment and Other Military
Records - www.worldvitalrecords.com >
Record Types

Free at Family
History Centers.

US Army Heritage Center – *FREE*
www.ahco.army.mil

A digitized collection
of 23,000 Civil War
photographs (MOLLUS
collection) consi-
dered by historians
to be the best and
most extensive
collection in the world. Also contains: personal
papers, oral histories, letters and diaries of
veterans, military units and associations,
images of historical property, and
military publications.

National Archives –
www.archives.gov/genealogy/military/#have *FREE*

Holds Federal
military service
records from the
Revolutionary
War to 1912 in
Washington, D.C.
Another main
repository for military records is the National
Personnel Records Center (NPRC) in St. Lewis,
Missouri. Your research path will depend on:
what branch of service your ancestor was in,
which conflict, what dates, whether Regular
Army or a volunteer unit, whether your
ancestor was an officer or enlisted personnel,
and whether there was a pension application.

U.S. Military Records Chart

War	Conflict Years	Approx. Birth Years	Locate Records at	Look for
Revolutionary War (250,000+ servicemen, 50,000+ casualties)	1775-1783	1726-1767	www.HeritageQuestOnline.com (check with your local library, available at some Family History Centers) **FREE**	Muster Rolls Pension Files Bounty-land Warrants (applications)
			www.Footnote.com **$**	Muster Rolls, Pension Files, Service Records
			www.Ancestry.com > *Military Collection* **$**	DAR Linage Books Bounty Land Warrants
			www.Dar.com **FREE**	DAR Patriot Index
			www.RoyalProvincial.com **FREE**	Loyalist Records: Muster Roll Index, Regimental Documents, Land Petitions, Postwar Settlement Papers
War of 1812 (530,000 servicemen, 2,000 casualties)	1812-1815	1762-1799	www.Ancestry.com > *Military Collection* **$**	Service Records Pension Application Index Bounty-land Warrants
			www.FamilySearch > *Search Records > Record Search > Browse All Collections*	Louisiana, War of 1812 Pension Lists
Mexican War (100,000 servicemen, 13,000 casualties)	1846-1848	1796-1831	www.archives.gov/research/ military/mexican-war.html **FREE**	Microfilmed indexes to military service and pension files available from your local Family History Center
			www.militaryindexes.com **FREE**	
			www.olivetreegenealogy.com > Military **FREE**	
Civil War (2.8 million+ servicemen, 510,000+ casualties)	1861-1865	1811-1848	Civil War Soldiers and Sailors System - www.itd.nps.gov/cwss **FREE**	Service Records, Regimental Histories, Battle Descriptions Prisoner Records
			www.Ancestry.com > *Military Collection* **$**	Soldier Index, 1890 Veterans Schedules (partial records only), Pension Index
			www.Footnote.com **$**	Confederate Service Records Union Pension Records (click: Browse by Historical Era > Civil War > Title > Civil War Pension Index)
			www.familysearch.org > *Search Records > Record Search > View All Collections*	NARA Confederate Service Records, Civil War Pension Index
			www.CivilWarData.com **$**	Pension Indexes, Rolls of Honor, State Rosters
			www.Archives.gov/genealogy/military > *Civil War* **FREE**	Union Pension Index links Confederate Pension Records (by State Archive links)

Spanish-American War (280,564 servicemen, 2,061 casualties)	1898	1848-1881	www.spanamwar.com *FREE*	Rosters Historical info
			www.accessgenealogy.com > *military records* *FREE*	Spanish American War
			Archival Research Catalog http://arcweb.archives.gov *FREE*	Spanish American War
Philippine Insurrection (125,000+ servicemen, 4,200 casualties)	1899-1902	1849-1885	www.ancestry.com >*Military Collection* *$*	1900 Census (use Military & Naval Forces as the state of residence)
			FREE www.heritagequestonline.com (thru your library or Family History Center)	Use Military & Naval Forces as the state of residence
			www.Archives.gov/genealogy/ military > *Philippine Insurrection* *FREE*	Phiippine Insurrection information
World War I (24 million+ registered for draft; 4.7 million+ served, 116,516+ casualties)	1917-1918	1872-1900	www.ancestry.com >*Military Collection* *$*	WWI Draft Registration Cards
			www.Archives.gov/ genealogy/military > *World War I* *FREE*	Draft Registration Cards
			http://gravelocator.cem/va/gov *FREE*	Burial locations of veterans nationwide
World War II (16.5 million+ servicemen, 400,000+ casualties) The majority of WWII records are not publicly available yet.	1941-1945	1877 1925	www.ancestry.com >*Military Collection* *$*	WWII Draft Registration Cards Army Enlistment Records POW Records
			www.FamilySearch.org > *Search Records > Records Search Pilot* *FREE*	United States, WWII Draft Registration Cards (In process)
			www.Archives.gov/ *FREE* genealogy/military >*World War II*	Army Enlistment Records
Korean War (33,642 casualties)	1950-1953	1900-1936	www.Archives.gov/genealogy/mi litary >*Korean War* *FREE*	Electronic records - The majority of records are not publicly available yet.
Vietnam War (110,000+ casualties)	1964-1972	1914-1955	www.Archives.gov/genealogy/ military > *Vietnam War* *FREE*	Casualty Lists
			http://go.Footnote.com/vietnam *FREE*	Vietnam War Collection

Ancestry, Footnote and HeritageQuest are free at some Family History Centers. HeritageQuestOnline is also searchable free through subscribing libraries; check your local library whether you can log on from home via the library's Web site using your library card.

National Archives Guides –
www.archives.gov/publications/
finding-aids/guides.html

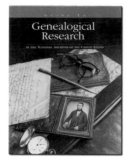

NARA Published Guides provide researchers with detailed information on general and selected subjects documented in the holdings of the National Archives. Included are: Guide to Federal Records in the Archives (2428 pages $95), Black History (397 pages, $15), Records for the Territorial Period 1804-1912 (140 pages, $12), Civil War Guides (The Union, The Confederacy) (733 pages $25), and more. The *Genealogical Research Guide* (420 pages, $25), is an indispensable aid for researching family genealogy, local history, and social trends. Beyond its extraordinary reference value, it inspires a deep appreciation of America's rich documentary heritage.

Veterans Affairs GraveLocator – FREE
http://gravelocator.cem.va.gov

Search 5 million internment records for burial locations of veterans and their family members in VA National Cemeteries, state veterans cemeteries, various other military and Department of Interior cemeteries, and for veterans buried in private cemeteries when the grave is marked with a government grave marker. A map of the cemetery is also displayed, showing the section where the grave is located. VA operates 128 national cemeteries and 33 soldiers' lots and monument sites.

GenealogyBank.com –
www.genealogybank.com

Find millions of U.S. military records, casualty lists, Revolutionary and Civil War pension requests, widow's claims, orphan petitions, and land grants from 1789-1980. This unique content provides critical

Best Military Records in Individual State Archives

Alabama Archives – FREE
www.archives.state.al.us

Search the Thomas McAdory Owen's Revolutionary War Soldiers in Alabama, Confederate service cards and WWI deaths.

Louisiana State Archives – FREE
www.400.sos.louisiana.gov/archives/
gen/cpa-alpha.htm

Search a 49,000-name online index to 152 rolls of microfilmed Confederate pension applications.

Maryland Archives – FREE
www.aomol.netwww.aomol.net

Provides access to muster rolls and other service records from the Revolutionary and Civil War records from both sides; also home to land and probate records.

New York Civil War Soldiers – FREE
www.archives.nysed.gov > *Research* > *Geneology*

Search more than 360,000 New York soldiers.

Pennsylvania State Archives – FREE
www.digitalarchives.state.pa.us/archive.asp

Search veterans from the Revolutionary War to the Spanish-American War, and WWI medal applications.

Texas State Library – FREE
www.tsl.state.tx.us/arc/genfirst.html

Search more than 54,000 Confederate pension applications, the Confederate Indigent Families Lists, and the Index to Texas Adjutant General Service Records, 1836 to 1935.

Virginia Library – www.lva.virginia.gov > *Using the Collections* FREE

Provides a 34,402-name Virginia Military Dead Database, 250,000 Virginia World War II Separation Notices, and an index to names in Confederate Veteran magazine.

Suggested Activities

Look at your pedigree chart and determine if you have any ancestors who may have served in the following wars: French and Indian War 1754-1763; Revolutionary War 1775-1783; Indian Wars late 18th and 19th centuries; War of 1812, 1812-1815; Mexican-American War 1846-1848; Civil War 1861-1865; Spanish-American War 1898; Philippine Insurrection 1899-1902; World War I 1917-1918; World War II 1941-1945; Korean War 1950-1953; Vietnam War 1965-1973.

access to important military records to help discover and honor the veterans in your family. U.S. Military Registers from the Army, Navy and Air Force provide the name, birth date, location, rank and date of death of every U.S. military officer that served. Provides details that are difficult to find anywhere else. 30-Day trial $9.95

Footnote Military Records -
www.footnote.com/military

An online repository for original historical documents relating to the Revolutionary War, Civil War, WWI, WWII, US Presidents, historical newspapers, naturalization documents, and many more. The documents are made possible by their unique partnership with The National Archives. They recently released the first ever interactive World War II collection, which includes an interactive version of the USS Arizona Memorial, WWII Hero Pages, and WWII photos and documents previously unavailable on the internet. Their Hero Pages is an easy way to create a tribute or memorial to war heroes. It features an interactive timeline and map, a place to upload photos, documents and letters, and a place to share stories about individuals who fought in WWII. All the indexes are free to search which includes names, places, topics, a list of documents and a small image of the document, but a

membership is required to view the full image. Free at Family History Centers. $11.95/month, $69.95/year.

Ancestry Military Collection -
www.ancestry.com

Discover the heroes in your family tree in their U.S. Military Collection - the largest online assortment of U.S. military records, covering more than three centuries of American wars and conflicts. With more than 100 million names and 700 titles and databases in military records from all 50 U.S. states, there are countless opportunities to learn the stories of courage and sacrifice in your family tree.

2 Add New Branches

American War of Independence (1775-1783)

American Revolution - www.lineages.com

Revolutionary War - www.revwar.com

United States Military Records -
www.rootsweb.com/~rwguide/lesson14.htm

Cyndi's List: Military Resources -
www.cyndislist.com/milres.htm

Virtual Museum of the Revolutionary War -
www.home.ptd.net/~revwar/museum.html

The War for American Independence -
www.home.ptd.net/~revwar

National Archives and Records Administration -
www.nara.gov/genealogy/genindex.html

Sons of the American Revolution -
www.sar.org

Daughters of the American Revolution -
www.dar.library.net

Web Links to Major Repositories -
www.familysearch.org > Search Records > Web Sites

Library of Congress - www.lcweb.loc.gov

Libraries, Archives and Organizations

Rich Sources of Unique Information

Even though the Internet contains a seemingly endless depth of information for tracing your own family roots and stories, sooner or later you will need to visit a library or archive to find records that you can't find as yet on the Internet. It's difficult to physically visit the library in every town in which your ancestors may have lived, but most libraries around the world now have their library catalogs and collections online, so their information is becoming increasingly available to us. You can quickly know whether that library has the information or title you want, if it's available by interlibrary loan, or found in a nearby branch library. It's fast, convenient, and time-saving.

The Family History Library -
www.familysearch.org

The library houses a collection of genealogical records that includes the names of more than 3 billion deceased people. It is the largest collection of its kind in the world, including: vital records (birth, marriage, and death records from both government and church sources); census returns; court, property, and probate records; cemetery records; emigration and immigration lists; printed genealogies; and family and county histories.

National Genealogical Society -
www.ngsgenealogy.org

Founded in 1903 as a non-profit organization, the National Genealogical Society (NGS) is a dynamic and growing membership of individuals and other groups from all over the world that share a common love of genealogy. Whether you're a beginner, a professional or somewhere

in between, NGS can assist you in your research into the past. The NGS is one of the important genealogical societies in the U.S., and is an excellent site for learning genealogy standards and methods.

National Archives - www.archives.gov

Your can search for military, immigration and other records at the archives of the US government. This site offers two digital databases into the archives' holdings. The ARC (Archival Research Catalog) indexes 6.4 million records and includes 153,000 digital records. The AAD (Access to Archival Databases) lets you search more than 85 million historical records, such as: photos, maps, immigration records, and over 9 million WWII enlistment files. Scroll down to *Online Databases* on the home page.

Library of Congress - www.loc.gov *FREE*

The Library's mission is to make its resources available and useful to the American people and preserve a universal collection of knowledge and creativity for future generations. Since its founding in 1800, it has amassed more than 119 million items and become one of the world's leading cultural institutions. Just a few of the vast sections of the library include:

American Memory - http://memory.loc.gov *FREE*

A gateway to rich primary source materials relating to the history and culture of the United States. The site offers more than 7 million digital items from more than 100 historical collections.

America's Story - www.america'slibrary.com (FREE)

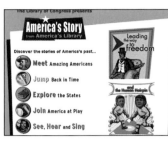

Here you can discover what Abraham Lincoln had in his pockets on the night he was assassinated. Or you can read about Buffalo Bill Cody and his "Wild West" show; the heroism of Harriet Tubman, who helped many slaves escape bondage; the music of jazz great Duke Ellington; or the inventions of Thomas Edison. Click on *Jump Back in Time* and find the settlers who landed on Plymouth Rock. Or jump to a more recent age and read about bebop, a type of music invented long before hip-hop. Do you know what happened on the day you were born? You can find out here.

Research Tools - www.loc.gov/rr (FREE)

Offers many databases and links to resources. Specifically, you should access the *Local History and Genealogy* page - www.loc.gov/rr/genealogy.

American Treasures - www.loc.gov/exhibits/treasures (FREE)

An unprecedented permanent exhibition of the rarest, most interesting or significant items relating to America's past, drawn from every corner of the world's largest library.

Allen County Public Library - www.acpl.lib.in.us

One of the (FREE) leading genealogy departments in a public library.

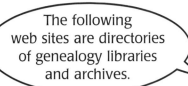

The following web sites are directories of genealogy libraries and archives.

Library Directories

Cyndi's List - www.cyndislist.com/lib-b.htm (FREE)

Directory of Genealogy Libraries in the U.S. - www.gwest.org/gen_libs.htm (FREE)

The Family History Library - (FREE) www.familysearch.org

The library houses a collection of genealogical records that includes the names of more than 3 billion deceased people. It is the largest collection of its kind in the world

National Archives & Records - www.nara.gov

NARA is America's national record keeper. (FREE) It is the archives of the Government of the United States.

Library of Congress - www.loc.gov (FREE)

One of the world's leading cultural institutions. You should look at American Memory which offers more than 7 million digital items from more than 100 historical collections, America's Story, and American Treasures, an unprecedented permanent exhibition of the rarest, most interesting or significant items relating to America's past.

Godfrey Memorial Library - ($) www.godfrey.org

The Library offers access to many premium databases. It's a good resource for historic newspapers, including the London Times, 19th century US newspapers, and early American newspapers. $80/year

WorldCat - www.oclc.org > *WorldCat* (FREE)

The window to the world's libraries. WorldCat is a global network of library content and services.

LibDex - www.libdex.com (FREE)

An easy-to-use index to 18,000 libraries worldwide, library home pages, Web-based library catalogs, Friends of the Library pages and library e-commerce affiliates.

Add New 2 Branches

FREE

Major Family History Libraries

Family History Library, Salt Lake City, Utah - www.familysearch.org. The largest genealogical library in the world houses 2 million rolls of microfilm and more than 270,000 compiled family histories.

Library of Congress, Genealogical Room, Thomas Jefferson Annex, Washington, DC - http://lcweb.loc.gov/rr/genealogy/

U.S. National Archives and Records, Washington, DC - www.archives.gov/index.html

U.S. National Archives Library, College Park, Maryland - www.archives.gov/research_room/genealogy/index.html

National Genealogical Society Library, Arlington, Virginia - www.ngsgenealogy.org

New England Historic Genealogical Society Library, Boston, Massachusetts (Specializes in data about New England and NY, and the states to which they migrated.) - www.newenglandancestors.org

Daughters of the American Revolution Genealogical Library, Wash., D.C. - www.dar.org/library/library.html

Palatines to America National Library, Columbus, Ohio (ancestors from all German-speaking lands) - www.palam.org

New York Public Library, New York, New York - www.nypl.org

Newberry Library, Chicago, Illinois - www.newberry.org

Allen County Public Library, Ft Wayne, Indiana - www.acpl.lib.in.us

Become familiar with local libraries, historical and genealogical societies, and Family History Centers in your area.

Use state and national resources after you have thoroughly explored what is available to you locally which will save you time and money.

Making of America - http://moa.umdl.umich.edu and http://moa.cit.cornell.edu/moa

FREE

This is a joint project between the University of Michigan and Cornell University which provides free access to a large collection of 19th century books, journal articles, and imprints available on two websites. Two separate online archive sites put digitized books at your fingertips. The first collection contains some 10,000 books and 50,000 journal articles; the second site covers 267 monograph volumes and more than 100,000 journal articles.

Canadian Genealogy Centre - www.collectionscanada.gc.ca/genealogy

FREE

Library and Archives Canada collects and preserves Canada's documentary heritage including publications, archival records, sound and audio-visual materials, photographs, artworks, and electronic documents such as websites. It offers genealogical content, services, advice, research

tools and searchable databases for vital, census, immigration and naturalization, military, land and people records, all in both official languages.

BYU Family History Archives – FREE
www.lib.byu.edu/fhc

A collection of published genealogy and family history books. The archive includes histories of families, county and local histories, how-to books on genealogy, genealogy magazines and periodicals, medieval books, and gazetteers. Combines family history books from the collections of the Family History Library, the Allen County Public Library, Houston's Clayton Library, the Mid-Continent Public Library Midwest Genealogy Center, the BYU Harold B. Lee Library, the BYU Hawaii Joseph F. Smith Library, and the LDS Church historical library.

DenverLibrary Western History – FREE
http://history.denverlibrary.org

The collection includes 200,000 cataloged books, pamphlets, atlases, maps, microfilm titles, 600,000 photographs, 3,700 manuscript archives, and a remarkable collection of Western fine art and prints. You can order photo prints and digital photos on line for a fee.

New York Library Collections – FREE
www.nypl.org/collections

Collections include more than 14 million books, 400 databases, 700,000 images digitized, 30,000 ebooks, music, and video items, and 66,000 linear feet of manuscripts. It covers American Indian portraits, African-American history and migration, historical photographs, surveyors of the American West, Holocaust memorial books and much more.

Online Archive of California – FREE
www.oac.cdlib.org

Compilation of historical materials from museums, historical societies and archives. You'll find more than 170,000 images, 50,000 pages of documents, letters and oral histories, and 8,000 guides to collections.

WorldCat.org – FREE
www.worldcat.org

Search the collections of libraries in your community and thousands more around the world; more than 10,000 libraries worldwide with more than 1 billion holdings. There's no better tool to identify obscure or out-of-print books to borrow on interlibrary loan.

DAR Library - http://dar.library.net FREE

Daughters of the American Revolution library, one of the largest genealogical libraries in the world, is an essential destination when researching your family history. Since its founding in 1896, the library has grown into a specialized collection of American genealogical and historical manuscripts and publications.

Repositories of Primary Sources - FREE
www.uidaho.edu/special-collections/other.repositories.html

A listing with Internet links of over 5300 websites describing holdings of manuscripts, archives, rare books, historical photographs, and other primary sources for the research scholar.

2 Add New Branches

A Rosetta Stone

William Alexander Haley, chairman of the Alex Haley Center, said,

"The Freedman's Bank records may be more than just an historical record. They may be the Rosetta Stone – the piece that allows you to go in and make the connection."

It's difficult for us who are not the descendants of slaves to fully comprehend the sense of pain and loss of identity for African-Americans. We have never tried to piece together our ancestry from families who howled in pain as they were sold away from each other. Or who cannot find their grandparents in a census because they were considered only a possession. Or had no surname except for one they borrowed from a 'master' who claimed them as property.

LibDex - www.libdex.com **FREE**

An easy-to-use index to 18,000 libraries worldwide, library home pages, Web-based library catalogs, Friends of the Library pages and library e-commerce affiliates.

African American Roots

Many people have interesting challenges in doing ethnic research. This may be particularly true of African American research. However, many African Americans, believing they are descendants of slaves, falsely assume that records relating to the lives of their ancestors

are non-existent. This is not necessarily the case today due to the availability of new information on the Internet and the compilation of records by thousands of people. For example, the 1870 Federal Census was the first to name all Blacks.

FreedmensBureau.com - **FREE**
www.freedmensbureau.com

U.S. Freedmen Bureau Records of Field Offices, 1865-1872. This database contains African-American records relating to the Freedmen's Bureau from the following field offices: Washington, D.C., Florida, Georgia, New Orleans, North Carolina, Tennessee, and Virginia. Information available in the database includes: name, record type, year, and field office location.

Freedman's Bank Index - **FREE**
www.heritagequestonline.com –and– www.familysearch/org > Search Records > Records Search

Freedman's Bank Records is a unique searchable database documenting several generations of African Americans immediately following the Civil War. You can access the Heritage Quest database for free using your local subscribing library online (and your library card), or access Heritage Quest for free at your local Family History Center. Or you can search the records for free at http://search.labs.familysearch.org >*Browse Collections.* You can also purchase the CD for a nominal fee at www.ldscatalog.com > (do a quick search for *Freedman*). $6.50

Congress chartered the Freedman's Savings and Trust Company in 1865 with the primary objective to assist former slaves and African-American soldiers with their new financial responsibilities. Ideally, this bank would be a permanent financial institution for savings deposits only and assist families with the challenges they faced in their transition from slavery to freedom. It was also designed to provide a place, safe from swindlers, to deposit money while individuals learned personal finance management skills. But mismanagement and outright fraud caused the bank to collapse in 1874, dashing the hopes and dreams of many African Americans. Bank deposits totaling more than $57 million were tragically lost.

Reginald Washington of the National Archives and Records Administration said, *"An idea that began as a well-meaning experiment in philanthropy had turned into an economic nightmare for tens of thousands of African Americans."*

A Silver Lining

Now, over 145 years later, there is a silver lining to the disaster. In an effort to establish bank patrons' identities, bank workers at the time recorded the names and family relationships of account holders, sometimes taking brief oral histories. Many of the records documented family relationships and relatives who were sold into slavery to other locations. In the process, they created the largest single repository of lineage-linked African-American records known to exist.

It contains more than 480,000 names, documenting several generations of former slaves. Remarkably, the records of an institution that caused so much pain among African Americans following the Civil War now hold keys for their posterity to discover their roots. For the 8 to 10 million Americans who have ancestors whose names are recorded in the Freedman Bank Records, these records now cast a new light on their ancestry.

GenealogyBank.com -
www.genealogybank.com

The leading provider of digitized historical and recent newspapers for family history research, including over 300 African-American newspapers from1827-present. An especially rich resource for historical newspapers containing runaway slave ads, estate sale notices and Post-Emancipation obituaries; it offers fascinating insights into African American

history, culture and daily life, and provides a vivid snapshot of virtually every aspect of the African American experience. You will find firsthand perspectives on notable Americans from Frederick Douglass to Martin Luther King, Jr., as well as obituaries, advertisements, editorials and illustrations. New content added daily. You can search for free, but you need to subscribe to view the details. $9.95/month, $69.95/year.

Afro-American Historical and Genealogical Society - www.aahgs.org

Strives to preserve African-ancestored family history, genealogy, and cultural diversity by teaching research techniques and disseminating information throughout the community. Their primary goals are to promote scholarly research, provide resources for historical and genealogical studies, create a network of persons with similar interests, and assist members in documenting their histories.

African-American Genealogy Group - *FREE*
www.aagg.org

A valuable resource for searching African-American roots.

> Begin at home to find information about yourself and work back one generation at a time.

Research Tip

Interview relatives for family history stories. Enter the information that you have gathered on a pedigree chart, family group record and research log. Join an African American genealogical society. Learn about African American history and the records that are available to you.

Add New 2 Branches

Cyndi's List.com - www.cyndislist.com FREE

Perhaps the best known index website; lists over 265,000 links to sites to help you with research; over 180 different categories. Contains hundreds of links to websites for doing African American research (search *"African American"*). The general site links are categorized as follows: General Resource Sites; History & Culture; How To; Libraries; Archives & Museums; Locality Specific; Mailing Lists, Newsgroups & Chat; Maps, Gazetteers & Geographical Information; Military; Newspapers People & Families; Professional Researchers, Volunteers & Other Research Services; Publications, Software & Supplies; Records: Census, Cemeteries, Land, Obituaries, Personal, Taxes and Vital; Slavery; and Societies & Groups. Each category is helpful, but the *"How To"* category helps you find a place to get started.

Footnote African-American Collection - $

http://go.footnote.com/blackhistory

View more than a million photos and documents from the National Archives found nowhere else on the internet. These newly digitized records provide a view into the lives of African Americans that few have seen before and cover subjects including slavery, military service, and issues facing African Americans dating back to the late 18th century. These records will help you to better understand the history and sacrifice that took place in this country. 7-day Free trial, $11.95/month. Free at Family History Centers.

AfriGeneas.com - www.afrigeneas.com

A searchable database of surnames for researching families of African ancestry. They offer a guide

to family history resources around the world, and a mailing list of information about families of African ancestry. They also have impressive links to other websites to do research.

African American Cemeteries - FREE

http://africanamericancemeteries.com

Listing of African American cemeteries created by the Millenium Project Coalition.

Christine's Genealogy Website - FREE

www.ccharity.com

An excellent site about African-American history and genealogy.

Guide to Black History - FREE

http://search.eb.com/blackhistory

Encyclopedia Britannica's *Guide to Black History* features a timeline, Eras in Black History; a numerous collection of articles; related Internet links to history, culture, literature and music; and a study guide.

National Archive Resources - FREE

www.archives.gov/genealogy/heritage/index.html

Directory of web links to African-American resources.

Articles at Ancestry.com > *Featured Collections (scroll down) > African American Family History* -

www.ancestry.com/learn/ContentCenters/content Center.aspx?page=AfricanAm&sp=articles FREE

Dr. Roseann Hogan has written a 3-part series of articles called *African American Research.* She says that searching for African American families involves two distinct research approaches which

correspond to the change in the legal status of African Americans in the U.S. before and after the Civil War. The first two articles discuss basic and general research techniques. In the third article, several case studies are presented to illustrate useful resources in building an African American family history. These case studies show that it is possible to discover precious information on African American families.

African American Research Guide - FREE
www.familysearch.org > *Research Helps* > *Articles*

FamilySearch and the Family History Library have developed a comprehensive, 18-page *Research Guide* about African American research: *Finding Records of Your Ancestors: African American 1870 to Present.* This publication explains the best ways to search public records to find African American ancestors as well as U.S. ancestors of

Suggested Activities

■ Regardless of your ethnic background, historical events affected the lives of your ancestors, and learning about those events can help you in your family history search. Using the dates and places on your pedigree chart, create a simple time line that shows some of the historical events that your ancestors may have experienced, such as the Civil War, or the Great Depression.

■ Locate history books about those events that will help you better understand the lives and experiences of your ancestors. For African American research, three main historical eras influenced African American records:

• Civil War and Reconstruction (1861-1877)

• Segregation (1896-1954), and

• Civil Rights Movement (1954-1970).

any heritage. Covering 1870-present, it explains the most useful records for that time frame, provides an introduction to basic research tools and strategies for finding records, and gives a case study that illustrates each step of the research process.

You can download and print it online for *free* at www.familysearch.org. Click on the *Research Helps* >*Articles* button on the top bar, click on *Sorted by Title* in the left hand column; find *African American: Finding Your Ancestors* and click on *PDF.* They also offer a 6-page *Quick Guide to African American Research* at the same web site location. It describes strategies for discovering your ancestors in various periods of history, the most useful records and indexes to search, and specific information you need to trace your ancestors.

Article on Using Federal Census Indexes – FREE
www.africanaheritage.com/ Federal_Census_Indexes.asp

Tom Blake has written a valuable article about Using Federal Census Indexes to Find an 1860 Slaveholder.

1860 U.S. Federal Slave Schedules – FREE
www.familyhistory101.com/research-census/slave_1860.html

This database details those persons enumerated in the Slave Schedule of the 1860 U.S. Federal Census and are linked to the actual images of the Census.

Slave Voyages.org - www.slavevoyages.org FREE

The Trans-Atlantic Slave Trade Database has information on almost 35,000 slaving voyages that forcibly embarked over 10 million Africans for transport to the Americas between the sixteenth and nineteenth centuries. It offers a chance

Add New 2 Branches

2 Add New Branches

to rediscover the reality of one of the largest forced movements of peoples in world history. It documents the slave trade from Africa to the New World from the 1500s to the 1800s. The names of 70,000 human cargo are also documented (slaves' African names).

MySlaveAncestors.com - FREE
www.myslaveancestors.com

A small resource center by profession-al genealogists who understand the needs of beginning researchers. They offer a sound strategy for tracing your African-American roots, plus some professional help if you desire.

Lowcountry Africana.net - FREE
http://lowcountryafricana.net

This free site focuses on records that document the family and cultural heritage of African Americans in the historic rice-growing areas of South Carolina, Georgia and extreme northeastern Florida, home to the rich Gullah/Geechee culture. It will be a treasure trove of primary documents, book excerpts and multimedia for exploring and documenting the dynamic cultural and family heritage of the Lowcountry Southeast.

Afro-Louisiana History and Genealogy - FREE
www.ibiblio.org/laslave

A free site providing information on 100,000 Louisiana slaves 1719-1820 compiled by Gwendolyn Midlo Hall, Ph.D.

Documenting the American South - FREE
http://docsouth.unc.edu

This rich site from the University of North Carolina is especially strong on the African-American experience, including such collections as The Church in the Southern Black Community, Colonial and State Records of North Carolina, and North American Slave Narratives. It provides access to texts, images, and audio files related to southern history, literature, and culture. It currently includes twelve thematic collections of books, diaries, posters, artifacts, letters, oral history interviews, and songs.

Afriquest.com - www.afriquest.com FREE

A new free database (beta) for African and African American genealogy and history which is a cooperative volunteer effort by The USF Africana Heritage Project, WeRelate, and IDEAS4.

Hispanic American Roots

There are lots of great resources for tracing your Spanish language heritage family roots and stories especially in Spain or Latin American countries. Tens of millions of Spaniards emigrated from Spain to Mexico, Puerto Rico, Central and South America, Latin America, North America and Australia. Tracing your Hispanic roots may, eventually, lead you to Spain, where genealogical records are among the oldest and best in the world.

Mexico Research Guide - www.familysearch.org > *Research Helps > Articles* FREE

The Family History Library has also developed a comprehensive 68-page *Research Outline* about Mexican family history records to search.

FamilySearch Hispanic Resources – FREE
https://wiki.familysearch.org/en/Portal:-_Hispanic_Family_History_Resources

A portal (in both English and Spanish) with links to search digital records, databases, and microfilm records for millions of people with Hispanic ancestors. You can search by specific database or by region: Caribbean, Central and South America, México, and Spain. Microfilm civil and church records are listed by country. You can also link to free downloadable research outlines (for Argentina, Chili, Latin America, Mexico and Peru), related websites that are particularly useful for Hispanic research, and educational videos, among other resources.

Cyndi's List of Hispanic Sites - **FREE**
www.cyndislist.com/hispanic.htm

Catalog of genealogical sites arranged by topic and country. Includes web links to Internet sites; mailing lists; people and families; news groups; publications, and transcriptions of records; societies; and villages, and colonies.

Mexico GenWeb - www.rootsweb.com/~mexwgw

Index of helpful **FREE** genealogical sites arranged by region and country.

Hispanic Genealogical Resources - **FREE**
www.genealogiahispana.com

Directory of Hispanic web links in Spanish and English.

Hispanic Genealogy.org -
www.hispanicgen.org/links.html **FREE**

Valuable web links to Hispanic genealogy by the Colorado Society of Hispanic Genealogy.

Historical Map Collection - **FREE**
www.davidrumsey.com

The David Rumsey Historical Map Collection has over 18,460 maps online. The collection focuses on rare 18th and 19th century North American and South American maps and other cartographic materials which can be used to trace your family roots.

Spain and Latin America Archival Guide -
http://aer.mcu.es/sgae/index_censo_guia.jsp

In Spanish.

FREE

Hispanic Roots Television -
www.rootstelevision.com > Hispanic Genealogy (right hand column) **FREE**

An online television network featuring on-demand videos absolutely free. The Hispanic Roots Channel features free genealogy family history videos focused on Hispanic, Latino, South American, and Mexican research.

Society of Hispanic Ancestral Research - **FREE**
http://home.earthlink.net/~shharmembers/networking.htm

A non-profit all-volunteer organization with the specific goal of helping Hispanics research their family history.

Genealogy of Mexico - http://members. **FREE**
tripod.com/~GaryFelix/index1.htm

A comprehensive resource of Spanish genealogy

information including lists of soldiers and settlers serving in expeditions as far back as 1519, conquistadores serving under Cortez, and names of the first Spanish settlers in California.

Native American Roots

The history and heritage of the Native Americans who inhabited the American continent is a significant part of the American story.

Searching for American Indian ancestors has become much easier today, but much of the information may be inaccurate or incomplete. First, determine the tribal affiliation of your ancestor(s), and do some basic homework on tribal history. Then, search for your ancestor in official records created by the numerous Indian agencies. These are the primary sources for documenting that your ancestor was recognized by the federal government as a member of a tribe.

How to Trace Indian Ancestry - FREE
www.doi.gov/ancestry.html

U.S. Department of Interior's website on tracing your Indian ancestry.

Indians.org - www.indians.org FREE

List of federally recognized U.S. tribes and locations.

Carolyne's Genealogy Helper - FREE
www.angelfire.com/tx/carolynegenealogy

Valuable articles and a blog by a professional genealogist on tracing your Native American roots.

Cyndi's List.com - www.cyndislist.com > Native American FREE

Numerous links to web sites for tracing your Native American family roots.

Native American Genealogy - FREE
www.accessgenealogy.com/native

Free message boards, searchable Indian rolls, and maps.

American Indian Help Center - FREE
www.amerindgen.com

Native American Indian help for all tribes for beginners and experienced researchers.

Footnote.com Native American -
http://go.footnote.com/native_americans $

Footnote is an online repository for original historical documents. Some areas are free, while others can be freely searched and then viewed with a paid subscription. They have nearly 900,000 Native American records currently. Free at Family History Centers. $11.95/month.

Native American Internet Index - *FREE*
www.hanksville.org/NAresources

Directory of web links and blog for Native American web sites.

Access Genealogy - www.accessgenealogy.com

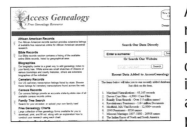

A free genealogy resource with tons of links, this portal also offers census, vital, immigration, cemetery and military records; plus Native American and African American essentials. *FREE*

Asian American Roots

Map Resources - http://geography.about.com/od/findmaps/u/maps.htm *FREE*

The Internet is home to a vast collection of world maps, country maps, state maps, city maps, street maps, road maps, physical maps, political maps, and every type of map possible. This page provides resources for maps along with information to learn how to best use maps and map tools.

Cyndi's List.com - www.cyndislist.com/asia.htm

Numerous links to web sites for tracing your Asian family roots and history. *FREE*

Early Arrivals Records - *FREE*
http://casefiles.berkeley.edu

Online searchable index to casefiles for early immigrants to San Francisco and Hawaii. You won't find the actual case files on this

website; you will have to travel to the NARA office in San Bruno, California to see the records themselves.

Asian-American Web Links - *FREE*
www.archives.gov/genealogy/heritage/index.html#asian

From the National Archives and Records Administration.

AsiaGenWeb - www.worldgenweb.org > AsiaGenWeb *FREE*

Part of the WorldGenWeb, this site links to genealogical information sources in 26 Asian countries.

Angel Island.org - www.angelisland.org *FREE*

Describes the processing of Asian immigrants through Angel Island in San Francisco Bay. Learn the history of this California port and locate and search passenger lists.

Chinese Americans - www.angel-island.com *FREE*

An oral history of Chinese American detainees.

Japan GenWeb -
www.rootsweb.ancestry.com/~jpnwgw *FREE*

This web site contains links to Japanese genealogical web sites in English, Spanish and Japanese. Research on Japanese family heritage can also be done according to Japanese prefecture.

Japanese Research -
www.genealogy.com/00000376.html **FREE**

Contact information, web sites, and books to assist in Japanese genealogy research.

Jewish Resources

JewishGen.org - www.jewishgen.org **FREE**

Searchable data bases for Jewish given names in fifteen nineteenth century European regions, including links to the new local vernacular names adopted in ten foreign countries. Thus, for each European region, these databases include the Hebrew, Yiddish, and local and other-European-country secular names used, as well as new names in foreign countries. These databases of linked European and foreign- country given names allow Jewish genealogists to define all of the Jewish and vernacular names which an ancestor may have used in Europe and in his new country of immigration. Their *Family Tree of the Jewish People* contains data on over 3 million people.

Jewish Shoah Foundation Holocaust Survivors - http://college.usc.edu/vhi **FREE**

An archive of nearly 52,000 videotaped testimonies from Holocaust survivors and other witnesses videotaped in 56 countries and in 32 languages.

Jewish Holocaust Memorial - **FREE**
www.yadvashem.org

Yad Vashem, Jerusalem, is the Jewish people's memorial documenting the history of the Jewish people during the Holocaust period, preserving the memory and story of each of the six million victims. Contains 68 million pages of documents, nearly 300,000 photographs along with thousands of films and videotaped testimonies of survivors, and 112,000 titles in many languages, and thousands of periodicals.

Center for Jewish History - www.cjh.org **FREE**

A Jewish historical and cultural institution to foster Jewish knowledge and to make the historical and cultural record of the Jewish people readily accessible to scholars, students and the broad public.

Jewish Genealogy Publisher - **FREE**
www.avotaynu.com

The leading publisher of products and information of interest to persons who are researching Jewish genealogy, Jewish family trees and Jewish roots.

Jewish Cemetery Association - www.jcam.org

Provides free **FREE** access to more than 50,000 Jewish names for genealogy searches or visitation information. You may search by individual name (first or last).

The Best LDS Web Sites

Millions of people who are interested in genealogy and family history around the world owe a great deal to The Church of Jesus Christ of Latter-day Saints (casually known as the LDS or Mormon Church) due to its unique collection of billions of records

Mormon Temple, Salt Lake City, Utah

worldwide spanning more than a century, and then making the records available to everyone for *free*, regardless of religious affiliation.

Unique Beliefs Drive Search for Ancestors

Latter-day Saints are actively involved in family history, but they are involved for unique reasons. The Church emphasizes the importance of the family and the value of learning about their heritage. They believe that family and marital bonds can last eternally. The primary purpose of their temples is to "seal" or unite families together for eternity, and that their ancestors who have died may also be sealed and united with their spouse and family for eternity. Thus, LDS members feel strongly motivated to seek information about their deceased ancestors and participate in temple rites in their behalf. These unique believes drive their collection of billions of records worldwide to better be able to search for their ancestors.

To help members in tracing their genealogies, the LDS Church has microfilmed vital records throughout the world, and continues to collect billions of records worldwide. They are currently in the process of digitizing and indexing them for access by everyone. They provide access to these records through the Family History Library in Salt Lake City and in over 4,600 local Family History Centers worldwide. They have also developed large databases of genealogical information which is available at http://www.FamilySearch.org. And fortunately for us, they make the records available to everyone for free to our great benefit.

The following collection of the best LDS Web sites is not meant to be a comprehensive

listing, but is a selection of pre-screened, *key* web sites. *See Chapter 5 for more information on FamilySearch.*

Cyndi's List of LDS Records - **FREE**
www.cyndislist.com/lds

A comprehensive list of LDS related websites organized by the following topics: Family History Centers, Family History Library, FamilySearch, history of the LDS Church, Mailing Lists, Miscellaneous Genealogy Resources, Professional Researchers, Publications/Software, Queries and Lists.

FamilySearch.org Web Links - www.family-search.org > *Free Online Resources* (Listed under *Start Your Family History*) **FREE**

Web links to Census records, Vital records, Immigration records, Military records, and Other Key Web Resources.

Genealogy Links.org - **FREE**
http://genealogy-links.org

US & Canada census indexes, immigration, birth, marriage, death, cemetery, obituary, maps, colonial ancestors, LDS info, Paf, Legacy. Contains many LDS/Utah references including information on history, genealogy, and immigration.

Allen's Mormon Site.org - **FREE**
www.mormonsite.org > *Links*

LDS Web links created by Allen Leigh on a wide variety of different topics, including some genealogy links.

LDS and Utah Records -

http://uvpafug.org/classes/dons/
dons-lds&utahrecords.html

FREE

Web links and
notes by Donald
Snow, family
history instructor,
categorized under
the following
headings: Major web sites, Utah and Arizona
Vital Records, LDS Church records, LDS family
history CD, and Miscellaneous.

Book: *A Guide to Mormon Family History Sources* - www.kipsperry.com $16.95

$

A comprehensive
list of LDS family
history websites,
databases, and
much more in
one book by Kip
Sperry, an author,
lecturer, and Professor of family
history at BYU. Available to
purchase online from
www.Ancestry Store.com.

Tracing LDS Families - http://wiki.family-search.org > Search for *'Tracing LDS Families'*

FREE

Research
Outlines detail the
strategies and
records that can
help you learn
more about your
ancestors from
around the world who
were members of the LDS
Church. It helps you decide
which types of records to
search. In addition to this
outline, you will also need
to use the research outlines available
for the state, province, and nation where your
ancestor lived. For example, the *Utah Research
Outline* and the *United States Research Outline*
would help locate many records about Church

members in those places. Go to
www.FamilySearch.org > *Research Helps >
Articles,* and click on 'PDF' under each article.

Early Latter-day Saints.com - www.earlylds.com

This site provides **FREE**
information about
the lives and families
of pioneer Latter-day
Saints (over 61,000
names) who lived
in the more than 90
settlements of Latter-day Saints in the Missouri
Valley, across the state of Iowa, and Winter
Quarters in Nebraska from 1830–1868. You will
find individual and family information in family
group, pedigree and descendant reports some
with photographs as well as biographies,
settlement histories, maps, cemeteries, and
timelines that will help you understand their
lives and times. It also contains an index of
over 100 books found in the Pioneer Research
Library at the Mormon Trail Center at Historic
Winter Quarters, and links to Census records
and other research sites. Click *'Help'* to view
the introductory information.

Early LDS Church Membership -

www.worldvitalrecords.com > *Record Types >
Popular Collections > LDS Collection*
–or– http://www.worldvitalrecords.com/
indexinfo.aspx?ix=usa_il_nauvoo_early_
lds_members

$

A database of birth,
marriage, and death
records comprised
of a 50-volume list
(about 113,000
names) of people
who were members
of the LDS Church from 1830 to 1848 and who
lived in the United States, Canada or Great
Britain. The database created by Susan Black
was compiled using more than 300 primary and
secondary sources on early Latter-day Saints, but
it does not necessarily include every member of
the Church who lived during the time period.
This site includes other LDS databases of value

2 Add New Branches

and allows you to *browse* the list for free. But at Family History Centers you can also browse and view the actual databases for free.

Early Church Information File - FREE

https://wiki.familysearch.org >
(Perform a search for this title)

An alphabetical index of individuals on 75 rolls of microfilm. It contains about 1,500,000 entries from over 1,200 sources about Latter-day Saints and their neighbors. The index is international in scope and should be among the first sources checked when searching for Latter-day Saint ancestors or persons living in areas heavily populated by Latter-day Saints. It mainly covers sources from 1830 to the mid-1900s; includes LDS Church records, LDS immigration records, cemetery records, biographies, journals, and some published books. Microfilm numbers for each individual are listed in the Family History Library Catalog.

Tracing Mormon Pioneers -

www.xmission.com/ ~nelsonb/pioneer FREE

Tips for tracing Mormon Pioneer ancestry from Europe, Scandinavia, Australia, and South Africa to Salt Lake City, Utah. Includes an index of thousands of references of those who migrated to Utah during 1847-1868, plus an index search tool for *Utah Census Records.*

Mormon Pioneer Overland Travel - www.lds.org > *About the Church > Church History > Library > Resources Available Online*

Or try: www.lds.org/churchhistory/library/pioneercompanysearch/1,15773,3966-1,00.html

The most complete index of individuals and companies that crossed the plains to Utah between 1847

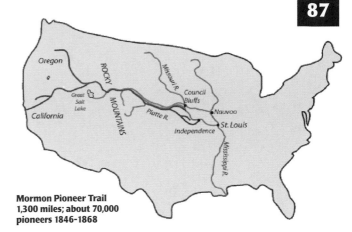

Mormon Pioneer Trail
1,300 miles; about 70,000 pioneers 1846-1868

and 1868. Includes transcribed excerpts from trail diaries, letters, and newspaper reports. The Pioneer Story - www.lds.org/gospellibrary/pioneer/pioneerstory.htm

OneClickTempleTrip.com - $

www.oneclicktempletrip.com

A new website (Beta) that focuses on one specific task, finding your next ancestor ready to take to the temple. It automates the long manual steps on new.FamilySearch.org to find missing ordinances. First, it searches all your direct ancestors to the end of each ancestral line or to the year 1500. It then searches the spouses, children, siblings and parents and shows all the ordinances that need to be done in your tree. Sign in using your new FamilySearch sign-in credentials. It searches your family tree for missing ordinances, reserves the ordinance for you, and generates your Family Ordinance Request. It took some time but it searched 19 generations for me, processing a total of 842 ancestors, saving me an estimated 28 hours of manual searching. Results: 18 different ordinances ready for the temple, and over 100 ordinances missing but not ready for the temple due to missing information. *Certified by FamilySearch.* $29.95/year.

Membership Card Index - FREE

www.xmission.com/~nelsonb/minnie

This unique card index (also known as the "Minnie Margetts File") indexes selected LDS Church membership records, primarily in the United States and England from 1839-1915.

Nauvoo Records of Baptisms - http://family history.byu.edu/publications/baptisms.html

A valuable seven-volume set of over 15,000 baptisms, not found elsewhere, that have been extracted, edited, and alphabetized from faded holographic baptismal records, including information on work done in the Mississippi River. $150

Mormon Immigration Index - FREE $
www.ldscatalog.com > *(do a quick search)*

This Index on compact disk documents the journeys of over 94,000 LDS Church converts who crossed the Atlantic or Pacific oceans to gather in Nauvoo, Illinois, or other frontier outposts, between 1840 and 1890.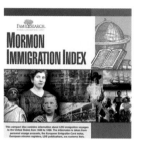
Includes the name, age, and country of origin of each passenger, ports of departure and arrival, approximate number of passengers on each ship, the assigned company leaders, often a brief history of the voyage, plus autobiographies, journals, diaries and letters of approximately 1,000 immigrant converts. These accounts provide a compelling view of those who crossed the oceans and then by land, rivers, and rails gathered in Salt Lake City. Search for free at Family History Centers. $6 to purchase.

Linkpendium.com - www.linkpendium.com > *Utah Genealogy* (listed under *Localities: USA*) FREE

A good statewide directory of about 4,500 family history web links.

Cyndi's List.com / Utah - FREE
www.cyndislist.com/ut.htm

Another good directory of about 1,500 web links.

Death and Marriage Notices - FREE
www.rootsweb.ancestry.com/~utsaltla/ obit_DeseretNews_1850s.html

Abstracts of Deaths and Marriages Notices in the *Deseret News Weekly* of Salt Lake City, Utah (1852-1900) made available by UtahGenWeb.

Utah Digital Newspapers - FREE
http://digitalnewspapers.org

Contains over 600,000 pages of Utah historical newspapers and other digital collections.

Utah Research Center - FREE
http://historyresearch.utah.gov

Research **Utah Death Certificates** from 1904-1956; research historic state and local government records from 1850 to today; and research manuscripts, photographs, books, maps, and online resources about Utah and the West.

Utah State History / Cemeteries - FREE
http://history.utah.gov/apps/burials/ execute/searchburials

Explore Utah's history and its place in the West, search

thousands of photographs, and find many of Utah's cemetery records online.

Utah Census Search - www.xmission.com/%7Enelsonb/census_search.htm **FREE**

Utah Census Search

An index for Utah Census records from 1850-1880.

Western States Marriage Index - **FREE**
http://abish.byui.edu/specialCollections/westernStates/search.cfm

A current ongoing project that contains about 700,000 marriage records to date from selected counties in California, western Colorado, Montana, Oregon, Utah, eastern Washington, Wyoming and New Mexico.

Washington County Pioneer Index -
www.lofthouse.com/USA/Utah/washington/pioneers/main.html **FREE**

An index of the names and vital information of Utah Pioneers who entered Washington County, Utah up to 1870. The resources include: U.S. 1860 and 1870 Census, early LDS Ward membership records, cemetery records, local histories, family group sheets, and indexes of land deeds.

Washington County Early Marriage Index -
www.lofthouse.com/USA/Utah/washington/marriage/index.html **FREE**

Contains over 2,000 marriages in Washington County, Utah from 1862-1919.

Salt Lake City Directories - **FREE**
www.rootsweb.com/~utsaltla/Directories/index.html

Links to early residential directories.

Utah Digital Collections and Indexes -
http://historyresearch.utah.gov/indexes/index.html

Salt Lake County death certificate images, 1905-1956

FREE

Daughters of Utah Pioneers - **FREE**
www.dupinternational.org

The members of the Daughters of the Utah Pioneers (DUP) have prepared and collected thousands of biographies of early pioneers (1847-1869). A pioneer is an ancestor who came to the Utah Territory/State of Deseret; died crossing the plains; or was born in the Utah Territory/State of Deseret before May 10, 1869, the coming of the railroad. Also available are photographs of many of the early LDS church members. You can search for a pioneer on their website and then request a copy of their biography.

BYU Family History Archive - **FREE**
www.lib.byu.edu/fhc

One of the greatest online genealogy resources available that is still relatively unknown. It currently includes a collection of about 20,000 diaries, biographies, family histories, Elders journals, oral histories, gazetteers, and a medieval section. However, they continue

2 Add New Branches

to add new volumes each week, and they are targeting over 100,000 published family histories and thousands of local histories, city directories and other related records all of which can be easily searched by surname, geographic area, book title, or author. You can simply browse all the family histories or view the full text of each. The best way to quickly find the histories most likely to be of use to you is to use the Keyword searches. This promises to become the most comprehensive collection of city and county histories on the Web. And it's free!

Trails of Hope: Overland Diaries and Letters - **FREE**
http://overlandtrails.lib.byu.edu

A collection of the original writings of 49 voyagers on the Mormon, California, Oregon, and Montana pioneer trails who wrote while traveling on the trail; includes maps, trail guides, photographs, watercolors and art sketches between 1846-1869.

Missionary Diaries - **FREE**
www.lib.byu.edu/dlib/mmd

A superb collection of over 63,000 pages of missionary diaries including some individuals fairly prominent in the LDS Church.

It provides an opportunity to read and understand the missionary experiences, the joys, the sorrows, the struggles that can change lives. The earliest missionary diary in the collection is a one–volume diary penned in 1832 by Hyrum Smith.

Journals of Early Members of the Church - **FREE**
www.boap.org/LDS/Early-Saints

Journals, diaries, biographies and auto-biographies of some early Mormons and others who knew Joseph Smith, Jr. and/or his contemporaries.

Biography and Journal Excerpts - **FREE**
www.signaturebookslibrary.org

Some biography and journal excerpts and resources on different topics about Utah, Mormonism and the West including the full text of some out-of-print books.

Biographical Registers - **FREE**
http://byustudies.byu.edu/Indexes/BioAlpha/MBRegisterA.aspx

A list of people in selected Mormon biographical registers.

Biographical Sketches - **FREE**
www.saintswithouthalos.com

A website devoted to the life and times of Joseph Smith from 1831 to 1839 (the Ohio/ Missouri period); includes biographical sketches of his contemporaries.

LDS Biographical Encyclopedia - **FREE**
www.lib.byu.edu/online.html > *All Collections* > *Misc. Books* > *Encyclopedic History of Church*

A compilation of over 5000 biographical sketches and more than 2000 photo-graphs of prominent men and women in the LDS Church, authored by Andrew Jenson, Assistant Church Historian. It comprises 4-volumes from 1901-1936 available on line in the special books collection at BYU. It includes accounts of all the general authorities and many of the presidents and bishops of the stakes and wards. This work is particularly valuable in providing brief histories of Church units from their beginnings up to 1930.

Mormons and Their Neighbors - **FREE**
www.lib.byu.edu/Ancestry

An index compiled by Marvin E. Wiggins in the 1970s (which took more than a decade to compile) of over 100,000 biographical sketches appearing in 236 published volumes; includes people living between 1820 and 1981 in northern Mexico, New Mexico, Arizona, southern California, Nevada, Utah, Idaho, Wyoming, and southwestern Canada. It is not a name index, only published works containing actual biographical information were indexed. Most of the titles are housed in the BYU Library. Copies of the biographies can be requested from your own public or university library via Interlibrary Loan.

Welsh Mormon History.org - **FREE**
www.welshmormonhistory.org

Contains journal excerpts, vital information, biographies, and photos. This site seeks to preserve and share information about the early converts to Mormonism in Wales, and is the product of Dr. Ronald Dennis' research.

Mormon Publications - **FREE**
www.lib.byu.edu/online.html Or try <http://contentdm.lib.byu.edu/cdm4/browse.php?CISOROOT=%2FNCMP1820-1846>

A digital collection in the BYU Library of early Mormon publications which includes books, missionary tracts, doctrinal treatises, hymnals and periodicals which helped define the doctrinal development and historical movements of the Mormon people in the 19th and 20th centuries.

Studies in Mormon History - **FREE**
http://mormonhistory.byu.edu

An online indexed bibliography that is being updated constantly. It includes articles, books, theses, dissertations, and diaries dealing with the history of the Church written from the time of its inception in 1830 to the present.

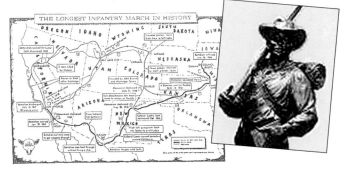

Mormon Battalion.com - **FREE**
www.mormonbattalion.com

Contains a brief history of the U.S. Mormon Battalion along with a documented, researched roster, photographs, and maps.

LDS Families Info - www.sedgwickresearch.com > *Family Website Links* **FREE**

Biographical information on many well-known LDS families.

Add New 2 Branches

Historical Documents of the LDS Church - FREE
www.centerplace.org/history

From the Evening and Morning Star, Messenger Advocate, and Times and Seasons.

FarWestHistory.com - www.farwesthistory.com

Interactive map and history of Far West.

FREE

Mormon Frontier Foundation - FREE
www.jwha.info/mmff/mmffhp.htm

History of early settlements in Missouri.

BYU Winter Quarters Project - FREE
http://winterquarters.byu.edu

Searchable pioneer database and information on the settlements in Nebraska.

Mountain West Digital Library - FREE
http://155.97.12.155/mwdl

An aggregation of digital collections from universities, colleges, public libraries, museums, and historical societies in Utah, Nevada, and Idaho.

Early Mormon History Articles -
www.sidneyrigdon.com/dbroadhu/artindex.htm

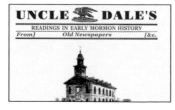

Old newspaper articles on the Mormons indexed by region.

FREE

Utah State Historical Society - FREE
http://historyresearch.utah.gov

Thousands of photographs, books, manuscript collections, maps, newspapers and periodicals on Utah's history.

BYU Library Photo Collection - FREE
www.lib.byu.edu/dlib/historic_photos

Over 30,000 historic photographic collections.

Isle of Man Mormon Coverts - FREE
http://isle-of-man.com/manxnotebook/mormon

Biographies of some Mormon converts.

Perpetual Emigrating Fund -
www.mormonhistoricsitesfoundation.org >
(do a search)

Names of persons and sureties indebted to the Perpetual Emigrating Fund Company from 1850 to 1877.

 FREE

BYU Immigrant Ancestors Project - FREE
http://immigrants.byu.edu

An ongoing project sponsored by BYU's *Center for Family History and Genealogy* uses emigration registers to locate information about the birthplaces of immigrants in their native countries, which is not found in the port registers and naturalization documents in the destination countries.

Other Ethnic Resources

See also the Best International Websites pages 175-188.

National Archive Resources - *(FREE)*
www.archives.gov/genealogy/heritage/
index.html

Directory of web links to various ethnic resources. Includes: United Kingdom and Ireland; Australia and New Zealand; Canadian and French-Canadian; Eastern European and Russian; Hispanic: Central and South America, Mexico, Caribbean, West Indies; Jewish; Western European; and more.

Cyndi's List.com - www.cyndislist.com > *(FREE)*
Topical Index > Ethnic Groups and People

Numerous links to web sites for tracing many Ethnic heritages.

Federation of East European Family History Societies - http://feefhs.org *(FREE)*

An umbrella organization that promotes family research in eastern and central Europe without any ethnic, religious, or social distinctions. It provides a forum for individuals and organizations focused on a single country or group of people to exchange information.

Russian & East European Studies - *(FREE)*
www.ucis.pitt.edu/reesweb

Directory of Internet resources for the Balkans, the Baltic states, the Caucusus, Central Asia, Central Europe, the CIS, Eastern Europe, the NIS, the Russian Federation, and the former Soviet Union.

Directory of Irish Genealogy - *(FREE)*
http://homepage.tinet.ie/~seanjmurphy/dir

Information, links, FAQ, advice, and articles about tracing Irish ancestors.

WorldGenWeb.org - www.worldgenweb.org *(FREE)*

A non-profit, volunteer based organization dedicated to providing genealogical and historical records and resources for world-wide access.

Additional Ways to Do Research Online

Here are additional ways to do research, gather information, and share your family roots, stories, photos, and heritage using the Internet.

Social Networking Sites
One of the Newest Connection Tools

Social networking refers to a class of web sites and services that allow you to connect with friends, family, and colleagues online, as well as meet people with similar interests. You can connect with your family, swap stories and recipes, share family photos, and build collaborative family trees. Your extended family can collaborate and share information on your shared family tree. Some of the sites use advanced technologies like wikis, RSS, mapping, and online family tree building to help you connect with your family and ancestors. All of these family history social networking sites have great appeal, wonderful capabilities, and are private and secure. Here are the most popular social networking sites to explore.

Book: Social Networking for Genealogists - *($)*
www.genealogical.com

This book by Drew Smith describes the wide array of social networking services that are now available online and highlights how these services can be used by genealogists to share information, photos, and videos with family, friends, and other researchers. From blogs and wikis to Facebook and Second Life, it shows you how to incorporate these powerful new tools into your family history research. $18.95

Facebook.com – www.facebook.com

A free social networking website where you can add friends and send them messages; connect and share with the people in your life. Anyone can join. You can join networks organized by city, workplace, school, and region. It currently has more than 350 million active users worldwide, and has become so ubiquitous that the generic verb "facebooking" had come into use to describe the process of browsing others' profiles or updating one's own. One of the most popular applications on Facebook is the *Photos* application where users can upload an unlimited number of photos; 14 million photos are uploaded daily. You can also "tag", or label users in a photo. The instant messaging application (*Chat*) allows users to communicate with friends. *Gifts* allows you to send virtual gifts to your friends. *Marketplace* lets you post free classified ads which are only seen by users that are in the same network. Because of the open nature of Facebook, several countries have currently banned access to it including Syria, China, Iran, and Vietnam.

Geni.com - www.geni.com

This free, simple interface allows you to create a family tree online and then invite family members to join the family tree and add other relatives. Family members can share photos and work together to create profiles for common ancestors. New features including video sharing and tree merging. Combined with existing features such as photo sharing, calendar, timelines, and news, the site provides a complete suite of free tools for families to build their family tree, preserve their history, and stay in touch in a private, secure environment.

GenealogyWise.com - www.genealogywise.com

A new web site that combines community interaction with tools and resources for people

who are interested in researching and sharing their family history with others. It's an open network that allows anyone to join and create social groups within the genealogy-focused community. The innovative and easy-to-use platform opens the doors of social networking to millions around the world who are interested in sharing their passion for family history and in meeting new people that share that passion. The free service allows users to join surname groups, explore ancestral records, share photos, video, and family trees. Users can create a profile to tell others about their research interests, to receive and respond to emails from other users without publishing an email address, to create online family trees and personal research pages, and to collaborate with other users.

FamilyLink.com - www.familylink.com

A free application on Facebook to help you stay in touch with your families through photo sharing, a news feed, birthday reminders, etc. You can also build your family tree.

MyFamily.com - www.myfamily.com

In a secure, password-protected environment, you can create online family photo albums, share family news, maintain a calendar of family events, and more. There's also a toll-free phone number to record your family stories and memories. The basic site is free which includes uploading 100 MB per member per month (with unlimited storage space) and complete backup protection. You can upgrade for extra features such as: Ad-free, professionally-designed and customizable themes, your custom domain, and 1 GB per member of monthly uploads (10x more than basic) for only $29.95 per year total.

MyHeritage.com - www.myheritage.com (FREE)

A host of free genealogy tools enable you to create your family's own meeting place on the Internet where you can share family photos, post your family tree online, trace the family's medical history and keep track of important family events. Plus, free genealogy software and a genealogy search engine help you expand your family history research. Home to more than 28 million family members, 5 million family trees, and 300 million profiles available in 34 languages.

GeneTree.com - www.genetree.com (FREE)

A DNA-enabled networking site designed to help people understand where their personal histories belong within the greater human genetic story. Creates unparalleled opportunities for unlocking genetic heritage and identity, connecting with ancestors and living relatives, and sharing meaningful information and experiences to help preserve family histories. You can build and collaborate on family trees, and share digital videos, photos and memories. This site also offers a genealogy DNA testing service, and notifies you of a DNA connection with others in the database, providing the opportunity to make a connection with that individual if you wish.

Genes Reunited.com - www.genesreunited.com

The UK's no.1 (FREE) family tree and genealogy site with over 10 million members. It's free to build your family tree online, search for your ancestors in 650 million names in family trees, census, birth, marriages, death and military records, and send messages to other members to discover a shared family history and find new relatives.

Our Story.com - www.ourstory.com (FREE)

Allows you to create a visual timeline, collaborate with family and friends, and document every moment of your loved ones' life with video, pictures, and storytelling. The site also offers ways to share with anyone you want and backup these memories on CD, DVD and books.

WeRelate.org - www.werelate.org (FREE)

Wiki-based Web site—sponsored by the Foundation for On-Line Genealogy in partnership with the Allen County Public Library—allows you to easily create profile pages for your ancestors. Others can view these pages and add information, or add profiles for their own ancestors. Source citations and scanned images of original documents can be added to document the information.

KinCafe.com - www.kincafe.com (FREE)

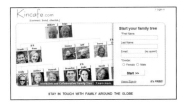

A free family network to connect, bond and cherish loved ones. You can build and link family trees together, remember birthdays and anniversaries, share your photo albums, family calendar, blogs and other family treasures with all who care most. You manage whether to allow your friends and relatives to see your family's content.

Famiva.com - www.famiva.com (FREE)

This free social network for families offers a secure, password protected place for you and your relatives to connect and collaborate. You can share photos and stories, work together to build an online family tree, explore family maps, and more.

Mailing Lists

Share Info with Others with a Common Interest

RootsWeb Mailing Lists - **FREE**
http://lists.rootsweb.ancestry.com

Mailing lists are free discussion groups where individuals with a common interest share information with each other by e-mail.

All subscribers can send e-mail to and receive e-mail from the list. There are thousands of family history / genealogy mail lists. This is the oldest and largest index of family history mail lists (about 30,000 currently) which is organized in categories: Surnames, USA, International, and Other.

Newsgroups

Discussion Groups with Common Interest

Discussion groups are stored on the Internet until you request the messages. There are dozens of newsgroups and tools that will search these messages. For more information, see the following web pages:

> www.rootsweb.com/~jfuller/gen_use.html
> www.genhomepage.com/communications.html
> www.cyndislist.com/newsgrps.htm

Surnames and Family Associations

Individual Family Surnames

RootsWeb Surname List - **FREE**
http://rsl.rootsweb.com

Allows you to register the surname you are currently researching. By checking these lists, searchers often find others looking for the same surnames. Every day, dozens of connections are made between relatives using these lists. Contains over 1,200,000 surnames.

Finding Your Ancestors - **FREE**
http://genealogy.about.com/library/weekly/aa041700a.htm

A guide to internet search techniques for the surnames in your family tree. There are many

wonderful family history Web pages on the Internet which remain undiscovered because people just don't know how to locate them. These pages may contain just the valuable information that you are looking for - family trees, stories, photographs, cemetery transcriptions, wills, etc.

Surname Finder - www.surnamefinder.com

Providing easy access to resources **FREE** for 1,731,359 surnames.

Queries

Requests for information about a specific ancestor, couple, or family. Besides accepting queries, most sites allow you to search the queries left by others. These include www.usgenweb.org, www.genforum.com, and www.query.genealogytoolbox.com.

Help (or Lookup) Lists

USGenWeb.org - www.usgenweb.org **FREE**

Provides e-mail addresses of people for each county in the U.S. willing to look up information for you at no charge. These are volunteers who do quick searches in various books, records, and record offices as a public service.

Random Acts of Genealogical Kindness - **FREE**
http://raogk.org

A global volunteer organization with over 4000 volunteers in every U.S. state and many international locations have helped thousands of researchers. Their volunteers take time to do everything from looking up courthouse records to taking pictures of tombstones. All they ask in return is reimbursement for their expenses (never their time) and a thank you.

CHAPTER 3

3-Easy Steps
Follow These 3-Easy Steps to Begin Building Your Family Tree

STEP 3 - Connect With the Lives of Your Ancestors

DISCOVER YOUR FAMILY HERITAGE, STORIES, AND PHOTOS

Family history is more than just names and dates. You should learn more about who your ancestors really were, where they lived, and what they did. You should try to gain information and an understanding of each of your ancestors if possible. Finding your roots and stories helps you gain a sense of belonging, and an understanding of who you are and where you come from.

The Internet is the perfect tool for opening a window to the past and connecting with the lives and stories of your ancestors. Discover more than you ever imagined about the lives of your ancestors that made you who you are today.

3 Connect with Ancestors

Suggested Activities

1. Consider ways your family can best honor and pay tribute to your ancestors and inspire your children to know them.

2. Establish a new tradition in your family for honoring your ancestors which can be perpetuated from generation-to-generation.

3. Create a timeline of one or more of your ancestors lives combined with historical events to get to know the times in which they lived.

4. Visit the cemetery and gravesite of an ancestor(s) to better connect with them.

Family History Insights - 3

Alex Haley

Knowing Who You Are

"Knowing who you are and what responsibility you have towards your family forces your behavior to be consistent with your family values. It passes right down across the generations." Alex Haley, press conference, Freedman's Bank CD, 2001

Daniel Webster

Connecting the Past with the Future

"Those who do not look upon themselves as links connecting the past with the future do not perform their duty to the world." Daniel Webster (1782-1852), statesman

Helen Keller

A King Among Your Ancestors

"There is no king who has not had a slave among his ancestors, and no slave who has not had a king among his." Helen Keller (1880-1968), American author, political activist and lecturer

Boyd K. Packer
© by Intellectual Reserve, Inc.

Finding the Time to Connect to Your Ancestors

"There somehow seems to be the feeling that genealogical work is an all-or-nothing responsibility. That is not so. Genealogical work is another responsibility for every [one]. And we may do it successfully along with all the other responsibilities that rest upon us. ... You can fulfill your [ambition to trace] your kindred dead... without forsaking your other responsibilities. ... You can do it without becoming a so-called 'expert' in it.

There is an old Chinese proverb which states: 'Man who sits with legs crossed and mouth open, waiting for roast duck to fly in, have long hunger.'

Once we started, we found the time. Somehow we were able to carry on all of the other responsibilities. There seemed to be an increased inspiration in our lives because of this work. But the decision, the action, must begin with [you]. ...

The process of searching...[is] worth all the effort you could invest. The reason: You cannot find names without knowing that they represent people. You begin to find out things about people. When we research our own lines we become interested in more than just names. ... Our interest turns our hearts to our fathers—we seek to find and to know and to serve them." Boyd Packer, Bookcraft, 1980, pp. 223-30, 239-40

Monte J. Brough
© by Intellectual Reserve, Inc.

Finding Joy in Family History

"Thirty-five years ago I was... in England. My mother had been pursuing her grandmother's family history, but she knew nothing more than that her grandmother had been born in a little place called Philly Green, England. My mother had never been able to locate this town. ... As I was driving...I saw a little sign that said "Philly Green." Several weeks later, I returned and drove down a winding country lane until I came to a quaint little village with a church that had been built in 1174. I went out into the cemetery and looked at each headstone. During the next few hours, I had the privilege of finding the headstones of my great-grandmother's family members. I'll never forget how I felt that day standing in that cemetery in that beautiful place in England. I felt a connection with my ancestors, particularly with my great-grandmother, who as a seventeen-year-old girl left her family in England and moved to [America]. What a great experience! This kind of joy really can come to every[one]." Monte J. Brough

Connect With the Lives of Your Ancestors

DISCOVER YOUR FAMILY HERITAGE, STORIES, AND PHOTOS

Published family histories can help you make connections between generations. Timelines of your ancestor's lives in context with historical events–along with photographs of the times in which your ancestors lived–can provide an interesting perspective and add life to your story. Historic newspapers and periodicals provide unique insight and a rare opportunity to understand the culture and customs of how your ancestors lived. Online gazetteers (geographical dictionaries) and place databases help you discover the geographic location of the place your ancestors called home–their village or town and cemetery.

Discovering your ancestor's health history can be a useful tool to aid you in interpreting patterns of health, illness and genetic traits for you and your descendants. Learning how to care for your precious photos will help preserve the past for future generations. And perhaps discovering that you descended from royalty or related to someone famous may just 'make your day'.

Finding your family roots–and the stories, values and traditions about your ancestor's lives–can help you better understand them. But it also helps you better understand yourself, and gives you a

Benefits of Connecting With the Lives and Stories of Your Ancestors

- **Knowledge** of your forebears will increase
- **Better Understand** your ancestors and yourself; the opportunity to learn more about your kindred dead will bless lives
- Gain a **Greater Appreciation** of your heritage, the sacrifices your ancestors made for you, and a better understanding of what their life was like
- **Gain Strength** from learning about how your ancestors met challenges in life
- Unite, weld, and **Strengthen Bonds** between family members forever; your family will grow closer
- Promote a **Sense of Belonging** that ties generations together, and foreshadows your belonging in the eternal family of God; your desire and willingness to honor your beloved ancestors prepares you to belong to Him who is our Father
- **Discover** within yourself a reservoir of patience, endurance, and love that you will never find without the deep commitment that grows from a sense of real belonging
- Gain a **Sense of Identity and Purpose in Life**
- Draw yourself and your family **Closer to God**
- Your ties with the eternal world suddenly become very real, **Sharpening Your Life's Focus** and lifting your expectations
- Exerting such immovable loyalty to your forebears **Teaches You More About How to Love Others.**

greater appreciation of your heritage and the sacrifices they made for you. Many of your ambitions and challenges in life are the same as theirs. You gain strength from learning about how your ancestors met life's troubling challenges.

Doing family history work helps unite your family, and strengthens bonds between your family members.

Knowledge of your forebears will increase, your family will grow closer, families will be strengthened, and the opportunity to learn more about your kindred dead will bless lives. As you learn more about your ancestors, you weld eternal family links, and draw yourself and your family closer to God. It's a wonderful opportunity to find your family identity. And help promote that identity in your children and grand children.

Appreciating Your Heritage

Reflecting on the Past

Who were your ancestors? Each of us has hundreds of thousands of ancestors as part of our unique heritage. And each and every one of your ancestors had to exist in order for you to exist. Each one of them and everything they were have contributed to your being. Their genes are in you; their blood runs in your veins. You not only inherited their genes, but many of their physical traits, values and attitudes have been passed down to you from one generation to another showing up in the way you look, think, and act. The choices made by your ancestors over the generations have influenced the way you live and think. In many ways, your ancestors have affected your life and molded your destiny. They are a part of who you are today. It took thousands of years of people having children with the right person at the right time to get to your existence.

Your ancestors are more than just a bunch of lifeless names and dates on a chart. They made a huge difference in who you are. And still do! The Best way to know who you are is to know where you came from. But it is strange how little most

of us know about them or the times in which they lived. Most certainly, many of your ancestors lived a life of deprivation and hardship. Most of them sacrificed much for their posterity. Many left behind beloved family members, plush homelands, and previous possessions to come to often a barren, undeveloped strange land so that their descendants could have a better life. By tracing your own family roots and stories, you can come to appreciate your heritage more and more, and know and honor your forefathers as you discover what their lives were like.

Some people find great joy in discovering an ancestor's diary, journal or letter to help find their roots and collect their family traditions and stories. But usually it's the small bits of information from many different sources that help bring your ancestors to life. Everyone has his own unique history and family stories. And finding your family roots and treasured stories is one of the most meaningful ways you can honor your ancestors. You can honor those who have gone before by learning more about them and following in their footsteps. And you should be grateful for the rich abundance you enjoy today because of their great sacrifices and efforts. They helped forge a life that is so much better for you than anything they might have even dared dream about for themselves.

Your ancestors labored long and hard, built their own home with their own bare hands, and raised a family and created their own livelihood. They became pilgrims and pioneers and cowboys who etched out a new life for themselves. They had great dreams and aspirations which wielded a profound influence on the future, just like you. You should honor your forbears for who they were, what they accomplished, and even the mistakes they made. One of the great lessons—maybe the principal lesson—of doing family history is learning from the mistakes of your ancestors. Tracing your family roots and connecting to your ancestors can be one of the most intellectually stimulating, absorbing, and fulfilling ways you will ever find to spend your valuable time.

Your ancestors deserve your recognition and honor for the determination and fortitude they portrayed in leaving the comfort of their home and emigrating to the New World to forge a new life.

Tools to Help Reflect on the Past

Here are some good tools that may help bring your ancestors to life. They can help you gain an insight into understanding their heritage, lifestyle, traditions, and what it was like "way back when".

Making of America -
http://moa.umdl.umich.edu and
http://moa.cit.cornell.edu/moa

This is a joint project between the University of Michigan and Cornell University which provides free access to a large collection of 19th century books, journal articles, and imprints available on two websites. Two separate online archive sites put digitized books at your fingertips. The first collection contains some 10,000 books and 50,000 journal articles; the second site covers 267 monograph volumes and more than 100,000 journal articles.

Library of Congress - *FREE*
www.americaslibrary.org

The Library of Congress in Washington, DC is the largest library in the world and has millions of amazing things that will surprise you. This is a site that teaches American history in a manner that is appealing to both adults and older children. Their **"America's Story"** section contains many documents, letters, diaries, records, tapes, films, sheet music, maps, prints, photographs, digital files, and other materials from the past, and wants you to have fun with history while learning at the same time. They want to show you some things that you've never heard or seen before. You can look at pictures of American inventors, listen to Thomas

Edison's voice extracted from an early recording, watch vaudeville acts filmed about 100 years ago, and even watch a film clip of Buffalo Bill Cody's Wild West show made in 1902. Their **American Memory Collection** at http://memory.loc.gov/ ammem offers more than seven million digital items from more than one hundred historical collections.

Generation Maps.com -
www.generationmaps.com

An easy to use, very affordable, genealogy chart design and printing service. They offer personalized working charts, beautiful decorative charts, custom heirloom charts, and a printing service for charts you've created. Now you don't have to fill in a chart yourself — just send your genealogy computer file and/or your digital photos, tell them how you want it to look, and it arrives on your doorstep for a very reasonable price. They can help you get your research out where you can see it and surround your family with a sense of their heritage. It's also a wonderful, easy way to explain to your family members the research that has been accomplished.

Reminisce.com - www.reminisce.com

A nostalgia magazine, written by its readers from around the country and published bi-monthly. Advertising-free with real-life stories and family album photos—recalling times from the Roaring Twenties to the Fabulous Fifties—take a trip down memory lane. A magazine that brings back the good times. $14.98

Everyday Life Book Series -
www.writersdigest.com

Everyday Life in Colonial America from 1607-1783 describes home life, agriculture, cooking, transportation, dealing with the natives, and details about their courageous

struggles to carve out a new life for themselves in North America. (Dale Taylor, Writers Digest Books, Cincinnati, Ohio, 2002). $16.99

Everyday Life in the 1800s discusses homes, furniture, travel, money, occupations, health and medicine, amusement, courtship and marriage, slavery, crime, and cowboy life out West. (Marc McCutcheon, Writers Digest Books, Cincinnati, Ohio, 2001) $16.99

Everyday Life during the Civil War describes many aspects of life in both the North and South, including housing, clothing, military uniforms, weapons and insignia, camp life, newspapers, etc. (Michael J. Varhola, Writers Digest Books, Cincinnati, Ohio, 1999) $16.99

Honoring Your Ancestors

Every human being alive has ancestors: parents, grandparents, great-grandparents, and so forth. Knowing who your Ancestors are is fundamental to knowing who *you* are. Your ancestors DNA runs in your blood. All of your Ancestors are inside of you – whether you know them or not – so honoring them is honoring yourself.

What Does it Mean to Honor Ancestors?

According to the dictionary, to *honor* means to regard with great respect, to have an attitude of admiration or esteem, to revere, and to manifest the highest veneration in words and actions.

© Intellectual Reserve, Inc.

Revering ancestors can support you in your life's journey because your ancestors are a source of wisdom. When you seek to connect with your ancestors, you connect with forbears who love you and are interested in you. Ancestors help you to know who you are. To know who you are and where you're going, you need to start at the beginning. Connecting with your ancestors is a way to trace your identify back through time. Knowing your past empowers you to make wise choices about your future.

Ancestors unite us with all of humanity. Virtually all of the human family are, on some level, our "cousins", no matter how near or distant. Recognizing this common connection with all segments of the human family is a powerful doorway into universal brotherhood and peace. When we acknowledge our relatedness to the entire human family it helps us to treat others as our kindred.

We honor our ancestors for many reasons but also because they were brave, courageous men and women who fought stalwartly for our future destiny. For example, during the American Revolutionary War they were outnumbered, outgunned, and ill-equipped, yet they successfully defeated the greatest military and naval power of the 18th century. Our forefathers believed that *"all men are created equal, that they were endowed by their Creator with certain unalienable rights, that among these are life, liberty and the pursuit of happiness."*

They believed in consent of the governed, the right to bear arms and self-defense, and in limited interference by government. They were good people who believed in the sovereignty and guardianship of Almighty God. Their motto became *"In God We Trust"* which was later declared on all of our national coins.

How to Honor Your Ancestors

Once you get to know your ancestors, you invariably develop a sense of belonging to them. So it's natural and right to want to pay tribute to and honor them. You may write a family history or plan a family reunion which helps you reach out to others and ensure that the memory of your ancestors will survive. But there are countless ways you can pay tribute to the valuable insight and wisdom of those who have gone before you.

Learn About Them and Share

Learn about your ancestors: trace your family roots back a few generations. Make a family tree

Someday, each of us will be someone's ancestor. How would you like to be honored?

with your children. Collect interesting family stories about each person and write them down with a photo and some details. Visit their hometowns or homelands. Study the language or culture of your ethnic roots. Share what you learn with your children. You might even assign a report on an ancestor to each child.

Keep a Memento

One idea for celebrating mothers and grand-mothers on Mother's Day – and honor the special women in your family – is to create an online photo gallery. Your ancestors will be pleased to know that their smile can be viewed by family members everywhere. Gather family members together while visiting graves. Keep a memento, such as: Your grandfather's cufflinks, your grandmother's silk handkerchief or precious china keepsakes.

Have an Ancestor Feast

One way to honor your departed ancestor on the anniversary of their birth or death is to have an ancestor feast. Set an extra plate at the table, lit by a candle, and surrounded by a photo of your ancestor. Serve that person's favorite dishes, their signature recipes, or foods that reflect their cultural heritage. What were some of the special dishes they made that left a lasting impression on you? Have your children help in selecting and preparing foods for this commemoration. The flavors and aromas associated with a relative's favorite foods are a concrete way to keep memories alive. And if not an entire meal, baking or cooking something just like mom, dad, or grandma did can be just as effective a way to pass something of that person along to your own children.

Plant a Garden

Here's a lovely and lasting tribute. Plant a small garden in honor of an ancestor. Consider having a small tree, such as a Japanese maple or weeping cherry as the centerpiece. Designate an annual tradition of adding something to the garden in the late spring or early summer of each year. If space allows, place a bench near this garden for sitting, meditating, and remembering.

How Would You Like to Be Honored?

Is it enough to just keep up the gravestones and monuments to our ancestors? That must undoubtedly be done, but it's only a part of the honor that we owe to our gallant ancestors. What would honor them the most of all?

John Weaver wrote: *"The greatest honor that we could bestow upon our ancestors is to follow them in their faith, maintaining their cause, and fighting for the same truths and principles they tenaciously held. The greatest honor my grandchildren and great grandchildren can bestow upon me is to follow in the faith, principles, and truth that I communicate and teach."* (Pastor John Weaver, Freedom Baptist and Dominion Ministry; http://www.virginials.org/honoring.htm)

Live a Honorable Life

One of the best ways to honor your ancestors is by loving and caring for yourself, and living a respectable, honorable life since you are the carrier of their genes. Take care of yourself. Stay healthy, keep your body whole and hearty. After all, it is a gift from them. Ancestors generally wish the best for you and your family. They take pride in your accomplishments, just as they did when they were living.

We honor best those who have gone before when we serve well in the cause of right, goodness and truth. We should walk as they walked and embrace the goodness they embraced. It is not enough to just care for their grave sites and monuments. We should emulate their lives, their goodness, and their faith.

Megan Smolenyak's Books -
www.honoringourancestors.com

Megan Smolenyak has been an avid genealogist for 30 years. She was the lead researcher for the PBS *Ancestors* series, and did most of the research for PBS's *They Came to America.* She also wrote the companion guide to the new NBCTV series, Who Do You Think You Are? She is skilled in many aspects of family history research, and is the author of several best-selling books on family history, including:

Who Do You Think You Are? $24.95
Honoring Our Ancestors $12.95
In Search of Our Ancestors $3.50
They Came to America: Finding Your Immigrant Ancestors $14.80

In her book, *Honoring Our Ancestors,* Megan discusses ways in which different cultures honor their ancestors and heritage. You'll find stories of people who built a Viking ship and sailed across the Atlantic, devoted decades to collecting slavery memorabilia, passed a diaper down through four generations, conducted ancestral scavenger hunts, and painted an 80 by 30 foot mural. She offers suggestions on many possible ways to creatively honor and pay tribute to our own ancestors and learn to appreciate our heritage. The heartwarming stories found in her book will inspire you in your quest for your own roots.

Shouldn't we honor the ancestors who touched our lives and pay tribute to the loving people who came before us? And shouldn't we help inspire our children to honor our ancestors so that they can also gain strength from the past?

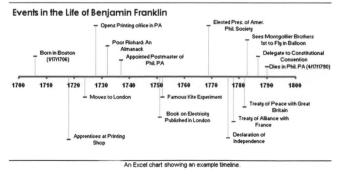

Sample Timeline

Timelines and History
Add Life to Your Family Story

Timelines are chronological listings or graphics of historical events. Timelines are a great visual way to put all your historical research into perspective and discover the "rest of your family's story", but can also help you identify gaps where you may need more information on your ancestor's life. You may want to place each ancestor in a timeline at least once in every decade of their lives using some kind of official documentation. See if a major world event or disaster may have affected the lives of your ancestors. Check out these exciting software tools to help you quickly and easily create and customize historical timelines. Historical events help you place your ancestor's lives in context with history so you can get to know the times in which they lived.

Genelines -

www.progenygenealogy.com/genelines.html

A powerful research and story-telling tool, lets you SEE your ancestor's lives in time. By bringing together elements of time, history and family relationships on visual timeline charts, Genelines can bring your family history to life, and even help you find new directions for your family. Different versions of the software let you use the visual timeline charts with various popular genealogy software programs, including Legacy, Ancestral Quest, Family Tree Maker, Personal AncestralFile and GEDCOM. $29.95

Timeline Creator.com -

www.timelinecreator.com

See history unfold with this easy-to-use software that enables you to easily and efficiently create historic timelines. You add you own events, choose fonts and icons, and add clipart images if you wish. $29.95

Timeline Maker.com -
www.timelinemaker.com

A robust software application to build quality timeline charts instantly. Features include: Unlimited chart themes/styles, seamless integration with Microsoft PowerPoint®, exclusive sharing capabilities, and output to a range of graphic files, PDF and HTML. Not specifically designed for genealogy, though many do use it for that. $49.95 download. Free Trial.

OurTimeLines.com - www.ourtimelines.com **FREE**

This site helps you create free, personalized timelines for your ancestors that show how their life fits into history. You can generate as many timelines as you like, and if you're into creating your own family web site, you can insert the timelines into your own pages.

WhoWhatWhen Timelines - **FREE**
www.sbrowning.com/whowhatwhen

A database of key people and events from 1000 A.D. to the present which allows you to create graphic timelines of periods in history and of the lives of individuals for free.

U.S. Twentieth Century Timeline - **FREE**
http://history1900s.about.com/library/weekly/aa110900a.htm

A free decade-by-decade timeline of the entire U.S. 20th century.

Timeline Template – **FREE**
http://www.vertex42.com/ExcelArticles/create-a-timeline.html

A template that creates a free timeline using Microsoft's Excel, and a hands-on article that describes how to create a timeline.

Din Timelines.com - www.din-timelines.com

A large world **FREE** history timeline that follows the rise and fall of civilizations all over the world, from circa 5000 BC to the 1940s.

Time Capsule: On This Day in History - **FREE**
www.dmarie.com/timecap

What was it like back then? Go to this website and learn what happened on any date. They currently have data online for the years 1800 through 2005, although data for the years 1800 - 1875 may be spotty. You can select specific headlines, birthdays, songs, TV shows, toys, and books for the selected date.

World History.com - www.worldhistory.com

A new web site that offers interactive maps, timelines, videos, geocoded **FREE** photos, museum artifacts, genealogy and much more. Their goal is to compile the history of the world and display it in such a manner that people of all ages and backgrounds can be interested in history. It's organized as events, people, groups, places, and artifacts; all of which can be interconnected, and displayed in unison; the content originates from www.wikipedia.org, visitors who join, museums, historical societies, and other organizations. Visitors can upload GEDCOM files which will geocode the information, and display it on an ancestor map and timeline. This gives a unique perspective of your own personal history. Not only can you see your ancestors on a map with a timeline, but you can see the nearby events that occurred and the famous contemporaries of your ancestors.

Mayflower History.com - *FREE*
www.mayflowerhistory.com

The Internet's most complete, thoroughly researched and accurate web site dealing with the *Mayflower,* the Pilgrims, and early Plymouth Colony.

Finding Mayflower Families -
www.genealogymagazine.com/finmayfam.html

An excellent *FREE* magazine article on how to do research on your pilgrim ancestors. Several good books are mentioned, to help further your study.

eHistory.com - www.ehistory.com *FREE*

Serves up more than 130,000 pages of historical content, 5,300 timeline events, 800 battle outlines, 350 biographies and thousands of images and maps. A favorite resource here for Civil War buffs is, incredibly, the searchable 128 volumes of *The War of the Rebellion: A Compilation of the Official Records of the Union and Confederate Armies.* This series is the authoritative reference to army operations during the Civil War.

HyperHistory.com - www.hyperhistory.com

An interactive *FREE* combination of lifelines, timelines, and maps covering over 3,000 years of world history, plus numerous web links to other sites.

Best of History Web Sites.net - *FREE*
www.besthistorysites.net

An award-winning portal that contains annotated links to over 1000 history web sites

(the best sites for Prehistory, Ancient/Biblical History, Medieval History, American History, Early Modern Europe, World War II, Art History, Oral History, and maps) as well as links to hundreds of quality K-12 history lesson plans, history teacher guides, history activities, history games, history quizzes, and more.

How Old Was I When ...? - *FREE*
www.frontiernet.net/%7Ecdm/age1bd.html

Do you need help putting your life into perspective? Go to the *Age Gauge* and enter your own birth date. You'll quickly learn how much older or younger you are than assorted celebrities, how old you were when Kennedy was assassinated, when man first walked on the moon, etc.

European History - *FREE*
http://eudocs.lib.byu.edu/index.php/Main_Page

These free links from BYU library connect to European primary historical documents—ancient, medieval, renaissance, and modern times—that shed light on *key historical happenings* within the respective countries and within the broadest sense of political, economic, social and cultural history.

Western History Photography Collection -
www.photoswest.org *FREE*

This searchable selection of over 120,000 images from the collections of the Denver Public Library and the Colorado Historical Society documents the history of Colorado and the American West. Bring your Old West family history to life with scenes of American Indians, pioneers, railroads, mining, frontier towns, ranch life, scenery, news events and more.

Library of Congress.com - www.loc.gov *(FREE)*

The Library of Congress is the nation's oldest federal cultural institution, and serves as the research arm of Congress. It is also the largest library in the world, with more than 119 million items on approximately 530 miles of bookshelves. The collections include more than 18 million books, 2.5 million recordings, 12 million photographs, 4.5 million maps, and 54 million manuscripts. The Library's mission is to make its resources available and useful to the Congress and the American people and to sustain and preserve a universal collection of knowledge and creativity for future generations.

America's Story Online - *(FREE)* www.americaslibrary.org

The Library of Congress has millions of amazing things that will surprise you. This is a site that teaches American history in a manner that is appealing to both adults and older children. The Web site contains many documents, letters, diaries, records, tapes, films, sheet music, maps, prints, photographs, digital files, and other materials from the past, and wants you to have fun with history while learning at the same time. They want to show you some things that you've never heard or seen before. You can look at pictures of American inventors, listen to Thomas Edison's voice extracted from an early recording, watch vaudeville acts filmed about 100 years ago, and even watch a film clip of Buffalo Bill Cody's Wild West show made in 1902.

American Memory Collection - *(FREE)* http://memory.loc.gov/ammem

Perhaps you're curious to look at the world through your ancestor's eyes. Thanks to the *American Memory Collection* of the Library of Congress, now you can. This site offers more than seven million digital items from more than one hundred historical collections.

More Library of Congress *(FREE)*

Catalogs, Collections, and Research Services - http://lcweb.loc.gov/library

Online Exhibitions - http://lcweb.loc.gov/exhibits

Manuscript Collections - *(FREE)* http://lcweb.loc.gov/coll/nucmc/nucmc.html

National Union Catalog of Manuscript Collections.

Economic History - *(FREE)* http://eh.net/hmit/ppowerusd

To determine the value of an amount of money in any year compared to another.

Daughters of the American Revolution.org - www.dar.org *(FREE)*

A volunteer women's service organization dedicated to promoting patriotism, preserving American history, and securing America's future through better education for children.

Sons of the American Revolution.org - *FREE*
www.sar.org

A historical, educational, and patriotic non-profit corporation that seeks to maintain and extend the institutions of American freedom, an appreciation for true patriotism, a respect for our national symbols, the value of American citizenship, and the unifying force of e pluribus unum that has created, from the people of many nations, one nation and one people.

American Civil War - http://sunsite.utk.edu/ *FREE* civil-war and www.cwc.lsu.edu

A comprehensive portal to everything about the civil war dedicated to preserving America's cultural heritage.

Civil War Soldiers and Sailors - *FREE*
www.itd.nps.gov/cwss

CWSS is a database and historical information about servicemen who served on both sides during the Civil War; a cooperative effort by the National Park Service and partners. It enables you to make a personal link between yourself and history.

U.S. National Archives.gov - www.archives.gov

The National *FREE* Archives and Records Administration (NARA) is America's national record keeper. It is the archives of the Government of the United States that is responsible for safeguarding records of all three branches of the Federal Government. NARA provides ready access to essential records of what the Federal Government does--why, how, and with what consequences.

UK National Archives - *FREE*
www.nationalarchives.gov.uk

UK government records and information; 180,000 microfilm and microfiche, and 300,000 commercial trade catalogs.

National Archives Online Catalogue - *FREE*
http://catalogue.pro.gov.uk

Ellis Island.org - www.ellisisland.org *FREE*

Contains some 22 million immigration records from 1892-1924 available for free searching. You'll find passenger records, original manifests, and ship information, often with a picture, giving the history and background of each ship that brought the immigrants. *(See more details in Chapter 3.)*

The Smithsonian Institution Libraries - *FREE*
www.sil.si.edu

The most comprehensive museum library system in the world unites 20 libraries into one system supported by an online catalog. The Libraries offers its treasures to the nation through book exhibitions, lectures, special tours, and a well-designed public website. Collections include: 1.5 million printed books, of which 40,000 are rare books, 2,000 manuscripts, 180,000 microfilm and microfiche, and 300,000 commercial trade catalogs.

Color Landform Atlas - *FREE*
http://fermi.jhuapl.edu/states/states.html

You can also view new U.S. maps and imagery that have never before been posted to the internet. You will see 3-D maps, high resolution maps, registered maps, as well as maps of Mars, Europe, Asia, all of the continents, and more.

U.S. Census Bureau.gov - www.census.gov **FREE**

Serves as the leading source of quality data about the nation's people and economy.

U.S. Citizenship and Immigration Services - http://uscis.gov **FREE**

The History, Genealogy and Education section provides interesting information about immigration history, about immigration in our history and about how to find out more about immigrant relatives.

Ancestry.com - www.ancestry.com > *Search* **$**

You can search their vast *Historical Records, Stories and Publications, Photos and Maps,* and *Other Resources* databases. You can also search the Allen County Public Library's famous periodical database, *Periodical Source Index, the Genealogical Library Master Catalog,* bibliographic references to over 200,000 family histories, genealogies, town and county histories, and other records held by libraries across the United States. There is a fee to become a member. Available free at regional Family History Centers.

U.S. Geological Survey - http://geography.usgs.gov

Confronts some of the most pressing natural resource **FREE** and environmental issues of our Nation. Observing the Earth with remote sensing satellites, geographers monitor and analyze changes on the land, study connections between people and the land, and provide society with relevant science information to inform public decisions. Geographic names information.

Founders Documents – **FREE** http://rotunda.upress.virginia.edu/founders/ FOEA.html

The National Historical Publications and Records Commission (NHPRC) and the University of Virginia have put online 5,000 previously unpublished documents from the founders of America. Included are letters, papers, and diaries of George Washington, Benjamin Franklin and Thomas Jefferson amongst others.

GenealogyBank.com - **$** www.genealogybank.com

With millions of records added monthly, Genealogy-Bank now has over 323 million family history records and an estimated 1 billion names found in: Historical Newspapers (1690-1980) 2,500 titles, America's Obituaries (1977-Today) – over 130 million obits from over 4,000 newspapers, Historical Books & Documents (1789-1980), Social Security Death Index (1937-Today) – more than 85 million death records. Most comprehensive SSDI site online! You can search for free, but you need to subscribe to view the details. $9.95/30 day trial.

Making of America - http://moa.umdl.umich.edu and http://moa.cit.cornell.edu/moa **FREE**

This is a joint project between the University of Michigan and Cornell University which provides free access to a large collection of 19th century books, journal articles, and imprints on two websites.

Photographs, Videos and Scrapbooking

Preserving the Past for Future Generations

See also "What Are Your Memories Worth?" beginning on page 206.

Google's Photo Organizer - FREE
http://picasa.google.com

Find, organize and share your photos. Picasa is a *free* software download from Google that helps you: Locate and organize all the photos on your computer, edit and add effects to your photos with a few simple clicks, find, organize and share your photos.

PicaJet.com Photo Manager - www.picajet.com

Award winning digital photo album software with powerful sharing features. PicaJet offers direct import from your camera, image sharing via email or Web gallery, automatic photo enhancement, personal ratings and categories, as well as printing features. The photo organizer allows you to view your images by rating, keyword, or date/timeline and you can categorize your images by simple drag and drop. In addition, it offers editing features to correct red-eye, cropping, image sharpening, and level adjustment. Additional features include direct CD/DVD burning, an image search engine, slide show maker, and a tool to generate a Web gallery.

Western History Photography Collection - www.photoswest.org

This searchable selection of over 120,000 images from the collections of the Denver Public Library and the Colorado Historical Society documents the history of Colorado and the American West. Bring your Old West family history to life with scenes of American Indians, pioneers, railroads, mining, frontier towns, ranch life, scenery, news events and more.

Ancestor Photo Archive.com - FREE
http://ancestorarchive.com

Free collection of vintage family photos, for sharing, or reuniting with their families.

RoxioCreator - www.roxio.com $

Besides helping you transfer your old records and tapes onto CD, DVD, iPod, or PSP it can also help you edit videos, make calendars, postcards, and help you get the most out of your digital videos, music and photos. $79.99

Pinnacle Studio – $
www.pinnaclesys.com

Watch your memories come alive by transforming your videos and photos into amazing movies. You can mix your media together: photos, video, and music to create a Hollywood-style movie, and then archive and publish them on YouTube or burn them to DVDs. $49.99-149.99

Dead Fred.com - www.deadfred.com FREE

The original online orphaned-photo site has grown to more than 92,000 old pictures and over 16,000 surnames. Your ancestors might be waiting for you here.

Ancient Faces.com - www.ancientfaces.com

A visual genealogy website that has **FREE** thousands of old photos that adds a face to your lists of names and dates.

Genealogy Photo Archive - FREE
http://genealogyregister.com

A free genealogy database of family photos containing online vintage photographs. Many of these photos have been submitted by visitors to help you find your ancestors and surnames. Others were found in antique stores and flea markets, and posted here in hopes of reuniting them with family members. Your ancestors could be among these genealogy photos.

Family History Photo Gallery - FREE
http://jsmagic.net/kith

A gallery of free family history graphics and photos for your own family web site and other uses.

Caring for Your Collections - FREE
www.loc.gov/preserv/careothr.html

Need advice on the care of books, photos, videos, and other media in your collections? The Library of Congress site contains publications that answer many questions about the care, handling and storage of your valuable collections.

Talking Story.com - http://talkingstory.com $

A professional video service that assists you in preserving your loved one's important memories

and stories for generations to come on Video and DVD. The service is high quality and low pressure. They work with you and/or your loved ones to ensure that the process and the product are wonderful keepsakes. Pricing varies.

Family Photoloom.com - www.photoloom.com $

A dynamic web application that connects your photos, genealogy, stories, and documents to create truly seamless family history. You can organize your pictures around your family history (and into albums), index family relationships, and tag faces and resource documents. You can literally browse your pictures by simply clicking on an individual and every picture of him/her will appear in the portrait window. Plus it helps protect your family photos and documents from loss or damage by storing them on secure servers to give you security and peace of mind. Private, safe and secure. Unlimited image uploads and invited guests. 5GB storage space. Free trial. $39/year.

Newspapers and Periodicals

What Was Their Life Like?

Historical newspapers, magazines and other periodicals can open a window to the past about the lives of your ancestors, and are excellent sources of information about their heritage and stories. They provide a wonderful, untapped resource for events not recorded elsewhere, and affords you a rare opportunity to understand the times in which your ancestors lived and their daily activities.

For example, *obituaries* may include place and date of birth, names of siblings, parents, and other surviving relatives, occupation, and military service. *Society news* columns may include such tidbits as birthdays, job promotions, wedding announcements, and personal news. You might find in *public announcements* information on forced land sales, professional services, runaway slaves, and missing relatives. *Legal notices* may include proving of wills, divorce proceedings, proving of heirs, and the settlement of estates. *Military news* and *school news* are additional columns that you should also consider.

Historical newspapers can also add context through the breaking news of the day, gossip columns or local news, entertainment listings, and advertisements. Don't forget to evaluate the information you find against that provided from other sources.

Google Historical News Search -
http://news.google.com/archivesearch

Google enables you to search through more than 200 years of historical newspaper archives. Their News Archive Search provides an easy way to search and explore historical archives, and create a timeline of selected stories from relevant time periods arranged chronologically. These are web links to articles on other sites, both free and subscription. You may want to use *Advanced Search* to narrow the results.

GenealogyBank.com -
www.genealogybank.com

Features over 300 years of U.S. newspapers in all 50 states. Find obituaries, military records, marriage notices, photographs, hometown news and more. They make it easy to discover exciting details about your ancestors with unlimited access to: Over 1 billion names, over 4,000 newspapers (1690-today, about 300 million

articles), exclusive content, over 275,000 historical books, pamphlets and documents (pension records, land claims, military reports), and over 130 million obituaries and death records. New content added daily. You can search for *free*, but you need to subscribe to view the details. $9.95/month, $69.95/year.

WorldVitalRecords.com -
www.worldvitalrecords.com

They have two main newspaper collections: *Paper of Record* (450 million names, international newspapers from 1778) and *Newspaper Archive* (500 million names from over 800 newspapers). Free trial. $5.95/month. Free at Family History Centers.

Chronicling America Newspapers – **FREE**
http://chroniclingamerica.loc.gov

This site allows you to search and view select newspaper pages from 1880-1922 and find information about American newspapers published between 1690-present. This is a partnership between the National Endowment for the Humanities and the Library of Congress and will eventually include all U.S. states and territories.

NewspaperArchive.com –
www.newspaperarchive.com

Access to more than 95 million historical newspaper pages for the US, Canada, UK, Ireland, Denmark, Germany, So. Africa, and Japan, including rare content from small towns, currently over 1,000 million articles, and over 3 billion names. New content added daily. $17.99/month, $9.99/month annually.

Newspaper Abstracts.com – FREE
www.newspaperabstracts.com

Contains over 70,000 pages of abstracts (and growing) from historical newspapers in US, plus thousands of pages from other countries. Articles range in size from a single entry to an entire newspaper issue, all provided by site visitors and made available to everyone free of charge.

50states.com Newspapers – FREE
www.50states.com/news

Links to over 3,300 U.S. newspapers.

U.S. Newspapers List – FREE
www.usnpl.com

Lists with links to 3,900+ US newspapers, plus Canadian and African newspapers.

ABYZ Newslinks.com – FREE
www.abyznewslinks.com

A portal with links to online news sources from around the world. It is primarily composed of newspapers but also includes many broadcast stations, internet services, magazines, and press agencies.

Penn University Historical Newspapers –
http://gethelp.library.upenn.edu/guides/ FREE
hist/onlinenewspapers.html

A list of some of the historic newspapers that are available online for free or through subscription.

Library of Congress - www.loc.gov/rr/news

An extensive FREE newspaper collection of over 9,000 U.S. newspaper titles, 25,000 non-US newspaper titles, 7,000 current periodicals, 6,000 comic books, and 1 million government publications.

Godfrey Memorial Library - $
www.godfrey.org

Offers access to many historic newspapers, including the London Times, 19th century US newspapers, and early American newspapers. $10/day, $45/year (without newspapers), $80/year with newspapers).

Ancestry's Newspaper Collection - $
www.ancestry.com/newspapers

You can search about 1,000 of digitally available, large and small newspapers beginning in the early 1800s and some extending into the 2000s. They also have newspapers from Canada, Europe, Mexico and Australia. Membership is required. $19.95/month. Free trial.

The Olden Times.com - FREE
www.theoldentimes.com

Historic newspapers online for free from the 18th to 20th century from the U.S., England, Scotland, Ireland, and Australia. Search for your surnames in the index and click on the link to see complete scanned copies.

3 Connect with Ancestors

Cemeteries / Grave Sites / Obituaries / Death Records

Visiting cemeteries is a very rewarding part of connecting with the lives of your ancestors. Your ancestor's tombstone is one of the few remaining physical evidences of the life they lived. There is nothing in discovering your family roots and stories that will connect you to your ancestor more than to stand in the one place on earth which contains their mortal remains, and to touch their gravestone inscription. It is an once-in-a-lifetime, inspiring experience. Check out these free cemetery and obituary listings.

Find a Grave.com - www.findagrave.com *FREE*

Find the graves of ancestors, create virtual memorials, add 'virtual flowers' and a note to a loved one's grave, etc. Browse descriptions and photos of graves of thousands of famous people from around the world. The site also lists over 40 million grave records.

Tombstone Transcription Project - *FREE*
www.rootsweb.ancestry.com/~cemetery

Volunteers from across the U.S. have uploaded transcriptions and photos from thousands of cemeteries.

DeathRecords ObituarySearch.com - *FREE*
www.deathrecordsobituarysearch.com

Complete and accurate official U.S. death records and obituary records; more than 300 million records.

DeathIndexes.com - www.deathindexes.com

A directory of links to websites with online death indexes, listed by state and county. *FREE*

Included are death records, death certificate indexes, death notices & registers, obituaries, probate indexes, and cemetery & burial records.

National Archives.gov - *FREE*
www.archives.gov/research/alic/reference/vital-records.html

Hot links to vital records collections at the National Archives.

Distant Cousin.com - www.distantcousin.com *FREE*

A grab bag of newspaper obituaries, city directories, census records, ship lists, school yearbooks, military records and other resources. They provide access to more than 6 million records from 1,500-plus sources.

Interment.net - www.interment.net *FREE*

Provides free access to thousands of cemetery records, tombstone inscriptions and veteran burials, from cemeteries in the USA, Canada, England, Ireland, Australia, New Zealand, and other countries. There are currently 3.9 million cemetery records across 8,375 cemeteries available for searching on this site.

MortalitySchedules.com -
www.mortalityschedules.com

If your ancestor died within the 12 months preceding the 1850, 1860, 1870 or 1880 census

enumeration, you won't find them in the regular census, but you will find them in lists know as Mortality Schedules available on this site.

Veterans Gravesite Locator – FREE
http://gravelocator.cem.va.gov

Search for burial locations of veterans and their family members in VA National Cemeteries, state veterans cemeteries, various other military and Department of Interior cemeteries, and for veterans buried in private cemeteries when the grave is marked with a government grave marker.

Maps & Geography

Mapping Your Ancestry; Discover the Place Your Ancestors Called Home

Google Maps – http://www.maps.google.com

A popular, free web mapping service that offers street maps for much of the world, satellite maps for the whole world, and a hybrid map (satellite imagery with an overlay of streets, city names, and landmarks). It's easy to locate current places, such as small towns, libraries, cemeteries and churches. Their My Maps feature allows you to create your own personalized maps. You can plot multiple locations on a map; add text, photos and videos; and draw lines and shapes, and then share these maps with others.

Google Earth – http://earth.google.com FREE

Lets you fly anywhere on Earth to map your ancestors. You can view satellite imagery, maps, terrain, and 3D buildings; explore rich geographical content, save your toured places, and share with others. It also now includes historical imagery from around the globe.

Perry-Castañeda Map Collection – FREE
www.lib.utexas.edu/maps

Want a map of the 2010 Haiti earthquake or other maps of historical, general or special interest from around the world? How about a map of the British Isles 1603-1688, or Central Europe 980-1871, or England and France 1455-1494, or North America 1797, or Boston 1842? You'll find thousands of maps in this vast collection. Essentially all of the maps courtesy of the University of Texas Libraries are in the public domain, and you may download them and use them as you wish.

US Geological Survey – www.usgs.gov > FREE
Maps, Imagery

The National Atlas offers a wide variety of maps that you can print for free at home or play with. You can find maps of the US, as well as ones for your own state with county lines, cities, lakes, and rivers. Download or buy current maps, historic topographic maps from 1882, and aerial and satellite images. You can also use the Map Maker to make your own, custom, interactive map of the US.

Color U.S. Landform Atlas –
http://fermi.jhuapl.edu/states/states.html **FREE**

You can view new maps and imagery that have never before been posted to the internet. You will see 3-D maps, high resolution maps, registered maps, as well as maps of Mars, Europe, Asia, all of the continents, and more.

eHistory – http://ehistory.osu.edu > **FREE**
Maps & Images

This Ohio State University site contains hundreds of fully searchable historical maps and photos from the Civil War, WWII, and Vietnam.

Europe Aerial Photography – **FREE** **$**
http://aerial.rcahms.gov.uk

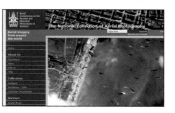

The Aerial Reconnaissance Archives (TARA) contains more than ten million declassified aerial reconnaissance images taken by Allied forces during the war which offers a fascinating way to view your ancestor's homes and landscapes. Aerial photographs circa 1940s are currently available for the following countries: Belgium, Croatia, Czech Republic, Denmark, France, Germany, Italy, The Netherlands and Poland. You can also access the extensive Scotland collection from this website. The site offers aerial images overlaid with modern satellite images. This is a very useful tool to help you locate your ancestor's home. Access to most low-resolution images is free; high-resolution photographs requires a subscription. £15/year (about $24)

Community Walk.com – **FREE**
www.communitywalk.com

A free website that allows you to create your own personal maps using Google Maps. You can add location markers and route markers, upload lots of photos and videos for each location, display content from other websites, leave comments, and show your map on a website or blog.

TriggerMap.com – **FREE** **$**
www.trippermap.com

A web service that allows you to put a flash based world map on your own website or blog. It automatically searches your photos at the free Flickr photo service for location information and plots the photos on your own map, on your own website. It works well for documenting family history travels and vacations. The free version is limited to 50 locations. $9.75/year

USGenWeb.org – www.usgenweb.org **FREE**

Contains resources and queries for a specific state or county in the USA.

Worldwide GenWeb – http://worldgenweb.org

Resources and **FREE** read/post queries that relate to a specific country.

Bureau of Land Management – (FREE)
www.glorecords.blm.gov

This is the place to start exploring land records, including more than 3 million federal land title records for Eastern public-land states (1820 to 1908) and images of serial patents issued from 1908 to the mid-1960s. Land east of the Mississippi that wasn't in one of the original colonies belonged to the U.S. government and was sold originally to the first settlers. Images of field notes and survey plats, dating to 1810, are being added on a state-by-state basis. Searching is fast and powerful, and you'll find plenty of help for understanding the records you locate.

Ancestral Atlas – (FREE) ($)
www.ancestralatlas.com

A new map-based site that enables you to add and share your family history events worldwide. It combines historical (Google) maps with social networking. You can: Attach your own family history to the map on the location where the event took place, and share it with everyone else; find out who else has family events in the same area and collaborate with them in a secure environment; and build your own atlas. Currently, they have integrated historical maps of England and Wales (circa 1900) and Ireland (circa 1840) as layers that you can turn on/off on top of the normal mapping. The USA Boundary maps show changes in states and counties in ten-year intervals from 1790-2000. A Life Map is a view of a number of related people or events connected together by lines on the map to help you to see where family members migrated around the world. You'll need a free registration to add your data; subscribers get additional benefits. £20/year (about $34).

Getty Research Institute – (FREE)
www.getty.edu > *Research* > *Conducting Research* > *Vocabularies*

Their Thesaurus of Geographic Names (TGN) is not just a gazetteer of current places; it is a searchable database of more than 1.1 million locales with historical spots from around the world.

UK Get-a-Map –
www.ordnancesurvey.co.uk > *Get a Map* (FREE)

Search for high-detail maps anywhere in the United Kingdom simply by entering the place name, full postal code or National Grid reference, then print the maps or copy for use on your own family history Web site.

Family Atlas Software – ($)
www.rootsmagic.com

Family Atlas Windows software is a fun and easy way to map your family history. Trace your ancestor's migration around the world and pinpoint the sites of important family events. Import your family data directly from your genealogy software, and then automatically add markers to create personalized maps. Print maps or save them to several graphics formats. $29.95

U.S. City Directories.com – (FREE)
www.uscitydirectories.com

City Directories, arguably one of the most over-looked resources by geneal-ogists, have been around since the

1700s. This web site attempts to identify all printed, microfilmed, and online directories, and their repositories, for the United States. Sponsored by Genealogy Research Associates.

Animated Map of U.S. –
www.edstephan.org/48states.html **FREE**

Watch the boundary lines of the U.S. change right before your eyes. Simple, educational animated map of the settlement and boundaries of the United States.

Zip Code Lookup – **FREE**
http://zip4.usps.com

Find a ZIP+4 Code for an address or all cities in a zip code.

Court, Land & Financial Records

Add Interest to Your History

Court and land records, wills and other financial documents are those kept by town, county, and state officials regarding property owned, sold, or bequeathed to others. Land records provide two types of important evidence for you. First, they often state kinships, and second, they place individuals in a specific time and place, allowing you to sort people and families into neighborhoods. Deeds, land grants, and land tax lists help distinguish one person from another.

Land Patent Records - www.blm.gov **FREE**

The Official Land Patent Records Site. This site has a searchable database of more than two

million Federal land title records for Eastern Public Land States, issued 1820-1908, including scanned images of those records indexing the initial transfer of land titles from the Federal government to individuals.

U.S. General Land Office Records - **FREE**
http://content.ancestry.com/iexec/?htx=List&dbid=1246

This database contains land patents from 1796-1907 for 13 U.S. states. Information recorded in land patents includes: name of patentee, issue date, state of patent, acres of land, legal land description, authority under which the land was acquired, and other details relating to the land given.

About.com Using Land Records –
http://genealogy.about.com/od/land_records/Land_Property_Records.htm

Learn how to research your ancestors using deeds and other land records, including how to decipher old deeds and draw a plat map. Plus, how and where to access land records online.

RootsWeb Guides –
http://rwguide.rootsweb.ancestry.com

Free guides to different subjects; no. 29 is American Land Records, and no. 30 is Court Records.

Cyndi'sList Land Records –
www.cyndislist.com/land.htm

Links to various online resources, how-to, and specific geographic sites.

Be sure to note *when* medical conditions occur. For example, did Grandpa have diabetes as a child, or did it develop later in his adult life?

Sources of Medical Information

Sources for medical information can include your memory, your living relatives, and medical records. For deceased ancestors, search the following resources:

- Death certificates (dates and cause of death)
- Obituaries
- Pension and insurance documents
- Social Security applications
- Family bibles
- Diaries
- Old letters, etc.
- Military records

Privacy Concerns

Remember to respect everyone's privacy as you gather medical information. The information is only for you, your health care professional, and your descendant's use. You shouldn't publish this information as part of your family web site.

World Vital Records.com -
www.worldvitalrecords.com Ⓢ

A collection of various court, land, and probate records. Membership is required, but is free at Family History Centers. $5.95/month

Freedman's Bank Records - FREE
www.heritagequestonline.com

www.familysearch.org > *Search Records > Record Search (select USA region)*

Includes information for nearly 500,000 African Americans from the post-Civil War era. You can search Heritage Quest by first logging onto your local library online.

Public Records Online - www.netronline.com Ⓢ

Links to available state & county Tax Assessors' and Recorders' offices. Online public records may include copies of deeds, parcel maps, GIS

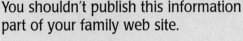

maps, tax data, ownership information and indexes. Some Recorders' offices have marriage and birth records available online. 3 days $2.95, $29.95/year.

Tracing Your Medical Heritage

A Useful Tool in Your Life

Tracing one's medical heritage is gaining more interest for people everywhere. What runs in your family? Long life? Twins? Blue eyes? Curly hair? Large nose? Perfect health? Cancer? Heart disease? Many of the factors that determine your health today were inherited from your ancestors. For some people, the answers to these questions can literally be a matter of life and death.

For example, what if both of your parents died of heart disease or cancer and you pieced together a medical family history that showed deadly cancers or heart disease going back several generations on both your mother's and father's lines. Or perhaps some of your family lived long active lives well into their 90s, and it was not unusual on another side of your family for some to pass away in their 60s. Why the difference? What caused their deaths? Are there common health characteristics in family lines? What does this mean to you and your descendants?

The information on your medical pedigree can show doctors not only what to look for, but exactly where to look, and may help provide preventive treatment to save your life. Experts say that about 3,000 of the 10,000 known diseases have genetic links, and that many diseases

How To Begin a Medical Pedigree

Start by writing down what you already know. Write down the health facts for yourself, and then go back one generation at a time. Consider recording the following information:

Birth and death dates

Cause of death

    Ethnic background (some genetic diseases occur in particular ethnic groups)

    Birth defects

    Major illnesses such as cancer, heart disease, diabetes, etc.

    General patterns of ill health, like respiratory problems

    Chronic health problems like asthma, diabetes, or high blood pressure

    General health routines (smoking, diet, overweight, etc.)

    Allergies (food-related and environmental)

    Emotional problems (depression, heavy drinking, anxiety, etc.)

    Vision and hearing problems

3 Connect with Ancestors

> Four-generations of medical information are usually sufficient for genetic counseling.

Tips

■ Gather medical information on living as well as deceased members of your family. Information from your horizontal line (brothers and sisters, aunts, uncles and cousins) may be as important as information from your vertical line (parents, grandparents, and great-grandparents).

■ Don't rely on family members' accounts of causes of death or illnesses in the family; document as much information as you can.

■ Treat the information that you gather with discretion.

■ Consult a physician or a genetic counselor if you have questions or concerns about the information you find in your family's medical history.

"run in families," including colon cancer, heart disease, diabetes, alcoholism and high blood pressure. Creating a family health history can be a useful tool to aid you and your health care provider in interpreting patterns of health, illness and genetic traits for you and your descendants.

Family Health History: Medical Genealogy

Learn how to get started creating your own medical family tree to help determine your genetic predisposition to certain diseases, genetic traits and more. Trace your family's medical history and become better informed about health conditions that may affect your own health and that of your loved ones with help from these websites: **FREE**

http://genealogy.about.com/cs/healthhistory
www.cyndislist.com/dna.htm
www.dcn.davis.ca.us/~vctinney/medical.htm

Suggested Activities

- Create a medical pedigree chart by listing the names of your ancestors, the illnesses from which they died, along with the dates of onset of the illnesses, and their death dates.

- Talk to your living relatives about what they remember the causes of death were for your ancestors.

- Verify the information they give you and find additional information for your medical pedigree by gathering death certificates. Copies of death certificates can usually be obtained through the public records office in the area where the death occurred.

- Look around your house for other records that will help you build a medical pedigree such as obituaries, insurance documents, hospital records, etc.

Organizing Your Health History

To organize your information, you can either enter it in your family history program as written text, or utilize special software program, such as *GeneWeaver*, (www.geneweaveronline.com) to create a medical genogram. A genogram is a schematic diagram of family relationships and diseases, which is used by your doctor to determine if there is a risk of inherited illnesses, which may lead to early detection and prevention.

Who knows, maybe the family health information you find today will help provide preventive treatment to save a life tomorrow.

Royalty and Nobility

Royal and Princely Families of the World

Records and other works about the genealogies, titles, and histories of the noble class: kings, dukes, duchesses, earls, etc.

Cyndi's List Royalty & Nobility - FREE

www.cyndislist.com/royalty.htm

Web links to over 220 indexed web sites of royalty and nobility.

Wikipedia Biographies & Genealogies - FREE

http://simple.wikipedia.org/wiki/Category: Royalty_and_nobility

Numerous web links to sites containing great biographies and genealogies of royalty.

Directory of Royal & Noble Genealogies - FREE

www3.dcs.hull.ac.uk/public/genealogy/royal

The genealogy of the British Royal family and those linked to it via blood or marriage relationships; contains the genealogy of almost every ruling house in the western world because of the intermarriage that took place between them; over 30,000 individuals. It also contains the genealogy of the U.S. Presidents, and links to other royalty sites.

About.com Royal Families - www.about.com >

(search for royal genealogies and medieval history) -or- http://historymedren.about.com/library/ who/blwwroyaldex.htm -or- http://genealogy .about.com/cs/royalgenealogies

Family trees and genealogy of kings, queens and royal families around the world; and Who's Who in Medieval History: Articles on Emperors, Kings, Princes, Dukes, Counts, Caliphs and others who governed cities, sovereign states, principalities or nomad nations.

The Crown of Russian Empire - *FREE*
http://sunsite.cs.msu.su/heraldry

An introduction to the *Russian Royal House.* Here, you will find pictures of the Russian tsars as well as the genealogical tree of the family.

Non-European Dynasties - $

www.almanach.be

A compilation of about 2500 non-European Sovereign Families and rulers, such as the Emperors of China, Morocco, and Turkey (over 700 countries), available by subscription. $9.95/month

Monarchs: Chronology and Genealogy – *FREE*
http://sitemaker.umich.edu/mladjov/
monarchs_chronology_and_genealogy

An attempt to provide a detailed and accurate account of the chronological and genealogical sequence of monarchs from earliest times to the present in various historically significant areas, such as Europe, UK, Far East, Mideast, Islam, and the New World.

Nobility Royalty.com - *FREE*
www.nobility-royalty.com

The International Commission on Nobility and Royalty works to authenticate that one has a royal or noble bloodline, or that one is a true member of a royal family.

ABC Genealogy.com -
www.abcgenealogy.com/Royalty_and_Nobility

Website devoted to royalty and nobility in *FREE*

countries outside of Europe.

Heraldry and Arms
Coat of Arms, Family Crests and Emblems

The study of coats of arms–including the art of designing, displaying, and recording arms–is called heraldry. A coat of arms (or armorial bearings), in European tradition, is a design belonging to a particular person or group and used by them in a wide variety of ways. Historically, they were used by knights to identify them apart from enemy soldiers. Unlike seals and emblems, coats of arms have a formal description that is expressed as a blazon (or symbols). Today, coats of arms still continue to be in use by a variety of institutions and individuals. Nearly every nation in every part of the world has its own coat of arms. The American Great Seal is often said to be the coat of arms of the United States.

Intro to Heraldry -
http://genealogy.about.com/cs/heraldry/a/
heraldry.htm -or-
http://genealogy.about.com/od/heraldry/ *FREE*
Heraldry_Coats_of_Arms_and_Family_Crests.htm

Learn all about coats of arms and family crests, including which people were granted the right to bear arms, what the designs and colors mean, and how you can use heraldry to prove family relationships.

American College of Heraldry.org - *FREE*
www.americancollegeofheraldry.org

Aids in the study and perpetuation of heraldry. Contains a lot of good information on heraldry and coats of arms.

3 Connect with Ancestors

College of Arms - www.college-of-arms.gov.uk

The official repository of the coats of arms and pedigrees of English, Welsh, Northern Irish and **FREE** Commonwealth families and their descendants. Learn more about heraldry and coats of arms, and help you locate your ancestor's coat of arms.

Rootsweb's Guide to Heraldry - **FREE**
www.rootsweb.ancestry.com/~ rwguide/ lesson19.htm

A good overview of heraldry (or armory) around the world.

Cyndi's List.com Heraldry -
www.cyndislist.com/heraldry.htm **FREE**

Contains about 120 indexed web links to heraldry web sites.

Fleurdelis.com -
www.fleurdelis.com/coatofarms.htm **FREE**

The meanings behind the symbols and a brief history of Heraldry.

Family Chronicle Article - www.family **FREE**
chronicle.com/CoatofArms1.htm

Halvor Moorshead explains the process of obtaining legitimate armorial bearings: *Acquiring a REAL Coat of Arms - Parts I &II.*

Heraldry & Genealogy -
www.acpl.lib.in.us/genealogy/11heraldry.pdf **FREE**

A document from the Allen County Public Library: Researching a

coat of arms, guides and glossaries, with descriptions and illustrations.

Augustan Society.org - $
www.augustansociety.org

An historical society working in the areas of European history, heraldry, genealogy and related fields. They maintain a Heraldry Collection including many rare books and pamphlets. In addition, the Society registers coats of arms and publishes a roll of arms. $25/4 issues.

Baronage Press - www.baronage.co.uk **FREE**

An electronic magazine devoted to genealogical and heraldic data. Not updated regularly.

Heraldic Artist -
www.calligraphyandheraldry.com **FREE** $

The studio web site and gallery of Neil Bromley, a Heraldic Artist, Calligrapher, and Medieval Illuminator.

Heraldic Dictionary -
www.rarebooks.nd.edu/digital/heraldry/index.html

A dictionary to **FREE** help understand written descriptions of armorials or coat of arms in order to identify the individual, family, or organization to which those arms belong.

3 Connect with Ancestors

Family History Insights - 3

The Seeds of Our Heritage

Rex D. Pinegar
© by Intellectual Reserve, Inc.

Etched in stone at the National Archives building in Washington, D.C., is this meaningful truth: *"The heritage of the past is the seed that brings forth the harvest of the future."* Two hundred years ago the seeds of our heritage were being planted by men and women of great spiritual drive and steadfastness of purpose. Seeds of devotion and willing sacrifice for a just cause, seeds of courage and loyalty, seeds of faith in God were all planted in the soil of freedom that a mightier work might come forth. In Richard Wheeler's *Voices of 1776* we read firsthand accounts of some of those who were engaged in this "planting" process. Their expressions stir our souls to a greater appreciation of the heritage we enjoy and upon which we must build. A young doctor of Barnstable, Massachusetts, recorded in his journal on the 21st of April, 1775, the following: *"This event seems to have electrified all classes of people … inspiriting and rousing the people to arms! to arms! … Never was a cause more just, more sacred, than ours. We are commanded to defend the rich inheritance bequeathed to us by our virtuous ancestors; it is our bounden duty to transmit it uncontaminated to our posterity. We must fight valiantly."* (Richard Wheeler, *Voices of 1776,* New York: Thomas Y. Crowell Co., 1972, pp. 33-34.)
Rex D. Pinegar

Unlock the Knowledge of Who You Really Are

James E. Faust
© by Intellectual Reserve, Inc.

"I encourage you...to begin to unlock the knowledge of who you really are by learning more about your forebears. ... Without this enriching knowledge, there is a hollow yearning. No matter what our attainments in life, there is still a vacuum, an emptiness, and the most disquieting loneliness. We can have exciting experiences as we learn about our vibrant, dynamic ancestors. They were very real, living people with problems, hopes, and dreams like we have today. In many ways each of us is the sum total of what our ancestors were.

The virtues they had may be our virtues, their strengths our strengths, and in a way their challenges could be our challenges. Some of their traits may be our traits. ... It is a joy to become acquainted with our forebears who died long ago. Each of us has a fascinating family history. Finding your ancestors can be one of the most interesting puzzles you...can work on. James E. Faust

Just by Chance?

"Having been brought up in an orphanage, I knew very little about my family... [but] I wanted to...learn about my ancestors. One day, as I was preparing to go on a business trip to Canton, Ohio, I...called an older half-sister and asked her if she knew our grandparents' names and where they had been buried. She gave me their names and told me that when she was a child she would visit them in a town in Ohio called Osnaburg.... I was amazed because this was only a few miles from where I would be going. I was very excited...I said a prayer that I would be guided if there was anything for me to find. I found myself in front of a small cemetery.... I saw an elderly man coming toward me on the sidewalk. I walked up to him and told him about my search for the grandparents of Fanny and John Robert Gier. He directed me to a house in town. When I went there, I found a woman in her 80s, Gurtie Baker.... When I said my maiden name was Irene Gier, she began to cry. She said she knew Uncle Bobby had remarried and had other children but that she never expected to see any of them. It turned out her mother and my father were brother and sister. I left the home with pictures... of my father, all his siblings and his mother and father. She also gave me all their birth and death dates and told me where my grandparents were buried. Throughout the visit, she said several times, 'This didn't just happen by chance.' I agree." Irene Durham

CHAPTER 4

A Directory of Family History Software

'Certified' Software

See a list of family history software programs that have been "certified" by FamilySearch to synchronize with *new FamilySearch* beginning on page 158.

Suggested Activities

1. Educate yourself about the different family history software programs available. Read the reviews of the various programs.

2. Try different free versions or demos if you wish. Make a decision on which one(s) you want to purchase.

3. Go on a treasure hunt. Discover some of your buried treasure in the web sites provided.

4. Persevere in searching for your ancestors and understanding what their life was like.

Family history has become a real passion and big-time hobby for millions of people today all around the world. Alex Haley called it "a hunger, bone-marrow deep, to know our heritage". Family history helps you discover a sense of identity and family pride in your life. It can also help unite and strengthen bonds between family members.

Whatever your reason for tracing your own family roots and stories, genealogy software can become one of your most valuable and indispensable tools. Software helps you discover your ancestors, organize and store your information (such as family photos, scrapbooks, health and personal data, reunions, etc.), measure the progress of your research, share your information with family and friends, provide tons of tools to make it easier, and much more. Software programs today are fun and interesting for the whole family, and no longer just about names, charts, and graphs.

In this Directory, you'll learn where to find comprehensive reviews that will help you make an informed decision about which software is right for you. Selecting the right software program can make all the difference in how much satisfaction and information you will derive from your family history quest. And the right software will help make your journey fun and much easier.

Family History Insights - 4

Gordon B. Hinckley
© by Intellectual Reserve, Inc.

Increases Sense of Identity

As I learn more about my own ancestors who worked so hard, sacrificed so much, it increases my sense of identity and deepens my commitment to honor their memory. Perhaps there has never been a time when a sense of family, of identity and self worth has been more important to the world. Seeking to understand our family history can change our lives and helps bring unity and cohesion to the family." Gordon Hinckley, *Deseret News,* 17 Apr 2001

Woodrow Wilson

Know Where You Came From

"A nation [or family] which does not remember what it was yesterday, does not know what it is today, nor what it is trying to do. We are trying to do a futile thing if we do not know where we came from or what we have been about." Woodrow Wilson, 28th President of the United States (1913-1921)

Boyd K. Packer
© by Intellectual Reserve, Inc.

A Feeling of Inspiration

"[Inspiration] comes to individual[s]... as they are led to discover their family records in ways that are miraculous indeed. And there is a feeling of inspiration attending this work that can be found in no other. When we have done all that we can do, we shall be given the rest. The way will be opened up." Boyd K. Packer

Frederick Douglass

No Progress Without Struggle

"If there is no struggle, there is no progress. Those who profess to favor freedom and yet renounce controversy are people who want crops without ploughing the ground."
– Frederick Douglass (1818-1895), Abolitionist, author, statesman & reformer

John H. Widtsoe
© by Intellectual Reserve, Inc.

Help From the Other Side

"Those who give themselves with all their might and main to this work...receive help from the other side, and not merely in gathering genealogies. Whosoever seeks to help those on the other side receives help in return in all the affairs of life." John A. Widtsoe, *Utah Genealogical and Historical Magazine,* July 1931, p. 104

Lee Iacocca

Love Your Family

"No matter what you've done for yourself or humanity, if you can't look back on having given love and attention to your family, what have you really accomplished?"
Lee Iacocca (1924-), former Chrysler CEO

Abraham Lincoln

Shall Not Have Died in Vain

"...from these honored dead we take increased devotion to that cause for which they gave the last full measure of devotion – that we here highly resolve that these dead shall not have died in vain – that this nation, under God, shall have a new birth of freedom – and that government of the people, by the people, for the people, shall not perish from the earth." Abraham Lincoln, (1809-1865) Gettysburg Address

Which Software is the Best?

The most often asked question today by people interested in family history software is *"which one is the best?"* This question is difficult to answer because what is right for me may not work as well for you. Everyone has different needs and preferences. There may be features in a particular family history program that I may not use, e.g. web-site creation or multi-media scrapbooking, but may be very important to you.

Some people even use more than one program to meet their needs. For example, you may prefer a primary, heavy duty program for your everyday use, and a different program to generate well-designed charts. Each program has its own strengths and weaknesses; each program does certain things well and other things not-so-well.

And they are always changing and upgrading. New features and options are constantly being introduced. They offer a wide variety of options including the way they format data, the types of charts they print, their ability to help you organize your research, and their capacity to store photographs and documents. They can even assist you in your research by letting you keep a research log or a to-do list with your family data. With dozens of software programs, and hundreds of features available, which program(s) should I choose?

Whether you're just starting out, or upgrading your existing software program take some time and effort to make your decision; it's well worth it.

You may want to consider making a list of features that you want or need, then prioritize that list to decide which are most important to you. As you gain more understanding and knowledge your list may change and grow.

Here are some things to keep in mind as you decide which features you may want or need.

Software Features

- **What do you want to do** with your family history information? Are you just looking for a basic program to organize names, dates and events? Some program basics may include: planning tools, data recording, analytical tools (search features, custom lists, flags, custom data fields, multiple note options, etc.), source documentation, reports, charts, publishing, multimedia, internet, portability, additional tools and convenience items.

- **What about charts and reports?** Do you want to create beautiful family trees to decorate your home; do you want to include photos, audio and video with your data? What kind of charts and reports would you like your software to be able to print?

- **Do you plan to create a family Web site** to share your information with family and friends? The popular software programs offer you the ability to upload your family tree data online right from your computer program, and help you create a simple family Web site.

- **Will you want to write a family history book** using your information? Some software programs offer more features for printing a family history book than others.

- **If you're a member of the LDS Church,** do you want to take your ancestors to the temple? If so, you will want to use software that helps track the special ordinance information.

Consider downloading one or more of the *free* family history programs, or trying the demo or trial versions of several programs   to see how each one works for you; download and use several different ones to find the one that feels right. Many software vendors have free trial or demo versions available to try out. Some software companies offer

their basic software for free, and then charge for the more advanced features. It won't take long for you to learn which ones offer the features you need and are the most intuitive for the way you work.

You may want to read reviews by experts and users' comments. You can do a Google search to find articles about a particular software program and read users' comments. Also, look at the publisher's Web sites for details and other web sites for users' message boards and e-mails.

There are many excellent family history programs available to meet your needs. Get the scoop on all

> You may want to read reviews by the experts on the dozens of software programs available before you purchase.

Software Reviews by Experts

Ten Reviews.com - FREE

http://genealogy-softwarereview.toptenreviews.com

Provides detailed product reviews, ranking, and side-by-side comparisons of ten family history PC software programs. They did not review or compare any free programs, web-based programs, or Macintosh programs, but they provide helpful buying guides, articles explaining how to get the most out of a product, and an easy way to buy them. Here's the criteria they used to evaluate the genealogy software they offer:

- **Ease of Use / User-Friendliness –** It's easy for beginners and experienced computer users alike; the program should be well organized and easy to navigate.

- **Ease of Installation & Setup –** The software should be straightforward and simple to install and setup on your computer, without any errors or confusing steps.

- **Feature Set –** It should include all of the features necessary to research and organize your family tree including reports, charts, searching capabilities, web access and insightful ways to store data.

- **Help/Documentation –** The developer should provide ample help in the form of FAQs, email and phone support, online

course and product tutorials so anyone can learn to use the program and conveniently access customer support.

FamilyTree Magazine Review -

www.familytreemagazine.com/ FREE
ResearchToolkit/SoftwareGuide

Reviewer Rick Crume rates 12 Windows programs and 5 for Mac. He says "the best choice for you depends on your personal preferences." Overall, he favors RootsMagic and Legacy Family Tree.

ConsumerSearch.com - FREE

www.consumersearch.com/genealogy-software

Reviews the best top 4 Windows software programs, Mac programs, mobile software (iphone and ipod), and free programs. It also ranks the various reviews for credibility.

GenSoftReviews.com - FREE

www.gensoftreviews.com

A new site that allows people to review and rate all the software packages.

the latest versions of the most popular family tree software programs in this software roundup.

Windows Family History Software Programs

Paul Nauta

Software Programs Make it Easy

"Once you start moving beyond your parents and grandparents in your personal research, I cannot imagine keeping track of your family tree and research efforts completely by hand or in paper files anymore. Great software programs are available that make it easy to build, organize, manage, share, and view your family history." Paul Nauta, FamilySearch Public Affairs Manager

Legacy Family Tree.com – 💲 *FREE*

www.legacyfamilytree.com

An easy-to-use, award-winning, full-featured, super-intuitive software program with numerous customizable features. You choose the options to reach the level of detail and accuracy you want. As your skills increase, Legacy's abilities and features are there to grow along with you. You have complete control as you decide which tools to use and how to use them. Their exclusive *Research Guidance* feature increases the odds of adding new ancestors to your family tree by guiding you step-by-step through the research process. And their *Chronology View* is the software's most powerful tool.

Using Legacy

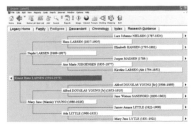

While Legacy's interface and usability suites the beginner, it is also robust enough to meet the demands of serious

researchers. It was created with the genealogist's needs in mind, and is designed to work with popular document retrieval and organizational systems. It uses the same *numbering system* as PAF (Personal Ancestral File) (RINs and MRINs) which is a well-known organizational system.

Features

Legacy is organized around four family tree views. Choose to import from a GEDCOM file or start a family tree from scratch. Add individuals on the *Family View* or on the *Pedigree View*; click to pull up the individual's information. Use the icons to add specific information like spouses, siblings and children. You have advanced color-coding options available to make it easier to trace ancestor lines. There is also a *Calendar Creator* that lets you create your own calendars, complete with pictures, birthdays, anniversaries and pictures.

Other standard features include: A wide variety of reports, global search and replace, auto-complete, powerful merge features, slide shows, multimedia, split-screen views, a Geo Location Database, and Master Location List Mapping . It automates the process of creating a family Web page, offers a good book feature and even helps you print out custom *Address Labels and Name Tags* (complete with pictures or three-generation pedigree charts) for your next family reunion.

Research Guidance

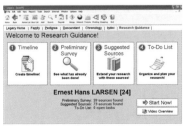

Built-in *Research Guidance* helps guide you step-by-step with the research process. You'll start with a *Timeline Review* and end with a *To-Do List* with detailed source tips along the way. The *Preliminary Survey* tab suggests sources, such as the best websites, message boards, and histories, and most are just a click away. If you want help with original research, click on the *Suggested Sources* tab where you can choose from one of the pre-defined goals of birth, death, marriage, parents, siblings,

At your direction, Legacy will produce a *Potential Problems Report* highlighting inconsistencies with your data.

You choose which problems to check and who to include in the report. You can also use the innovative *Missing Information Search* feature, which allows you to find those missing a specific piece of information, such as birth place or death date. Use the *U.S. County Verifier* to confirm the county associated with an event.

maiden name, or history. After selecting a goal, Legacy displays a list of the best records and websites to use to accomplish the goal.

It contains a very comprehensive directory of North American local and county histories which not only provide historical, geographical, religious, economic, and social information, but they are filled with extensive biographical information. *Research Guidance* analyzes the known information for an individual and provides prioritized suggestions based on your goals. Beginning researchers can appreciate the 24/7 assistance; professionals can benefit from the checklist-style approach to ensure you have covered everything.

Planning

The *To Do List* also acts as a Research Log. The tasks, which can be linked to each individual or to the family in general, can be filtered by category, location, status (open/closed), type (research, correspondence, other), and priority. The log reminds you what you have already looked at, contains bibliographical information about the sources searched, and records the results.

Chronology View

This is the software's most powerful tool. Viewing an ancestor's life in chronological order opens new doors and possibilities because of the different perspective. Clicking on this tab automatically gathers all known information about your ancestor – their vital information, custom events (residence, will proved, census, etc.), the births and deaths of their children and parents, etc. You can create your own historical timelines for analysis of obvious errors and combine with their extensive database of historical timelines which may suggest new avenues of research that had been overlooked.

Reporting

You can choose from many reports including Descendant Narrative, Family Picture Tree, and LDS Ordinances. Blank forms are also available. There are several unique reports that are helpful, and you can color specific boxes on pedigree charts to help the relationship stand out. Legacy can produce wall charts to display your family tree in a variety of formats, including DNA charts. You can also incorporate Microsoft's Virtual Earth to automatically pinpoint important locations and map your ancestors' migration. Their *Publishing Center* will combine multiple reports (pedigree charts, timelines, scrapbooks, calendars, etc.) and publish them in one combined book. It will automatically create a table of contents, index of names, preface page, etc. All reports can be printed, saved to files or PDFs for easy electronic sharing.

Certified by FamilySearch. Standard edition is *Free*, Deluxe edition $29.95.

RootsMagic.com – $ FREE
www.rootsmagic.com

*RootsMagic Essentials Free. Rootsmagic $29.95
Certified by FamilySearch*

RootsMagic Essentials

is a *free* genealogy program designed to help you easily start tracing your family trees. It shares many of the same features with the full RootsMagic software including clean and friendly screens, the ability to add an unlimited number of people and events, pictures and media management, the SourceWizard to write your source citations for you, powerful merging and clean-up tools, dozens of reports and charts, support for international character sets, FamilySearch integration, and the ability to share data with other people and software programs. The full version of RootsMagic is available for purchase and includes features not available in RootsMagic Essentials.

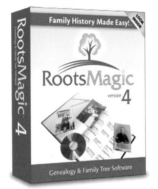

RootsMagic

is the award-winning genealogy software which simplifies researching, organizing, and sharing your family history.
A review in the popular *Family Tree Magazine* said, "Probably the best all-around genealogy program, RootsMagic offers a winning combination of features for both casual and serious genealogists." (July 2009 edition)

The Main Screen

RootsMagic has five main views (pedigree, family, descendants, people and WebSearch),

plus a sidebar for easier navigation. You switch between the views by simply clicking on the tab for the desired view. You can navigate between views using the mouse or arrow keys. Double clicking on a person's name brings up the data entry screen for that person. You can even open multiple databases side by side.

The Edit Screen

The edit screen lets you add an unlimited number of facts for every person (i.e. birth, death, marriage, occupation, religion, description, etc). If you want to add a fact type that isn't in their predefined list, you can simply create your own fact types. It also allows notes and unlimited source citations for every fact. Every piece of information on a person is available from this one screen... name, parent and spouse info, personal and family facts, DNA test results, alternate names, or LDS information. You can directly access the notes, sources, media, and more for every item.

The RootsMagic Explorer

The Explorer is the heart of RootsMagic' search system. It makes it easy to find and edit anyone in your file.
Quickly search by surname or given names, or perform sophisticated searches easily. Even find women by their married names. And you can easily edit any person in the search list with the click of a single button.

Document Your Family History

RootsMagic provides a powerful source list which lets you add, edit, delete, and print the sources of your information. Simply add the source once, then when you add a fact to a person and want to document where that information came from, you simply point to the source in the source list.

And best of all, their *SourceWizard* will help you write properly formatted sources regardless of your expertise. Quickly and easily create sources as defined by the experts. You can even create your own source types.

Print Charts and Reports

The program offers a large selection of printouts, all available from a single report dialog. Pedigree charts, family group sheets, wall charts, 7 styles of narrative reports (where it writes the sentences for you), numerous lists, mailing labels, calendars, relationship charts, individual summaries, and photo trees. And if that isn't enough, it even provides a custom report generator, so you can create your own specialized lists. Download a *free trial copy* of RootsMagic to try them for yourself.

Publish Your Family History

The *RootsMagic Publisher* lets you combine multiple reports and charts into a single document, and will automatically create a table of contents and full index for the book. You can include photos, notes, sources and other text in your book. You can even add cover and title pages, copyright page, dedication, and more. Send your book directly to your printer, or save it to a PDF file to burn on a CD or email to family members.

Create Spectacular Wall Charts

RootsMagic lets you create beautiful full-color ancestor, descendant, and hourglass wall charts. You have full control over the positioning, size, colors, fonts, and other aspects

of every object in the chart. With simple mouse control you can resize an individual's box, or drag it to another location on the canvas without breaking the family links. You can change colors of individual boxes, or change the font or color of the text in the boxes. You can even customize your chart by adding additional text, pictures, or shapes to the chart, and you can change the background image or color.

Make Shareable CDs

RootsMagic makes it easy to share your family history with your family and friends. Your *Shareable CD*™ will feature a custom home page with your own title, photo, description, and contact information, and will include a read-only version of RootsMagic to show off your data and multimedia items.

Map Your Family

RootsMagic 4 now lets you view your family on a map. Simply select a family member from the list and it will display the map (anywhere in the world), with pins where that person's events (birth, marriage, death, burial, etc) occurred.

Clean-up Duplicate Records

It provides a powerful and easy-to-use merge feature. It will automatically look for duplicate individuals and display them in a list with the most likely matches listed first. Simply click a button to merge the duplicate pair, or mark them as "not a match" so that they won't show up in any future merge sessions. Plus, it features *SmartMerge* technology to let you quickly merge all those "for certain" duplicates.

Create a Family Website

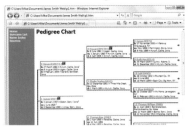

It can generate professional looking web sites automatically from your data, in narrative format, pedigree chart format, family group sheet format, or a combination pedigree / family group sheet format.

Synchronize with FamilySearch

RootsMagic allows you to search and optionally share data between your own data and the online *FamilySearch Family Tree* (an online system at www.familysearch.org that allows you to search for ancestors, contribute new persons and information, and retrieve missing information from a single, central database; *see chapter 5 for more information*). In fact, RootsMagic received an award for *"Easiest to Sync"* from FamilySearch. For LDS Church members, RootsMagic helps you reserve names and print ordinance requests for temple ordinances.

Web Navigation Features

One of its built-in intuitive features is a *Web Search navigation* tab at top. Using a drop-down list of genealogy databases you can search free websites (FamilySearch, Ancestry Message Boards, FindaGrave, Google, Live Search, Rootsweb, and Yahoo!), and subscription websites

(Ancestry, Footnote, GenealogyBank, and WorldVitalRecords). There's also a Custom Web Search feature which allows you to add a website to the search list. RootsMagic 4 may offer the easiest website access by any genealogy software program to date.

Take Your Genealogy Wherever You Go

RootsMagic To-Go lets you install and run RootsMagic on a USB drive so that you can take your data with you to a research facility, such as a library or archives, and view your data in the familiar RootsMagic program on a computer at that facility. Since you are running an actual copy of the program, you can update your data on the spot. When you return home, it will load your changed data files back onto your home computer.

Certified by FamilySearch. $29.95

Ancestral Quest -

www.ancquest.com

Certified by FamilySearch. 60-day Free trial. $29.95

An easy-to-use, full-featured family tree program used by novices and professionals alike. You'll get off to a quick start with the clear layout and friendly, conversational labels. Many users report they appreciate the completeness without a lot of seldom-used extra bells and whistles cluttering the screens. Entry of data is quick and efficient, and navigating family lines is straight-forward. Notes and sources can be easily entered and sources can be efficiently linked to individuals, families and events. Pictures, video and sound files and other documents can be added to individuals, allowing AQ to double as a family history scrapbooking and complete family documentation system.

Using AQ

When you start, you have several options: start a new family tree, use an existing file from your computer or access an online file with the collaborate option. A collaboration wizard will take you through this process. Data entry is a simple and thorough process. AQ offers 4 standard views: Pedigree, Family, Name List and Individual. The layout is intuitive and simple, input screens are thorough and easy to navigate. You can also opt to make events (immigration, census, etc.), individuals and relationships confidential. Sources are easy to add: just look for the "S" button next to each entry. You can even put AQ on a flash drive and take it with you wherever you go. Children can be properly identified as being the biological child of one parent, and the step or adopted child of the other parent.

Reports and Charts

Reports are clean and professional looking. From standard pedigree charts and family group sheets to wall charts, fan charts, book reports, listings, and more, AQ has a complete set of reports and charts. If you have linked original source images to the source records, AQ can even reproduce copies of original documentation with many of the reports. You can customize fonts, box colors and lines. Use the *Publish* icon to create a family book to print or save as a PDF file. Select *Internet* to use the Web Page Wizard to create a family history web site. You can also print birthday and anniversary calendars using your family file.

Unique Features

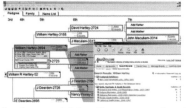

AQ has some unique features not found in other family tree software programs, including a *Collaboration* feature which allows you to share a common master family data file between siblings or cousins. You can also directly query the *Ancestry.com*

AQ offers integrated help to easily find the topic you have questions about.

Choose *Help* on your current view or search the entire help section. For Tech Support, contact by Email or phone. A video tutorial is available online.

databases for records or family trees. If you enable the interface with Ancestry.com, the number of trees and other records in Ancestry.com's collection, which feature a particular name on your tree will appear in the Pedigree View. You can search Ancestry.com while working on other tasks to effortlessly boost your outside research results. You can also link to *FamilySearch, World Vital Records* and your own favorite sites.

You can enable a detailed change log, which keeps track of every change you make to your data. You can also translate AQ into any language using a built-in translation tool. AQ has a unique Individual Summary view that lets you see all the information you have about any individual – standard events, notes, sources, DNA information, research tasks, parents, siblings, spouses, children, and more. You can click on most types of data on this screen to edit it, and you can click on a place name to see it on a map using an Internet mapping service.

AQ has a unique *"Advanced Filtering"* system for selecting groups of individuals to work with. Using this selection system, you can easily split your database, select groups to share with others, print various reports on just those people meeting your criteria, and more.

Award-Winning Program

Ancestral Quest was given an award from *FamilySearch* for having the *Most Comprehensive Syncing* tools for exchanging data with their system. AQ also received an award for having the *Best Listing Tool* – allowing you to view a list of all the data in your family file, sorted any way you can think of to help you find information. AQ recently received the *Editors Choice* award from *PC Magazine*.

The Ancestral Quest software has been licensed to other companies to be the base for other family tree programs. A decade ago, *FamilySearch.org* licensed AQ to be the base of the Windows versions of *Personal Ancestral File*. *Ancestry.com* licensed AQ from which it created Ancestry Family Tree in 2001. Ancestral Quest has been sold under different names by Individual Software for over 10 years, including *Family Ties, Family Trees Quick & Easy, Heritage Family Tree Deluxe, and Family Tree Heritage.* Users of any of these licensed products will recognize the similarities between their software and AQ, and will feel comfortable upgrading to the latest version of AQ. 800-825-8864. *Certified by FamilySearch.* 60-Day Free trial. $29.95

Personal Ancestral File – FREE

www.familysearch.org > *Download PAF*

PAF has been one of the most widely used and popular family history software programs. *It hasn't been updated for several years*, but it's a powerful, full-featured, user-friendly, quality product making it perfect for novice users. And it's *free*! It is produced by FamilySearch that pioneered the use of family history software. You can use it to record, organize, print, and share your family history information. It provides excellent reliable service. It has a nice selection of reports and charts and allows you to attach a person's picture with their information. It's easy to use, and has good support, including GEDCOM import and export.

PAF and New FamilySearch

You can still download a free copy of PAF from www.FamilySearch.org, but PAF does NOT synchronize data with new FamilySearch (nFS) and will *not* be upgraded. If you want to work and save your family history *only online* in new FamilySearch and not on your computer, then no other desktop software is needed. But if you want to keep a record of your own research on your computer, then you are required to use **PAF Add-in** software to enhance the various functions of PAF, **or** *purchase another software*

program. By doing this you will be able to connect directly with online databases, and receive research aid.

FamilySearch is certifying minimum requirements for other vendor's software to make it easier for you to understand what a vendor may or may not be offering you to synchronize your records with nFS. *See Chapter 5 for more information on FamilySearch Certified Affiliates.*

Family Tree Maker 2010 – $

www.familytreemaker.com $29.95

Millions of people have used Family Tree Maker (FTM) to discover and share their family stories. Now, with dozens of new features the latest version makes it easier than ever to explore your roots. Whether you're a seasoned pro or just starting on your family tree, FTM can help you create a family tree faster, easier, and better than ever before. A decade ago, FTM's frequent ownership changes and inconsistent product development began to erode their popular family history software, while other programs developed more powerful products. But the 2010 version has added popular new user-requested features and improved overall performance.

Using Family Tree Maker

It's easy to navigate and provides you with a wide variety of tools to create a detailed family tree. From the main *People Workspace* screen you can: customize an individual's profile, view a list of all the names currently entered and view the family tree chart. By subscribing to Ancestry.com for a fee, you will be able to do family research online. When you find information on family members through the web, you can simply click and drag the information on to the workspace and it will automatically link as a source. With help boxes

FamilySearch Certified PAF Add-Ins

These are programs that allow PAF users to access, print, update, and sync with online information in https://new.familysearch.org. These add-ins are intended primarily for those who wish to use your PAF 5 or Family Tree Maker program in conjunction with the online family tree at new FamilySearch.

FamilyInsight –

www.ohanasoftware.com

An essential tool for file management and a *FamilySearch Certified PAF add-in* that is currently compatible with: PAF (Personal Ancestral File), Legacy Family Tree, AncestralQuest, RootsMagic, Family Tree Maker, and GEDCOMs from any program.

Award-Winning Program

It was awarded the FamilySearch Software Award for *"Best Person Separator"* and *"Best Standardizer"* (finding multiple instances of a place name in your file and correcting all of them at once). One of the main purposes is to allow you to comfortably synchronize your personal family history research files with the new FamilySearch (nFS) website. The program includes some other unique and useful tools such as place editor, person separator, and LDS Church member features.

Synchronizes With New FamilySearch

The program starts by comparing your file to the information on the nFS website and bringing back records that are likely matches. Once you've decided which results really are matches,

you get to choose what information to save to your file. You also can choose to send information from your file to nFS for others to find. While you are filling in new information or sharing your information, the program uses your decisions to help combine duplicates and clean up the nFS database, thus helping you make progress on your own research, while still lending a hand in the group effort for nFS.

Sort and Rescue

Sometimes, while looking at nFS records, you may find that someone has incorrectly combined two dissimilar records. The *Separate* feature sorts the information so that you can quickly see the problem and pull out mismatches. Once you know which group of records don't belong, you can both separate them and recombine them into a second individual all at once.

One-Click Place Name Correction

The *Place Editor* is another big time saver. It lets you find all the instances of a place name and correct all of them at once. It also does an excellent job of finding duplicate records in your database so you can easily merge them.

"Guide Me" Button

This button provides click-by-click instructions as you use the program. Definitely a helpful feature for those of you who are new to computers. The program also contains lessons and other help documents simply by clicking on the 'Help' menu. There are also video tutorials on their website at: www.OhanaSoftware.com/VideoTutorials.

Free Web Classes

They offer free online classes (called webinars) which are great resources for researchers of all levels. The webinars cover trainings for their program, plus guest presenters each month on assorted valuable topics. Some are available in a video archive, but you may want to join the live classes whenever possible so you can interact and ask questions as they go along. You can sign-up for upcoming webinars at: www.OhanaSoftware.com/Webinars.

FamilyInsight is both Windows and Mac compatible and is currently the only Mac desktop program for quickly synchronizing files with nFS. It is also the ONLY program for synchronizing *Family Tree Maker* software with new Family Search.

Certified by FamilySearch. Free 60-day trial. $25.00

Ordinance Tracker –

FamilyInsight has added the ability to reserve LDS ordinances, and print out ordinance requests with their newest addition called *Ordinance Tracker*. It is part of the program or can be purchased as a stand alone program, and can be used with any of the current family history programs like RootsMagic, Family Tree Maker and Legacy. If you have decided to work directly from new FamilySearch, without a desktop program, it is a much needed tool to organize your reserved ordinances. $12.50, Mac and Windows compatible.

Certified by FamilySearch.

Ancestral Quest –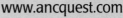

www.ancquest.com

A full-featured family tree manager created by developers of PAF for Windows. PAF 5 users will feel comfortable with the familiar look and functions of AQ. One of the many new features allows users to synchronize a PAF or other local database with the family tree on new.FamilySearch.org. AQ can be used by itself or as an add-in to PAF. *Certified by FamilySearch.* 60-day Free trial. $29.95

PAF Companion –

www.familysearch.org

A utility program for Personal Ancestral File, it is designed to print a variety of high-quality genealogy charts and reports from PAF files. Basic version is *Free*; full version $6.75.

Get My Ancestors – *FREE*

www.ohanasoftware.com > *Download*

Get My Ancestors

A new free utility that allows you to download your family tree from the FamilySearch Family Tree (you need to register) and save as a PAF database. It will contain FamilySearch IDs so that FamilyInsight can more easily synchronize any changes you make with FamilySearch. For a video tutorial visit their website.

Certified by FamilySearch.

at every step, FTM has a layout and design that will aid you through your research no matter how much experience you may have.

When there are possible duplicate individuals the software will link the information with all of the individuals who are associated with it, such as viewing both spouses in a marriage. To aid you in entering correct information, it will alert

you of any duplicate records or unlikely dates.

As your family tree becomes larger, you may want to use the *Places Workspace*. This allows you to review all of the locations that are linked to your family members. A simple click on the location will reveal all the facts associated with that site such as marriages, deaths or births. The map is powered by

Microsoft Bing. It may be viewed in three different ways; road map, satellite photograph (Bird's Eye), or a combination of the two.

Product Highlights

- A dynamic user interface that lets you quickly switch between important features.
- The ability to import data from other genealogy programs, including Personal Ancestral File, The Master Genealogist, and Legacy Family Tree.
- A Web Search that is integrated with Ancestry.com so you can easily add records and images from the millions of available historical records.
- Attractive charts and reports in a variety of formats.
- The ability to add photos and audio and video files to your tree.
- Timelines and interactive maps.
- Powerful sourcing tools that let you document—and rate—each citation.
- Family migration paths - View timelines and interactive maps highlighting events and places in your ancestors' lives.
- Better Performance - Experience faster load times and navigation.

Other Features

The combination of their new streamlined look and smoother integration with the Ancestry.com web service makes FTM an effective product, allowing you to quickly build a family tree in a refreshing way and bounce between branches and generations of your family with ease. This is a vastly improved program including better performance (faster load times and navigation), standard source templates (to help you enter the correct citation every time), ability to scan photos and documents directly into FTM, adding family picture and individual thumbnails photos to Family Group Sheet report, and a new tool to produce a map of the locations of an individual's life events.

Significant world events may be added to individual's time lines that will help you get a glimpse of what may have shaped their lives. To help you get a feel for what the locations really look like, there is a 3D option that allows you to see the height of buildings and other objects. There are a wide variety of charts and reports to choose from when printing. You can also create a personalized chart from a variety of backgrounds. Reports can be created for people, relationships, places, media and sources.

Help Support

By visiting their website, you will have access to a number of tutorials that can walk you through all of the latest features. You will receive a full length DVD with your software. Built-in prompts will aid you along your path as you create your family history. Online, you can search through the knowledge base for helpful hints of any subject and there is customer service contact information provided. $39.95

The Master Genealogist - 💲
www.whollygenes.com

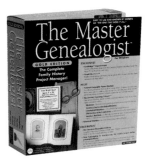

Known by experts as "the one that does it all." Although it is written with professional genealogical standards in mind, it comes with a tutorial and has more flexibility than its easy-to-use competitors. The learning curve is somewhat difficult, but it comes with everything you need to: manage volumes of research data, photos, and sources; organize a research trip, including "To Do" lists, reference material, charts, and forms; track your correspondence and expenses; be the hit of a family reunion; or publish a book, complete with table of contents, footnotes, multiple indexes, and bibliography. Silver $34.00, Gold $59.00

Genbox.com -
www.genbox.com

A complete, powerful and flexible genealogy software program that helps you organize your family genealogy research, store your family history data, enter proper source citations, and produce professional-quality family tree charts and genealogy research reports that you can preview and modify, then print or publish on the web on your own genealogy website. Offers you all the tools that you have been wishing for in your genealogy software with ability to link multimedia files to your family tree. Extensive data entry fields, customizable sources, helpful management tools, and beautiful reports and charts. The program seems to have essentially everything a genealogist needs, although due to its complexity beginners may find themselves somewhat overwhelmed. Someone with only basic skills may find it difficult to use. You can work with several databases at once, and the tools for helping you cope with different spellings of the same surname are excellent. Free trial. $29.95

DynasTree.com - *FREE*
www.dynastree.com

A new, fast-growing family network from the UK that offers free family tree software to create your family tree and stay in contact with your relatives.

Their *Home Edition* is a genealogy and family tree program that offers secure, state-of-the-art usability and technology in multiple languages.

Family Tree Legends.com - *FREE*
www.familytreelegends.com

Offers most of the features you would expect, but also offers an Internet-intelligent genealogy application. Their SmartMatching technology allows you to collaborate with other genealogists through a sophisticated, simple interface,

and intelligently matches the ancestors in your file to all the ancestors in the Gencircles Global Tree. It also includes: GEDCOM merge and find duplicates, lots of reports which can be exported to Adobe PDF format, Spell Check which quickly and easily checks your spelling in your notes and can add custom words to the dictionary, search and replace places, sources, repositories, and addresses in convenient list windows.

The Next Generation (TNG) -
http://lythgoes.net/genealogy/software.php

A genealogy program that runs on web servers. It has most all the features one expects in any modern genealogy program, including a powerful database, easy methods of adding new data, relationship charts, timelines, and more. The major difference is that TNG is installed on a Windows, Apple or Linux web server; to use this software you must have a Web server that supports PHP and MySQL and so *should not be considered by most people.* It also is multi-user: multiple people can access the database and even add new data simultaneously. $29.99

Brothers Keeper -
www.bkwin.org

A shareware program that will help you organize your family history information and let you print a large variety of charts and reports. It's available in 15 languages or so. You can download it for free and then decide if you want to keep it. It's one of the most respected and successful shareware genealogical programs, and has been around a long time and has many dedicated users. $45.

Web-Based Software

When you want to work together with other family members or researchers to collectively research a family tree, free Web-based family history software may be a good option. Check out the following considerations.

> FamilySearch Family Tree is a new single, universal family tree that all of us share and work on in common. It provides a free internet-based environment for everyone to collaborate. *It has been in Beta for several years and will soon launch to the public.*

Ancestry.com Online Family Tree – **FREE**
www.ancestry.com > *Start Your Tree*

This *free* service from Ancestry.com allows you to record, preserve, and share your family tree on the Internet without any additional software, in your own password-protected Online Family Tree. You can begin from scratch or upload a GEDCOM file to create your family tree and then invite multiple family members to join you in researching, editing and adding to the information.

AGES-online - **$**
www.ages-online.com

Build and manage your family tree from anywhere there is internet access. Whether you're at the local genealogy library, or on the other side of the world researching your tree, you can view or edit your data easily and quickly. Its password protected, so only you have access. You own the data, not the company. You decide who can view or edit your information. With their Share with Friends & Family feature, you can truly collaborate with others on the same family tree, with multiple family members, anywhere in the world and still maintain the necessary security. You upload your own GEDCOM file and a picture of each person in your tree and display on your web page. Recognized in Family Tree Magazine's "Top 101 Best Websites 2009" and "Top 10 for Storing and Sharing". 30-day free trial, $39.95/year Economy package.

ArcaLife.com – www.arcalife.com **FREE** **$**

This new site lets you build and share your family tree, and helps you record your life story. Features

FamilySearch Family Tree
http://new.familysearch.org (Beta) **FREE**

You cannot access this website yet, but since it will soon launch to the public we've included introductory info here. This *free* database allows you to record, preserve, and share your family tree on the Internet without any additional software. You can navigate from yourself, to your ancestors, and beyond. You and your family sharing the same family tree can collectively organize information into its appropriate branch on this shared tree which ultimately will link to all known information and documentation for each individual.

The ability to combine our family history data with online proof documents will *revolutionize* family history research collaboration and be a boon to tracing and sharing your family roots. When they begin to roll it out to the public soon it will greatly help reduce the duplication of research effort. It is temporarily located at the new.familysearch site, but soon will be relocated to the regular FamilySearch web site.

You can resize your family tree to show many generations on the screen to view your extended pedigree. When you hover the mouse cursor over someone in the tree, the path back to you is highlighted. This lets you more easily see how you connect to any person in your tree. You can also see descendants instead of ancestors.

You can also switch from the *Family Tree* view to the *Individual List* view or *Family Pedigree* with details view. When you switch from the Family Tree view to the list, the list contains the individuals in the Family Tree view. Once the list is displayed, you can sort the individuals by last name, first name, gender, birth date, birthplace, or person ID (PID).

include timelines, video and audio, a *"3-D* Life Cub"*,* plus you can import content from social networks such as Facebook. Basic membership is *Free,* or you can add storage space for a one-time fee starting at $20 for 10GB.

FamilyTree Explorer.com – FREE $
www.familytreeexplorer.com

 Free fully-featured family tree software (Beta) from FindMyPast.com that features online access to your research, photos and sources anytime, anywhere. Easy to use modern, simple, yet powerful design. Share and collaborate: invite nearby family or distant relatives to view and contribute to your tree. Options range from a free basic account to plans with varying annual fees.

AppleTree.com – www.appletree.com FREE

 Features a shared family tree; smoothly zoom and view the global visualization of the entire tree all at once. This is a Wikipedia-like approach to solving the master genealogical puzzle. You can upload all high-resolution photos, videos, audio and documents associated with people, events and places in order to preserve our history and memories. *Certified by FamilySearch.*

SharedTree.com - FREE
www.sharedtree.com

 An online family history and genealogy application that allows multiple people to collaborate on a family tree.

We Relate.org - www.werelate.org FREE

This free public-service Web site, created in partnership with the Allen County Public

Library, allows you to create Wiki pages for your ancestors, collaborate online with relatives, and upload photos, scanned images and GEDCOM files.

Family Pursuit.com - FREE
www.familypursuit.com

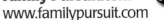 A new collaborative online genealogy management tool that allows people to work together in their efforts and to easily share their ideas and research. *FamilySearch certified.*

Genes Reunited.com - www.genesreunited.com

The UK's largest FREE $ family history and social-networking website. You can become a cyber detective by building your family tree and posting it on the site and investigating which ancestors you share with other members. It currently has over 10 million members worldwide and over 650 million names listed. Free membership allows you to use the family tree software, but to use all of the features you must upgrade. £9.95/month (about $15).

Family Tree Builder - FREE $
www.myheritage.com > *Downloads*

 A powerful software program that MyHeritage members can download and use for free to build family trees, research family history and add content like photos and videos. Their Smart Matching™ technology constantly compares new family trees to the database of more than 300 million profiles to find matches and discover long lost family connections. Basic (up to 500 people and 100MB) Free, Premium (up to 2500 people and 500MB) $3.95/month, Premium Plus (unlimited) $9.95/month.

4 Directory of Tools

Mac Software

MyHeredis.com - www.myheredis.com $

A full-featured, snazzy-looking family tree software program developed for Mac which benefits from all the latest technology of Mac OS X. It's a multi-file, multi-window application, with no limits to the number of individuals, or generations, or data entry. One of its greatest strengths is its ability to create an assortment of attractive, fully customizable charts. Free demo version available. System requirement: Mac OS X version 10.1.3 or later. $69.

Reunion - www.leisterpro.com $

Reunion is one of the easiest-to-use programs with superb charting capabilities and many features. It helps you to document, store, and display information about your family. It records names, dates, places, facts, plenty of notes, sources of information, pictures, sounds, and videos. It shows family relationships in an elegant, graphic form — people and families are linked in an easy-to-understand fashion. Reunion makes it easy to publish your family tree information. You can automatically create common genealogy reports, charts, and forms, as well as birthday calendars, mailing lists, questionnaires, indexes, and other lists. Reunion

even calculates relationships, ages, life expectancies, and statistics. It also creates large, high-resolution, graphic charts allowing complete on-screen editing of boxes, lines, fonts, and colors. Wall charts are one of its specialties. $99.

MacFamilyTree -
www.synium.de/products/macfamilytree $

A popular genealogy application that sports a stunning, configurable user interface, animated charts, editable reports, powerful print and export options, visualize migration of your ancestors over centuries and continents, and built-in support for Google Earth. The newest version features a new *VirtualTree* and an overhauled media library. Data can be viewed and compared in a number of useful ways. You get ancestor and descendant charts, timelines and family charts, as well as the more typical family tree. There's a powerful 3D view that maps family members with flags pinned to a rotating globe. Its main claim to greatness is its editing tools. The *Family Assistant* is the software's hub where you can access an animated family tree that zooms and scrolls as you navigate through its branches, adding new ancestors as you go. $49.

Handheld Software

See page 214 for information on handheld computer software.

See page 214 for information on handheld computer software.

Software Tools and Utilities

To Make it Easier

You can do much more than just keep track of your family tree with the following useful family history utility programs; including programs for writing your history, story-telling, creating timelines, creating your healthy history, smart research, organization, mapping, planning your family reunion, family tree charting, etc.

Personal Historian.com -
www.personalhistorian.com 💲

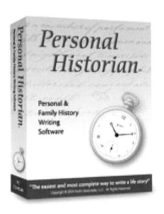

A complete system for writing personal and family histories. This exciting program imports names, dates and events from your family history software, and the powerful writing analysis helps you make your history readable and interesting to others. You can choose historical and cultural LifeCapsules to remind you of important events and give context to your history. The Timeline gives a visual description of your life in historical context. You can publish your completed history to your printer, word processor or PDF file. $29.95

Heritage Collector.com - 💲
http://heritagecollector.com

A comprehensive software management system that allows you to organize, work with, preserve, and find the many varied kinds of multimedia files you are using. It helps organize photos and documents, find anything in seconds, save hard drive space, achieve your information to CD/DVD, search your archive, create shareable slide shows, safeguard files with a backup system, unique photo identification, create "talking" photos,

and print in many different formats. It has an easy way to name everyone in the photo or create a caption by creating a photo "hot spot." You also get a free 200 page family history e-guidebook. Download $74.95

LifeSteps - www.allaboutfamily.com 💲

LifeSteps is a system of maintaining all the information about a family's situation. The easy-to-fill-out forms cover medical issues, real estate and financial holdings, an inventory of household and personal valuables, and more. A fun section on family traditions allows users to list birthdays and other special family events, including how they are usually celebrated. Included in this program are simple-to-fill-out forms that cover information individuals will need in the event of an emergency. $9.95

Genelines -
www.progenygenealogy.com/genelines.html 💲

One of the most powerful research and story-telling tools available, Genelines lets you SEE your ancestor's lives in time. By bringing together elements of time, history and family relationships on visual timeline charts, Genelines can bring your family history to life, and even help you find new directions for your family research. With Genelines you can create amazing timeline charts. Genelines gives you a suite of seven distinctive, fully customizable timeline charts. These eye-catching charts are created from two sources – your genealogy database and an extensive library of history files – to illustrate your family lines along with any fascinating facts and interesting events you've found in the course of your research. $29.95 (download)

YourFamily.com – www.yourfamily.com FREE

A place to go to find and reconnect to long lost relatives and even friends. They have helped hundreds of people locate lost relatives and ancestors through their Genealogy Message Board and Lost Family Bulletin Board.

VitalRec.com – www.vitalrec.com **FREE**

A comprehensive resource for locating U.S. vital records: birth certificates, death records, marriage licenses, divorce decrees, naturalization, adoption and land records from each state, territory and county. There is a fee for ordering vital records through them.

Passage Express - www.passageexpress.com **$**

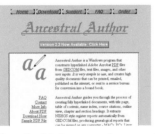

Software to transform your family history research into a professional looking multimedia presentation. Free Trial. $34.95

Ancestral Author - **$**
www.ancestralauthor.com

A program that constructs Adobe Acrobat PDF files from GEDCOM files, text files, images, and other sources of user input. It is used to create a family history and genealogy book based on the information stored in your files. It's simple to use, and creates high quality documents that you can print, email to family and friends, publish on the internet, or send to a printer for printing into a bound book. The end result is a family history 'book' PDF file that contains a customized document of your genealogical research. It automatically creates a name index, and a list of sources. One of the great things about Ancestral Author is that the sections are hyperlinked. Click on a name in the index, and you are brought to the page on which that person appears. $24.95

Clooz.com Filing Cabinet - www.clooz.com **$**

Clooz is a database for systematically organizing and storing all of the clues to your ancestry that you have been collecting over the years. It's an electronic filing cabinet that assists you with search and retrieval of important facts you have found during your ancestor hunt, showing you a complete picture of what you have and what you lack. Once you import your information, you can assign documents to each person. Then, a report will show you all the birth and death certificates, wills, deeds, diary entries, or other documents that pertain to each individual. $39.95

Family Tree SuperTools - **$**
www.whollygenes.com/supertools.htm

Offers powerful wall charting features and many other exciting add-ons to users of many popular family tree programs. It works directly with the data from many programs without the need of an intermediate GEDCOM file. $17.95

FamilySearcher - **FREE**
http://myweb.cableone.net/kevinowen3/familysearcher.htm

A windows program that can read a GEDCOM file and display a list of all names contained in the file in a spreadsheet format. It is then possible to search the Internet IGI (International Genealogical Index) and the other resources at FamilySearch.org web site for any matching entries.

GenSmarts - www.gensmarts.com

Works with your existing genealogy file and produces research recommendations. It helps you generate and track to do lists, print worksheets to record your search results, and plan research trips to libraries, court houses, etc. For online research sites, GenSmarts produces links that already have your ancestors name and specifics embedded - making it much easier to perform online record lookups. $24.95

GENMatcher -
www.mudcreek.ca/genmatcher.htm

Quickly compares two genealogy files for matches, or one genealogy file for duplicates.

I Felt Two Hands From Behind

Hildo Flores of Piura, Peru traveled to the town of Zorritos in northern Peru to find the death dates and final resting place of his great-grandparents. He walked down every vault aisle and read every inscription in the cemetery. Still nothing. He knelt and prayed, then repeated his thorough search pattern. For a third time, he was unable to find them and now it was getting late. He would have to leave without finding them. He turned toward the front gate, ready to leave the cemetery when something wondrous happened. "Just as I took my first step, I felt two hands take hold of my head from behind and turn it towards a certain spot. My eyes rested on a small, dirty headstone... I looked behind me to see who had grabbed my head, but no one was there." To his amazement, it was the very marker he was searching for!

It can show the comparisons side by side and save your work from session to session. $19.95

US Cities Galore - www.uscitiesgalore.com

Quickly find U.S. cities, towns, townships and counties. Copy and paste results into your genealogy program. Reads and writes GEDCOM. $29.95

AniMap Plus - www.goldbug.com

Just about every researcher deals with the problem of finding an old town that has long-since disappeared from the map. AniMap displays over 2,300 maps to show the changing county boundaries for each of the 48 adjacent United States for every year since colonial times. Includes all years, not just the census years. Maps may be viewed separately, or the program can set them in motion so you can automatically view the boundary changes. Maps of the full U.S. are also included showing all the changes in state and territorial boundaries from 1776 to the present. Each map includes a listing of the changes from the previous map making it simple to keep track of parent counties. $79.00

Map My Family Tree -
www.legacyfamilytree.com/ MapMyFamilyTree-1.asp

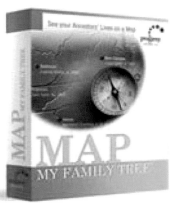

Genealogy mapping software that presents your ancestors' lives on a map. It plots all ancestral life events on customizable color maps. This allows you to see where your ancestors were born,

Directory of
4 Tools

married and died, plus track family migrations using the world and country maps. Then zoom into any part of the world to see detailed events in that particular location. $39.95

SmartDraw - www.smartdraw.com

Uses templates and drag-and-drop capabilities to make it easy to draw professional-looking family tree charts, diagrams, genograms, and flow charts. Free trial download for 30 days. $197.

SnapGenie.com - www.snapgenie.com (FREE)

Share the stories behind your photos. This program helps you easily build and share verbal narrated photo slide shows in a matter of minutes which you can share with family and friends. And best of all, it's free.

Politics and Family History

Mark Twain

"Why waste your money looking up your family tree, just go into politics and your opponents will do it for you." Mark Twain (Samuel Clemens) (1835-1910), Author & humorist

Genuine History

Thomas Jefferson

"A morsel of genuine history is a thing so rare as to be always valuable." – Thomas Jefferson (1743-1826), Founding Father, 3rd President

Standing on Ancestors Shoulders

The only way to look into the future is by standing on the shoulders of the past. – unknown

A Paper From Nowhere

Steve and Nancy Lealos made a trip to Delaware from their home in Alaska to spend two weeks researching Nancy's genealogy. They called and visited anyone and everyone with any information. They were at libraries, courthouses and other locations from the moment they opened until they closed. However, their hard work hit a dead end with Nancy's great-great grandfather and the time had come to go. "While I was taking some last photographs on a lawn, I happened to see out of the corner of my eye an older piece of yellow legal paper on the ground. As I picked up the paper, I was absolutely stunned to realize that I had in my hand a handwritten document that was at least 50 years old, written in ink without a smudge on it, that listed Nancy's great-great grand-father, his parents, his wife's family and continuing back even further with parents, husbands, wives and children, with dates, places, etc." To add to the amazement, they could find no reason for the paper to be there. "No one knew about it, no one claimed it." On a lawn in Delaware a piece of paper had appeared out of nowhere with the information they were seeking. Just coincidence? Steve Lealos

Preserve Your Journal for Posterity

Spencer Kimball
© by Intellectual Reserve, Inc.

"By now, in my own personal history, I have managed to fill seventy-eight large volumes, which are my personal journal. There have been times when I have been so tired at the end of a day that the effort could hardly be managed, but I am so grateful that I have not let slip away from me and my posterity those things which needed to be recorded." Spencer W. Kimball

CHAPTER 5

Best of the Internet

KEY FAMILY HISTORY WEB SITES

The internet contains a wealth of information and makes it easy to contact and stay in touch with others who might be working on your family roots. Whether you are experienced or a novice in tracing your family roots using the Internet, these personally-reviewed and singled-out-for-excellence web sites will empower you in your search for your treasured family heritage. A virtual *treasure trove* of empowering, irreplaceable knowledge and information—much of which had been essentially "lost" to mankind in dusty archives around the world—is now instantly available to you at your fingertips at any time.

Web sites come in all degrees of value, efficiency, and friendliness. And since everyone has different needs, not all are equally useful for every family historian, but each may have something of immense value to offer you and perhaps add an important piece to your family history puzzle.

This collection of key web sites is not meant to be a comprehensive listing of family history web sites available, as there are well-known web directories, such as *Cyndi's List*, that do this very well. Searching the various online genealogy databases can be time-consuming and even difficult. Rather, this is a valuable, easy-to-use selection of personally pre-screened, key web sites to save you valuable time, help you get started and get organized, and help you add new branches to your family tree, thus empowering you with the *Best of the Internet.* These sites and resources are **FREE** unless marked with an **$** to signify that access to some or all of the content requires a fee.

Opportunity in Difficulties

Winston Churchill

"A pessimist sees the difficulty in every opportunity; an optimist sees the opportunity in every difficulty." — Winston Churchill (1874-1965)

5 Best of the Internet

Family History Insights - 5

Spencer W. Kimball
© by Intellectual Reserve, Inc.

Help From the Other Side

"...my grandfather...searched all his life to get together his genealogical records; and when he died... he had been unsuccessful in establishing his line back more than the second generation beyond him. I am sure that most of my family members feel the same as I do–that there was a thin veil between him and the earth, after he had gone to the other side, and that which he was unable to do as a mortal he perhaps was able to do after he had gone into eternity. After he passed away, the spirit of research took hold of...two distant relatives. ... The family feels definitely that...our grandfather had been able to inspire men on this side to search out these records; and as a result, two large volumes are in our possession with about seventeen thousand names." Spencer W. Kimball

The Miracle of the Chinese Bamboo Tree

After the seed for this amazing tree is planted, watered, and fertilized regularly every year you see NOTHING for four years except for a tiny shoot coming out of a bulb. During those four years, all the growth is underground in a massive, fibrous root structure that spreads deep and wide in the earth. But sometime during the fifth year the Chinese Bamboo tree grows to EIGHTY FEET IN SIX WEEKS! Family history is much akin to the growing process of the Chinese bamboo tree. It is often discouraging. We seemingly do things right, and nothing happens. But for those who do things right and are not discouraged and are persistent things will happen. Through patience, perseverance, diligence, work and nurturing, that "fifth year" will come, and all will be astonished at the growth and change which takes place. Finally we begin to receive the rewards. To paraphrase Winston Churchill, we must "never, never, NEVER give up!"

Oliver Wendell Holmes

Where Are You Headed?

"The greatest thing in this world is not so much where we are, but in what direction we are moving." Oliver Wendell Holmes (1809-1894), Physician & professor

Henry David Thoreau

What Are You Doing?

"It is not enough to be busy; so are the ants. The question is: What are we busy about?" Henry David Thoreau (1817-1862), Author, poet & naturalist

Thomas A. Edison

Close to Success

"Many of life's failures are people who did not realize how close they were to success when they gave up." Thomas A. Edison (1847-1931), Inventor & businessman

Maya Angelou

Know Where You're Going

"No man can know where he is going unless he knows exactly where he has been and exactly how he arrived at his present place." Maya Angelou (1928-   )

David E. Rencher

Promptings that Help

"In this day and age of computer technology and computer wizardry there are things which do and do not work. We cannot overcome the promptings [we feel] and expect to find our ancestors. If we ignore that, above all else, we will not have the experiences which we continue to have if we listen to the promptings and go when and where we are told to go." David E. Rencher, AG, FUGA, Chief Genealogist FamilySearch

Pliny the Younger

Deserve to be Remembered

"It is a noble employment to rescue from oblivion those who deserve to be remembered." Pliny the Younger (AD 61-112), Author and philosopher

Best Top Ten Web Sites to Search for Your Ancestors

These *Best of the Internet* web sites can help you trace your family roots, connect to your ancestor's lives, and locate information about your ancestor's culture, traditions, homeland, and history.

There are literally thousands of Web sites available on the Internet to help you trace your family roots and stories which can become overwhelming if you don't know where to start. But some sites really stand out at providing the best information and records to get you headed in the right direction. Here's my list of the top sites.

Web sites can be categorized into different types. Explore all kinds of Web sites and bookmark the ones that seem the most helpful and interesting for you.

Web Site Categories

Huge Web portals or gateways - provide numerous links to collections of Web sites

Major collections of records - big Web sites, libraries, archives, public records, etc. that have parish records, censuses, wills, military and immigration records, maps, etc.

Support Web sites - local sites, how-to sites, blogs, podcasts, databases, maps, etc. that provide valuable information, keep you up-to-date, and help you collaborate with others who share your family tree.

EasyFamilyHistory.com

The Easiest Way to Your Family History™ **FREE**

The Internet is the place where some of the most exciting family history advances are taking place. You need to know about these valuable resources, and be able to conveniently and readily access thousands of web sites. So we created a companion website (or portal) to this guidebook so you can conveniently access all of these web sites with just a keystroke or two. No more typing in those lengthy website addresses. And every link to a website is LIVE, so just point and click to go directly to the website. And since *new* web sites become available constantly (and web addresses often change), we constantly scour the Internet and review all the new information and web sites to try to keep you up-to-date on changes.

EasyFamilyHistory.com - A *free*, user-friendly, up-to-date Internet directory of the best family history web sites as our way of saying thank you. Enjoy!

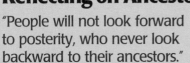

Reflecting on Ancestors

"People will not look forward to posterity, who never look backward to their ancestors." Edmund Burke (1729-1797), Irish statesman & author

Edmund Burke

1. FamilySearch.org (FREE)
New.FamilySearch.org

www.familysearch.org
http://new.familysearch.org

(New.FamilySearch.org has *restricted use* at press time; the worldwide rollout to the public will be announced soon.)

FamilySearch™ is one of the comprehensive, preeminent family history Web sites on the Internet, and the largest genealogy organization in the world. It provides online access to the world-famous Family History Library in Salt Lake City, Utah and the largest collection of free family history, family tree, genealogy records and resources in the world. It is the link to the world's largest repository of genealogical resources and a global network of research centers. Millions of people use FamilySearch online, or through over 4,600 family history centers in 132 countries, to learn more about their family history. FamilySearch is a nonprofit organization sponsored by The Church of Jesus Christ of Latter-day Saints (casually known as the LDS or Mormon Church).

FamilySearch Ongoing Major Projects

- Vastly improving their software and infrastructure
- Digitizing and indexing their extensive collection (of billions) of worldwide genealogical records held in the Granite Mountain Records Vault, currently viewed online at www.FamilySearch.org > *Search Records >Record Search pilot*. Although a billion names can already be accessed online free of charge, most of the vast collection of genealogical resources is yet to come online. FamilySearch is undertaking massive digitization and indexing projects to bring most of

Granite Mountain Records Vault

the additional collection of unique records online over the next few years.

- Adding millions of new records each year from its acquisition efforts
- Partnering with other libraries in digitizing their unique records
- Expanding their extensive collection of published family histories
- Upgrading their Family History Library catalog using new technology; you'll be able to view microfilms on your home computer. Right now, the online catalog allows you to see what microfilm and other holdings are at the library, and then order the films to be sent to one of the 4,600 family history centers nearest your home for viewing. About 100,000 rolls of microfilm are circulated to Family History Centers each month.
- Adding their new valuable wiki site
- Adding new searchable maps

A major, multifaceted project to improve *FamilySearch* has been in process for the past few years to upgrade their software and infrastructure.

What is "New FamilySearch"?

http://new.familysearch.org **FREE**

For several years, FamilySearch has been developing ways to make organizing, viewing, collaborating, and sharing personal family histories online easier, faster and more accurate for everyone. The Beta (or first) phase of this project is temporarily only available to members of the LDS Church because it primarily replaces an LDS tool called *TempleReady*. When the online Family Tree feature is made public it will be very attractive and valuable to everyone. It is temporarily called *"New FamilySearch"* (nFS) and is temporarily located at http://new.familysearch.org. But in the near future it will be relocated to the regular website and found under a *Family Tree* tab.

In addition, as part of the restructuring, the site will integrate all of the new technologies and record sets they've been working on (i.e. Record Search, Family Tree, Research Wiki, FamilySearch Indexing, searchable maps, etc.) into one easy to use experience. Instead of using these tools individually, you will simply go to FamilySearch.org to do extensive work on your family history.

Family Tree
Revolutionizing the Work

The new FamilySearch Family Tree is a single, universal family tree that all of us share and work on in common. It provides a free, multi-language, internet-based environment for everyone to collaborate as partners, and will eventually include capabilities to link scanned images of proof documents with each record.
It has the option to dispute and provide alternative lineages with notes and proof documents. The links to images of documents is a key component to compiling accurate lineages. This ability to combine our genealogy data with online proof documents will revolutionize family history

research collaboration and be a boon to tracing and sharing your family roots and stories.

Collaboration Is the Key to Successful Research

In the past, there has been no really effective way to collaborate with others, but nFS makes it possible to identify other descendants of your common ancestors and communicate with each other via email. Collaboration will allow you to build your family tree much faster and more accurately. When you register, you will have the opportunity to make your email address available for others to see *if you wish*. And you can always *Update Your Profile* on the home page. Email is a safe way to communicate. Providing your email address for collaboration purposes is essential if you contribute information to nFS or dispute data. You can create email addresses for free at many web sites, including www.gmail.com, www.hotmail.com and www.aol.com.

Limited Release of nFS

FamilySearch has begun to implement the new system worldwide in gradual phases, and at press time have issued a limited release. It is not available to the public quite yet, but this is a great way to work out all of the bugs with a relatively large user group before the major world roll-out. Hopefully this means that most of us will be spared the disappointment of slow access and the usual major problems of a gigantic new release, and that we'll be able to find support from experienced local Family History Center volunteers when nFS is available to everyone. Right now, it lacks some niceties considered standard in a major genealogy product, but many exciting new, exclusive features are coming. They make a new release to their web software quarterly, so it will incrementally become an increasingly valuable tool for everyone tracing their family roots.

FamilySearch Has a Lot Going On

On FamilySearch you can do significant research online and also discover what records you need to search to find your ancestors in record-breaking time. It provides easy access for the gathering, collaborating and sharing of family history information. They have been actively gathering, preserving, and sharing family history records worldwide for over 100 years. With vital records from over 110 countries and territories, FamilySearch is one of the top Internet sites for genealogical research. A lot is happening at FamilySearch and due primarily to the free access to billions of unique records, and their ongoing major projects, I've selected this as the number one overall family history Web site.

Intro to *New FamilySearch*

In time, the *FamilySearch* Family Tree feature will contain billions of records about individuals and readily help you see what information FamilySearch already has about you and your ancestors. In addition to names, dates, places, and relationships, you will also be able to see very

Combining all of the information about individuals and families into one place so everyone can see and work on it together has some real advantages.

- Spend less time searching for your ancestors since you need to look in only one place.
- Make tracing your roots easier by easily working together to evaluate the accuracy of the information. You can dispute incorrect information, make corrections, and add new information in one place.
- Helps eliminate the duplication of family history work.

comprehensive source citations, including links to source images provided by original contributors or collaborators. It will also include a mapping utility which maps locations where an individual has resided. By clicking on the link, a pop-up will display the events that took place at that location, i.e.: birth, marriage, death, etc. You can add new information and make corrections and work with other relatives on shared family lines. Information about each individual is combined, meaning all of the information is preserved; nothing is deleted or overwritten. Individuals are also organized into families and extended family lines. It also helps LDS Church members do temple ordinances for their ancestors.

For many years, FamilySearch has collected and published family history information in various computerized databases, such as: Ancestral File, Pedigree Resource File, International Genealogical Index, and church and vital records. Presently, these records are accessed separately at www.FamilySearch.org and through http://pilot.familysearch.org. When FamilySearch launches its new integrated website, you will conveniently access them from the single search option at FamilySearch's homepage.

The International Genealogical Index™ (IGI) FREE

Lists the dates and places of births, christenings, and marriages for more than 600 million deceased people. An addendum contains an additional 125 million names. The index includes people who lived at any time after the early 1500s up through the early 1900s. These names have been researched and extracted from thousands of original records. Most of these records are compiled from public domain sources. The IGI database makes otherwise difficult-to-access information readily available to you.

The new FamilySearch Family Tree feature is a *collaborative* or *shared family tree*; your family tree isn't all yours. You work with others as "partners" to make sure your family history is as accurate and complete as possible.

Working with Others on Shared Family Trees

The objective is that descendants of common ancestors will communicate with each other, share your information and your sources, jointly analyze the data and come to the most accurate information concerning your ancestors.

To make this possible, nFS keeps track of who contributes which information. Depending on how much contact information a contributor chooses to display, you may be able to contact him or her by email, standard mail, or telephone. As you look at your family history in nFS, you will find places where an ancestor is missing or has incomplete information.

Before adding a new individual or family, you should search nFS to see if someone else has already added that information. If you find it, you can just connect it to your family line. There is no need to enter it again.

Another way to see if someone else has already entered information about an individual is to see if nFS can find any possible duplicates. If it finds a possible duplicate, you decide if the information is about the same individual. If so, you can combine the information. All of the information will be preserved.

With an individual's information in the same place, everyone interested in an individual can more easily evaluate the accuracy of the information and make corrections if needed, and add notes and sources. After all of an individual's information has been combined, a is time to start adding new information and make corrections. New FamilySearch simplifies the process of building a family tree, and helps eliminate duplication of the work.

The Pedigree Resource File™ (PRF) *FREE*

A large collection of family histories submitted by individuals via the internet to help you identify and link your ancestors. Approximately 1.2 million names are submitted to this file every month. It is also a publicly-available method of preserving your genealogy on a computer database. The comprehensive index to PRF is available free on-line but the actual database files are currently only available on compact disc which you can either use *free* in Family History Centers worldwide, or purchase at a nominal cost.

(If you wish to purchase PRF, go to www.ldscatalog.com, click on *family history / software & databases* in the left column.) Each disc contains about 1.1 million names. Information is

You may want to send emails to other Contributors, particularly when you feel their information is wrong, and share your information and sources with them with the hope that your communication will result in your ancestors' records being more accurately reported.

Communicating With Others to Get it Right

You may need to Dispute data if the Contributor has not listed an email address or other means of contact. A "dispute" in nFS is simply a declaration for the benefit of other descendants that you think certain data is incorrect. Disputing is part of the cleaning-up process.

George W. Scott, a new FamilySearch instructor at the Lindon, Utah Family History Center has written a 74-page self-study guide available in PDF format for anyone to use for *free*.

How To Use New FamilySearch

www.usingfamilysearch.com

FamilySearch has a *Users Guide* to new FamilySearch. See more information on p. 157. George Scott's self-study guide is also very useful and he updates it whenever there is a significant revision in the program. The changes are identified and dated so you won't have to review or reprint the entire guide. He suggests the following 16 steps for using nFS to save you valuable time which are explained in detail in the guide. (*Two of the steps are specific for LDS Church members, but everything else is the same for everyone. Obviously, skip these steps if they don't apply.*)

Step 1. Register on nFS.

Step 2. Connect yourself with your family tree.

Step 3. Start the online training program, and learn where to find *Help*.

Step 4. Map out a plan for working with your family tree.

Step 5. Combine all the records for the individual.

Step 6. Separate out any records from the individual's *Combined Record* which don't pertain to that person.

Step 7. Clean the individual's *Summary* screen.

Step 8. Declare yourself the *Legacy Contributor* of your previously-submitted records, where appropriate, so you can make corrections.

Step 9. Search for family members missing in nFS.

[**Step 10.** LDS Members. Reserve family members for temple ordinances.]

Step 11. Correct erroneous data you submitted in the past.

Step 12. Make the necessary preparations for *Synchronizing* your family history software data with your nFS Family Tree.

Step 13. Synchronize your family history software file with nFS.

[**Step 14.** LDS Members. Reserve names for the Temple you added during Synchronization.]

Step 15. Make additional adjustments to the Summary screens, as a result of the data you copied from your family history software file to nFS during Synchronization.

Step 16. Send emails to Contributors whose data is incorrect. Dispute incorrect information if the Contributor lacks an email address.

organized in family groups and pedigrees, and is printed exactly as submitted and not combined with information from other submitters as is done in Ancestral File.

Ancestral File™ FREE

A collection of approximately 37 million lineage-linked names of people throughout the world that are organized into pedigrees and family group record forms. The information includes dates and places of birth, marriages, and deaths. It also contains names and addresses of the individuals who contributed the information. You can print copies of the records or copy them to your computer hard drive for use in

your family history database by creating a GEDCOM file (*see Chapter 4 for more details*). The site does not verify the accuracy of the information. It is simply a pool of information donated by thousands of people. The Ancestral File has not been updated since 2000 because of the major FamilySearch overhaul in process.

Providing Contact Information

When we are able to access the nFS Family Tree feature, you may want to provide your contact information so other people who are doing research on lines that connect with yours can contact you and share information they have gathered. You can also use contact information to get in touch with others who might be related to you. nFS automatically displays your contact name with every piece of information that you contribute, if you so choose.

Me and My Ancestors Tab

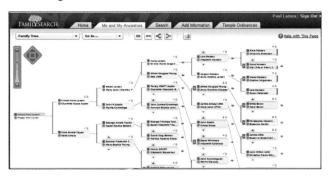

When you click the *Me and My Ancestors* tab, you can choose between two different forms of the pedigree chart: *Family Tree* and *Family Pedigree with Details*. You can switch between the two charts by clicking *Change View* in the upper left-hand corner of the screen. You can also see an *Individual List* of the people currently in the screen's view of your pedigree. You can sort the list by surname, given name, gender, birth date, birthplace, or PID (*Person Identifier*).

Family Tree View

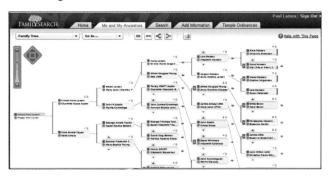

Family Tree is a new interface for FamilySearch which can handle a large number of users, larger files, and has great graphics capabilities. You can zoom in or out using the zoom bar in the upper left-hand corner; move the pedigree up or down or left or right using the pointers in the diamond; and see more generations in your pedigree chart by clicking the right arrow. You can also grab the pedigree using your mouse and move it up or down, left or right. When you hover your cursor over a person, the route back to you will be highlighted.

You can change the ancestral pedigree to a descendancy pedigree by clicking the *Descendants* icon at the top of the screen. You can switch back by clicking the *Ancestors* icon. When you click on a person in the pedigree their personal folder appears in the right column of the screen. In the folder, if you click *View Details*, a pop-up screen will

Figure out if you want to work on new FamilySearch beyond your own personal research.

Map out a Plan for Your Family Tree

It's easy to get lost in a large family tree and not know which branches you have and have not worked on. The easiest way to keep track of what you have done is to print off your pedigree chart and check off each family as you complete it in nFS. In addition, you need to decide how much of your family tree you will work on. Your lineages in nFS may stretch back further than your own records. Do you plan to work on nFS beyond the point of your own research? Generally, it is best to stay within the bounds of your own research and allow the researchers who submitted the records for earlier centuries to clean those records.

appear showing the person's record. You can click *Family Group Record* to view or print the person's Family Group Record.

You can *Add Parents* or a *Spouse* or a *Child* for the person by clicking the appropriate links. Doing so will open the *Search screen* so you can search for a record for the family member; you can also use that pop-up screen to *Add* the family member if the search does not produce a record for that individual.

The person's folder has a *Summary* icon and a *Family* icon. You can toggle those two icons to see either the person's Summary or a list of his family members. If you click on the name of a family member, a pop-up screen will appear with that individual's record.

New "Source" Standards

Currently, you can read, add, edit or delete *Sources*, which can be accessed from either the Summary or Details screen. However, it's largely a waste of time to enter your sources into new FamilySearch at this time because the Sources section will soon

There are great **helps** within the new FamilySearch website. Screens have a link entitled either *Help* or *Help with this page*. And the *Help Center* (bottom of page) is a valuable source of help.

be revamped. FamilySearch is currently working with major family history archives to develop a standardized digital source format so they will be able to submit large amounts of information with an automated source attached. Soon, greater attention will be paid to distinguishing among *good/bad/no* sources.

Add New Information and Make Corrections

In nFS you will find yourself in an environment where you can work with others to identify the correct information and preserve the most accurate information that can be found about your family. FamilySearch protects your information. When you contribute information,

In new FamilySearch, you can click on *Learn How To Use FamilySearch* to access different Overviews (videos) and Guides (PDF publications). The *Help Center* has a helpful e-Learning Course, and many Family History Centers offer free classes.

Help Center Overviews (Videos)

- Navigating and Finding Information
- Help Me Get Started with My Family History
- Introduction to FamilySearch
- Getting Help
- Adding Information about Individuals and Families
- Making Corrections to FamilySearch
- Transferring Information from Your Personal Computer to FamilySearch
- Resolving Possible Matches
- How Combining an Individual's Information Affects Your Family Line
- [LDS members] Doing LDS Temple Ordinances for Your Ancestors

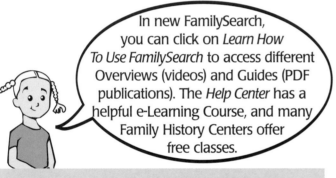

Help and Learning Assistance

You can search for answers using the Help Center's *Search* feature, or you can look for your question among the *Common Questions*. Also, at the top of the Help Center, there is a *Local Assistance* tab, which lists your free local Family History Consultants, their phone numbers and their email addresses. They will be happy to assist you for free if you can't find your answer in the Help Center. You can also call or visit your free local Family History Center, where Family History Consultants will be pleased to help you. Finally, you can call or email the FamilySearch Support team. You can email them for help using the *Send us feedback* feature at the bottom of most major screens. Or you can call them for free at (866) 406-1830.

only you can change or delete it. If other users contribute different information about the same ancestor, nFS keeps this new information in addition to your information. You can easily add new information. You can also correct the information that you added previously. Information about deceased individuals is available instantly to other users. If you contribute information about individuals who may still be living, only you will be able to see it.

Instead of providing other information, some users may indicate disagreement with a piece of information. This is called "disputing." You can easily communicate with the Contributor to correct the information, or dispute incorrect information if the Contributor lacks an email address. A user who enters a dispute should include a detailed explanation so that everyone can see why he or she believes the information is incorrect. The dispute can then start a discussion among contributors, which will ideally lead to the most correct information being identified and preserved and incorrect information being removed.

> Don't copy (download) all the records in your nFS Family Tree to your personal family history file, and don't upload a GEDCOM into nFS. That may sound strange, but here's why.

Protecting Privacy Rights

To protect the privacy rights of living people, nFS limits the amount of information that you can see about individuals who may still be

Help Center PDF Guides

- **What's New** in the New FamilySearch Web Site
- **A User's Guide** to the New FamilySearch Web Site

  Chapter 1: Introduction to the New FamilySearch Web Site

  Chapter 2: Navigating, Finding, and Printing Information

  Chapter 3: Adding New Individuals and Families

  Chapter 4: Correcting Information That Is Already in the System

  Chapter 5: Transferring Information between Your Personal Computer and the New FamilySearch Web Site

  Chapter 6: Combining Duplicate Records

- **Contributing a GEDCOM File** to the New FamilySearch Web Site
- **Getting Started** with the New FamilySearch Web Site
- **Printing** Family Pedigrees and Family Group Records

Specific Info for LDS Church members in the Users Guide

In the User's *Guide to the New FamilySearch Web Site* there is the following specific info for LDS Church members:

- Chapter 7: Performing LDS Temple Ordinances for Your Ancestors
- Policies for Preparing Names of Deceased Ancestors for LDS Temple Work
- A LDS Member's Guide to Temple and Family History Work
- Submitting Names to the LDS Temple Using the New FamilySearch Web Site

A Big Tip

Don't Copy All the Records in Your New Familysearch Family Tree to Your Own File

Your own family history file on your computer is your personal research, your niche. You may want to download a few records from nFS, but there is no benefit to copying all the records into your own file. You will never be able to keep it up-to-date, as your nFS family tree will change almost daily, so it is a wasteful effort to try to copy beyond the bounds of your personal research. It will be available (with all the latest research) on nFS anytime you want to peruse them. Allow nFS to serve as your super family tree over your niche, expanding your family tree beyond the bounds of your personal research.

Don't Upload a GEDCOM into New FamilySearch

As a general rule, it is best NOT to upload GEDCOM's into nFS, as it will almost invariably create many duplicate records. It will take you longer to combine all the duplicate records you create via a GEDCOM upload than it would take to synchronize your personal file with nFS. So, it is far better to *synchronize* than to upload a GEDCOM.

living. If you contribute an individual who might be living, only you can see him or her. Other users cannot, even close relatives and the individuals themselves. FamilySearch considers that an individual may be living if both of the following situations apply:

- He or she was born at least 110 years or married at least 100 years ago.
- The record contains no death information.

In nFS, you can easily identify individuals who may be living. In the details and on the family pedigree, the individual's name is displayed in *italics*. The text is lighter than the names of deceased people. In the details, the word *"Living"* appears next to the individual's name.

FamilySearch Certified Affiliates

www.familysearch.org/eng/affiliates/index.html

In order for any family history software to work correctly with new FamilySearch, it needs to make some enhancements or adaptations. Vendors of certified features are licensed to use the FamilySearch Certified Logo on the product packaging, website, and marketing literature.

FamilySearch certifies minimum requirements for product features, processes, or services from other vendors programs to make it easier for you to understand what they offer to synchronize your records with nFS.

At the present time, here are the certified software affiliates (third-party companies) that provide products and services with features that are compatible with FamilySearch programs. These products and services are independently developed and supported by their respective organizations, not by FamilySearch. You may want to check with the above web site for additional updates.

Certified Affiliates and Features*	Description
AllMyCousins (Web) FREE www.allmycousins.com Access, LDS Ordinance Status	View your relatives on New FamilySearch. See a summary of which relatives need LDS ordinance work and jump to nFS to combine duplicates or reserve LDS temple work.
AncestralQuest (Win) $ 60-day Free Trial / $29.95 www.ancquest.com Access, Helper, Multi-Language, PAF Add-in, Print, Sync, Update, LDS Ordinance Reservation & Ordinance Request	An easy-to-use, full-featured family tree program. PAF was created from AQ, so PAF users will feel right at home using the screens, reports, and other functions. PAF users can upgrade to AQ or continue to use PAF, supplementing it using the new features in AQ, including the ability to synchronize both AQ and PAF data with nFS.
AppleTree (Web) FREE www.appletree.com Access	Features a shared family tree; smoothly zoom and view the global visualization of the entire tree all at once. This is a Wikipedia-like approach to solving the master genealogical puzzle. You can upload all high-resolution photos, videos, audio and documents associated with people, events and places in order to preserve our history and memories.
Charting Companion (Win) $ $19.95 www.progenygenealogy.com Access, Print	View, customize, print and publish your nFS family history in more ways than ever imagined. Choose from an incredible variety of formats and more than 16-million color options. Lets you quickly and easily create amazing charts and reports from your family tree database.
Family ChArtist (Web) www.generationmaps.com/familychartist Access, Print FREE $	A simple-to-use website that helps you create custom charts of your family history; no software to learn or buy. Create your own chart directly from new FamilySearch. You can edit incorrect information, immediately add pictures, and create countless combinations with beautiful graphics. Print FREE 8.5x11 charts from your printer, or for a small fee, purchase either a poster-size archival print or high quality electronic image file.
FamilyInsight (Win & Mac) $ 60-day Free Trial / $29.95 www.ohanasoftware.com Access, Helper, Multi-Language, PAF Add-in, Sync, Update, LDS Ordinance Reservation & Ordinance Request	Designed specifically to help PAF and *Family Tree Maker* users synchronize with nFS. It ranks matches and highlights differences so you can quickly import or export data and get right back to your research. Also gives you the ability to merge, cleanup, and compare files with increased accuracy. Received FamilySearch Software Awards for its *Place Editor* and *Person Separator*.
FamilyPursuit (Web) FREE $ Free (Basic - Family Tree) /$19.95/yr. (Plus Version) www.familypursuit.com Access, Sync, Update	Enables families to work together by providing a centralized private and secure family tree website packed with features to maintain an up-to-date and accurate genealogy database, coordinate and document research efforts, and upload documents and photos. Intuitive drag and drop technology allows you to easily transfer information between your family tree website and nFS. The wiki-based approach enables you to monitor the entire database and easily undo mistakes. Unlimited members.

*See the Legend on their website at www.familysearch.org/eng/affiliates/index.html
for a full description of the different features for the various programs.

Certified Affiliates and Features*	Description
Generation Maps (Web) $ www.generationmaps.com Access, Print Service	A comprehensive genealogy chart printing service. Choose from inexpensive working charts that assist your research, or decorative charts suitable for framing. They will individually handcraft your chart or your genealogy/photo files. Quality and attention to detail is in every chart. And it's easy—just pick out your chart, and it arrives on your doorstep.
Genetree (Web) FREE www.genetree.com Access	A social networking site to build your family tree for free. Share photos and stories of your ancestors with other family members. You can also enter DNA results to be able to search their database and find possible genetic cousins.
Get My Ancestors (Win/Mac) FREE www.ohanasoftware.com Access, Multi-Language	Sprout your family tree with this free downloadable program from the makers of FamilyInsight. Helps you download a few generations of family records from nFS and save them as a PAF File. A quick and easy way to get started on the search for your ancestors.
Grow Branch (Web) $ $99. For 3 Tree Branches or Research Assistance www.usfamilytree.com Access, Update	Focuses on researching USA relatives for the LDS Temple.
Legacy FamilyTree 7.5 (Win) Free / $29.95 (2 versions) $ FREE www.legacyfamilytree.com Access, LDS Ordinance Reservation & Ordinance Request, Print	Software to organize, research, and publish your family's tree. You can print maps, get research suggestions, collaborate with other family members, cite your sources, publish books and shareable CDs and much more. Legacy makes it easy to work with FamilySearch and will measure your progress against the goals you set. Easily import from PAF and other programs.
LiveRoots (Web) FREE www.liveroots.com Research Wiki Access	A specialized search experience for genealogists; an information resource that assists you with locating genealogical resources, wherever they may be stored.
MagiKey Family Tree (Win) $ $29.95 www.themagikey.com Access, Helper, LDS Ordinance Status, Ordinance Reservation	GEDCOM based software that helps you organize family history, analyze researched data, and publish customized book-like searchable web pages. It is designed to access nFS from within the program and merge information without losing the format integrity. Advanced features: US census tracking, relationship calculator, task suggestions, find anomalies, and place normalization.
MobileTree (iPhone, iPod) FREE www.mobiltree.me Access	nFS content on your iPhone and iPod Touch using iTunes. See your family history, search for specific names and do family history research from virtually any location. Using the GPS and camera features of the iPhone specifically, you can capture images of people, places or sources and associate that rich media content with a specific individual and event.
OrdinanceTracker (Win/Mac) $ $12.50 www.ohanasoftware.com Access, LDS Ordinance Status & Request	Works directly from nFS and can be used along with any desktop genealogy program to trace LDS Ordinances.
RootsMagic 4 (Win) FREE $ Free / $29.95 (2 versions) www.rootsmagic.com Access, Helper, Print, Sync, Update, LDS Ordinance Reservation & Request	Winner of the FamilySearch award for "Easiest to Sync" makes working with nFS a breeze, including reserving LDS ordinances and creating temple trips. Intuitive and easy-to-use; import directly from PAF, nFS, and other programs. Special features: run directly from a USB drive, SourceWizard, integrated web search, creating Shareable CDs, and more.
TreeSeek (Web) FREE www.treeseek.com Access, Print	A fully automated service that creates unique high quality genealogy charts from FamilySearch data. You specify the starting person for your chart and they do the rest. No data entry, no waiting, no high prices, and no GEDCOM files.

Unlocking the Granite Mountain Records Vault

FamilySearch and The Family History Library are in the process of a new massive project called the *Scanstone Project*. They are scanning, digitizing and indexing their extensive collection of genealogical records held in the Granite Mountain Records

The Granite Mountain Records Vault currently holds 132 times more data than the U.S. Library of Congress which is the world's largest library.

Granite Mountain Records Vault

Vault, and seeking volunteer help for the project (see *Enlisting Your Help* page 163). This is a climate-controlled, underground storage facility to safeguard master copies of all their microfilm records. The storage facility, built literally into a mountainside, is located about 25 miles from downtown Salt Lake City, Utah.

Records contained in the Family History Library and in FamilySearch databases (which are safeguarded in the mountain vault) have been gathered from a wide variety of sources worldwide

FamilySearch Labs - FREE

http://labs.familysearch.org

Take a look at some of the new things nFS is working on. They are testing a variety of products such as Records Search, Standard Finder and Research Wiki. You can sign up as a beta tester and help them develop even better products for future use.

FamilySearch Records Search -

www.FamilySearch.org > *Search Records* FREE
Record Search pilot

You can search millions of new indexed records for your ancestors. These are the records from the Granite Mountain Records Vault. More records are being added every month by volunteers at www.familysearchindexing.org. This will be integrated into the regular web site in the near future.

FamilySearch Wiki - FREE

http://wiki.familysearch.org

Free family history research advice for the community, by the community. A large, on-line library where you can find thousands of articles and how-to instructions about doing family history. It assists you in finding your ancestors, and offers information on how to find, use, and analyze records of genealogical value for beginners, intermediate and expert researchers. Since this is a wiki Web site, you can add to existing articles or write new articles. This will be integrated into the regular web site soon.

FamilySearch Community - FREE

http://forums.familysearch.org

Unofficial discussion forums for new FamilySearch.org

FamilySearch
Community Trees *FREE*

http://histfam.familysearch.org

These are lineage-linked genealogies from specific time periods and geographic localities around the world which also includes the supporting sources. Each Tree is a searchable database with views of individuals, families, ancestors and descendants, as well as printing options.

The scope of "partner projects" may be a small, grass roots village or township working together to form a family tree of all the known residents of its community for a given time period. Some are genealogical and historical societies working with FamilySearch to index several sources of

data to link them to common, lineage-linked genealogies of a targeted geographic area of interest. The scope could also be focused on a particular record set and locality. The goal may be to identify and reconstitute all families of a particular place from a village, county, or even a country.

Many of the current projects were produced by FamilySearch's Family Reconstitution team and date back to the medieval times. GEDCOM downloads of the community trees may be available depending on any records access restrictions. No living information is available in this public view. Community Trees will be integrated into the regular web site in the future.

in an ongoing collection effort that has been under way for more than a century. Records have been filmed in over 110 countries, territories, and possessions. Most of the microfilm collection has been produced by microfilming original sources worldwide. In cooperation with legal custodians of records worldwide, The Family History Library currently has about 200 digital cameras photographing records in 47 countries and plans to expand this operation dramatically.

As part of this project, they are currently scanning over 32 million images per month or approximately 370,000 rolls of microfilm per year from their vault, *the equivalent of about 6 million 300-page volumes.* Volunteers extract family history information from digital images

Granite Mountain Records Vault

of historical documents to create indexes that assist everyone for free in finding their ancestors. With electronic help, each and every name and word in every record will be indexed so that we can find particular ancestors quickly. Names become the primary focus of the databases; localities and jurisdictions become identifiers. The project is expected to be completed within the next 5-10 years, and when it is completed an index to these records will be available online. The result will give you the ability to search and have billions of indexed genealogy records at your finger tips. You can access the newly indexed records right now for *free* at http://www.FamilySearch.org > *Search Records > Record Search pilot.*

5 Internet Best of the

Enlisting Your Help - FREE

http://familysearchindexing.org

FamilySearch is enlisting the help of thousands to index all those newly digitized records. *FamilySearch Indexing* is a worldwide, non-profit community effort to harness volunteers to gather, transcribe, and index records of genealogical significance. You can help create free public access to the U.S. census indexes and other records. The key life events of billions of people are being preserved and shared through the efforts of people like you. Using their online indexing system, volunteers from around the world are able to quickly and easily transcribe the records—all from the convenience of your home. The indexes

> Why not volunteer to help index a census project? It's easy, they train you, and you can work on your own schedule at home, as little as an hour each month. Your contribution is invaluable. Go to http://familysearchindexing.org for more information.

are then posted for FREE at FamilySearch.org.

Millions of rolls of microfilm provide census, vital, probate, and church records from over 100 countries for indexing projects. Governments, churches, societies, and commercial companies are also working to make more records available. YOU CAN HELP by volunteering to index one of the current U.S. census projects or the upcoming England and Wales census projects. It's easy, you can work on your own time, and they train you. You can get more info on their web site *http://familysearchindexing.org*.

Published Family Histories - FREE

www.familysearch.org > *Search Records* > *Historical Books*

The Family History Library has an extensive collection of published family histories and is digitizing more everyday – even faster. The effort targets published family, society, county, and town histories, as well as numerous other historical publications that are digitally preserved and made

accessible for free online. FamilySearch has nearly a million publications in its famous Family History Library, and there are millions of similar publications elsewhere in the United States.

Working with volunteers and select affiliate libraries, it plans to create the largest digital collection of published histories on the Web. It is helping to digitize and publish collections from the Allen County Public Library, Houston Public Library, and Mid-Continent Public Library Midwest Genealogy Center in Independence, Missouri. When all is said and done, there will be over a million publications in the digital collection online. It will be the largest free resource of its kind.

The Family History Library Catalog

The online catalog describes the books, microfilms, and microfiche in the Family History Library in Salt Lake City, Utah. The library houses a collection of genealogical records that includes the names of more than 3 billion deceased people. It is the largest collection of its kind in the world, including: vital records (birth, marriage, and death records from both government and church sources); census

returns; court, property, and probate records; cemetery records; emigration and immigration lists; printed genealogies; and family and county histories.

When you want to look at actual records of the people you are researching, you can visit a Family History Center nearest you (there are over 4,600 branches of the Family History Library worldwide) and order copies of the records from the main

Searchable Maps

FamilySearch will also be expanded with searchable maps. Partnering with the University of Austria Map Department, the maps of the Austro-Hungarian Empire (central Europe) were selected to add first. Jurisdictions overlap, several localities appear to have the same name, countries have been destroyed and wiped off the map, others have been created and added to the map, territory assigned to a new country carries a different name in each country—one place has two or more different names.

FamilySearch is indexing ancestor's names, the places where your ancestors are found, and the map reference. So with a click you can view and print the actual locality where your ancestors lived. This one feature alone will save you hours of research time. Then you can retrieve a copy of the record images to document your genealogy at a fraction of the time we spend today.

Free Research Assistance/Helps

FamilySearch offers two types of research assistance. The *Research Guidance* service is an online wizard that offers detailed research advice to a user based on his or her answers to a series of questions. *Research Helps* are research guides that can be read online or downloaded as a PDF. There are many guides available covering geographic areas and most types of genealogical records.

> **To use the Family History Library catalog,** search for your surname and various places that your ancestors lived, looking for information that might be relevant to your research. Choose from the following various search options.

Place: used to locate records for a certain place such as city, county, state, etc. Each jurisdiction has different records available, so it is important to search all jurisdictions for your area (i.e. both the city and county records).

Surname: used to locate family histories which include that surname or last name.

Author: used to search for a record by author.

Subject: used to search for a certain topic (based on Library of Congress subject headings).

Keyword: To find entries that contain a certain word or combination of words.

library in Salt Lake City for a nominal fee. To locate the nearest Family History Center, simply click on *Find a Family History Center Near Your Home* on the front web site page, or you may call 1-800-346-6044 in the United States and Canada.

Vital Records Index FREE

Collections of official birth, marriage, and death records from Mexico and Scandinavia. The official governmental records of births, marriages, and deaths in the United States and every Canadian province except Québec are called vital records. In other countries and Québec, official government records are called *civil registration*.

5 Best of the Internet

2. Ancestry.com $

www.ancestry.com

With more than 4 billion names and 27,000 searchable databases, Ancestry.com is the world's largest *online* collection of family history records, including the complete US Federal Censuses (1790–1930), US immigration records, vast military records, immeasurable passenger arrivals records at major U.S. ports, city directories, vital records, and many exciting collections from around the world. Ancestry users have created more than 14 million family trees containing over 1.5 billion profiles. And they have uploaded and attached to their trees over 32 million photographs, scanned documents, written stories and audio clips.

Even though Ancestry has relatively high subscription fees, users have access to hundreds of millions of fully searchable individual records, databases and family histories making the fees well worth your investment. You can search by record type, locality, or simply view scanned images of original historical documents. Access to these records is available through both free and premium subscriptions. With a paid subscription base of over 1,000,000 it is among the largest paid subscription

sites on the Internet and a premier resource to learn about your family history. Their service also provides a platform from which you can share your stories. You can invite family and friends to help build your family trees, add personal memories and upload photographs and stories of their own. And, with ongoing updates and new content always being added, you'll keep coming back to discover more.

Ancestry also has local web sites directed at nine countries, including U.K., Canada, Germany, Italy, France, Sweden, Australia, and China. 14-Day Free trial. U.S. Membership $19.95/month, $16.95/month for 3 months, $12.95/month for 12 months.

Ancestry WorldTree - *FREE*
www.ancestry.com/trees/awt

Rootsweb WorldConnect - *FREE*
http://wc.rootsweb.ancestry.com

Ancestry World Tree (and Rootsweb WorldConnect) is a free collection of user-submitted GEDCOMs (family trees). You can access World Tree and World Connect from two different websites, but either way, it is the same program and the same set of trees. The database contains more than 480 million names in family trees submitted by users. To search only World Trees or WorldConnect use the URL addresses above. Ancestry.com *general tree searches* includes other family trees not in World Tree, but general searches also includes World Tree only when searching for "EXACT matches only".

Ancestry.com is a private provider of a preeminent network of web sites for connecting families with their histories and with one another. The company's tools, content, and community help empower you to find the people most important to you and to share your unique family stories. By offering a variety of family websites, they give families all over the world a unique venue for keeping in

U.S. Social Security Death Index *FREE*

Contains information about persons whose deaths were reported to the Social Security Administration from about 1937 through current. The majority of the death records are from 1962 and later. This file provides birth and death dates and identifies the person's last place of residence and the place the death payment was sent. The Social Security number and the state of residence when the Social Security number was issued are also provided. This index contains vital statistics for over 86 million deceased individuals.

http://www.genealogybank.com/gbnk/ssdi

http://ssdi.rootsweb.ancestry.com

http://search.ancestry.com/search/db.aspx?dbid=3693

http://stevemorse.org/ssdi/ssdi.html

touch and strengthening relationships.

Ancestry.com and Rootsweb.com are two of the research sites that you will use the most. The Ancestry network includes:

RootsWeb.com - www.rootsweb.com
See RootsWeb site below for details.

Genealogy.com - www.genealogy.com **FREE**

 Provides the tools, resources (about 90,000 links to sites to help do research), and community that empowers you to uncover and share your unique family stories, and to research, organize and document your heritage. It produces the best-selling family tree software, *Family Tree Maker (see Chapter 5 for more details).*

MyFamily.com - www.myfamily.com

In a secure, password-protected environment, users can hold family discussions, create online family photo albums, maintain a calendar of family events and share family history information quickly and easily. Since 1998, myfamily.com has helped millions of people keep in touch with their family and friends by sharing photos, stories, news, family trees and more on their very own private web site.

DNA.Ancestry.com - http://dna.ancestry.com

 Expand your family tree, and discover ancient ancestry just by swapping your cheek. Learn about cheek-swab collection, DNA science and how to choose a test, order a DNA test, and see sample results.

UK Ancestry - www.ancestry.co.uk

This site maintains an extensive archive of 820 million searchable records from England, Ireland, Scotland and Wales, including England, Wales and Scotland Censuses, exclusive online access to UK birth, marriage and death records, plus a comprehensive selection of WW1 military, immigration and parish records.

Canada Ancestry - www.ancestry.ca

This site offers the largest number of Canadian family history records online, including more than 150 million names and the only fully indexed 1911 Census of Canada collection online, the Inbound Passenger Lists and Ontario and British Columbia vital records available in both English and French

German Ancestry - www.ancestry.de

The first website to host a significant collection of German family history records - currently more than 35 million, including the Hamburg Passenger Lists, both the German Phone and City Directories, plus international censuses, military and parish records with German relevance.

Australian Ancestry - www.ancestry.com.au

This site offers access to over 5 billion family history records worldwide, including more than 30 million Australian and 820 million UK family history records including the most comprehensive online collection of Convict and Free Settler records, the Australian Electoral Rolls, plus parish records, newspapers and more.

Italian Ancestry - www.ancestry.com.au

This site offers access to over 5 billion family history records worldwide, including more than 30 million Australian and 820 million UK family history records including the most comprehensive online collection of Convict and Free Settler records, the Australian Electoral Rolls, plus parish records, newspapers and more.

French Ancestry - www.ancestry.com.fr

Hosts more than 33 million French family history records including Paris vital records of births, deaths and marriages from as early as 1700s and other civil registration records from a variety of French provinces, plus international immigration and census records with French relevance.

Swedish Ancestry - www.ancestry.com.se

Hosts more than 11 million Swedish family history records including immigration records from as far back as the early 19th century, Varmland church records from the 1600s, plus international censuses and vital records with Swedish relevance.

Chinese Ancestry - www.Jiapu.com

Launched in 2008, hosts more than 3000 Jiapu – Chinese family histories bound in volumes – the earliest being from the 6th century BC and the most recent from the 1940s. The collection has been made available through an exclusive long-term partnership with the Shanghai Library, which holds the largest collection of Chinese family history records in the world. The site is in local language.

and Genealogy.org.

3. RootsWeb.com

www.rootsweb.com

FREE

A thriving, *free* genealogy community on the web (part of the Ancestry.com network) providing

a robust worldwide environment for learning, collaborating and sharing for the expert and novice alike. The site provides access to huge transcribed records from volunteer researchers, and contains extensive interactive guides and numerous research tools for tracing family histories. The site's *WorldConnect Project* contains more than 480 million ancestor names. Besides helpful advice such as the *RootsWeb Guide to Tracing Family Trees*, it boasts over 31,000 mailing lists, over 132,000 message boards, and the RootsWeb Surname List of more than 1.2 million surname entries.

It also hosts many major websites and sources of free data, such as: Cyndi's List, USGenWeb Project, the Obituary Daily Times (an index to published obituaries), National Genealogical Society, FreeBMD (the Civil Registration index of births, marriages and deaths for England and Wales);

4. Footnote.com

www.footnote.com

Through partnerships with some of the most

prominent archives in America including the National Archives, Footnote digitizes millions of documents, records and photos that paint a picture of our shared past that few have seen before. The collections include records relating to the Revolutionary War, Civil War, WWI, WWII, the Vietnam War, African American History, Native Americans, historical newspapers, naturalization documents, and city directories.

You can search the site for free: See all the index information and reasonably sized image thumb-nails, register and make any kind of contributions, including comments, annotations, Spotlights and Footnote Pages. You can even view millions of full images for free, it's just the full images in the Premium Titles that require a paid subscription.

Attracting over a million people to the site every month, Footnote goes beyond just making valuable documents available on the Internet. Tools on the site make it easy to engage with history. You can upload your photos and documents, make comments on documents and create your own web pages to display and share your discoveries.

Using Footnote

On the *Original Documents* page you'll find titles listed with short descriptions of the content at www.footnote.com/documents. If you want to see what they have available for a specific time period or record type, browse. www.footnote.com/browse.php. The tour page at www.footnote.com/tour.php reviews some of the things you can do on the site in more detail, and has a link to a search tutorial and a short video overview of the site. Free trial. $11.95/month, $79.95/year.

5. WorldVitalRecords.com

www.worldvitalrecords.com

A collection of over 1.4 billion records to help you build your family tree. By partnering with premier content providers throughout the world they are able to provide affordable access to genealogy databases and family history tools used by more than 258,000 monthly visitors and tens of thousands of paying subscribers. With thousands of databases they make it easy to fill in missing information in your family tree.

Databases include: Birth, marriage, and death records (from Colonial America to the 20th Century); family trees (featuring hundreds of millions of ancestors); family histories; census records (indexes for the 1860 and 1930 US Federal Census); court, land, and probate

records; cemetery, immigration and military records; newspapers (over 500 million names); directory lists; reference materials; and much more, including religious records.

Some of its partners include Quintin Publications, Archive CD Books Australia, Gould Genealogy, Immigrant Ships Transcribers Guild, Archive CD Books Canada, The Statue of Liberty-Ellis Island Foundation, Inc., Accessible Archives, Everton Publishers, Genealogical Publishing Company, Find My Past, Godfrey Memorial Library, Find A Grave, and FamilySearch.

Using WorldVitalRecords

They have many ways to search for your ancestors, such as a *Basic* and *Advanced* search engine, as well as the ability to browse their various databases by *Record Type, Place, Collection* and by *Database Title*. Each individual database can also be searched by going to the specific database and using the search engine found on the database's homepage. You can also search your ancestor's name by their exact name, soundex and double metaphone.

You may want to start your search by conducting a *basic* search for your ancestor (given name and surname only) and then narrow your search down, utilizing their advanced search engine. Limiting your search to a name, will provide more "hits" than by combining a name with other information.

The *Advanced Search Engine* allows you to search more than just a name. You can specify a year (a birth, marriage or death year) or location. One of the unique aspects of the search is the ability to add a keyword to your search, such as a newspaper, an occupation, religion or a spouse's name. As you use the Advanced Search feature and see what results you receive, remember the more information you provide to the search engine the fewer results you will receive. The *Keyword* on the Advanced Search allows you to narrow your search by typing in specific document types, alternate names or counties. For example, you may include terms such as: census, newspapers, Billy, Ada County, etc. In looking for vital records you could use it to add the name of a spouse.

If you find that the search engine has found no records for your ancestor, there can be a number of reasons. The search engine is going to look for records with the exact words that you type in (except in cases where you use the soundex or double metaphone search). Your ancestor's name may listed in any number of combinations, including initials for their first name, a different spelling, or the addition of a middle name or initial. If you are unable to find your ancestors, try searching in different ways, such as just searching the last name or typing in a first initial and last name. 7-day free trial.

U.S. Collection - $5.95/month, $39.95/year
World Collection - $14.95/month, $99.95/year

6. GenealogyBank.com

www.genealogybank.com $

Find the facts in four centuries of fragile, rare newspapers, books and documents. GenBank makes it easy to discover exciting details about

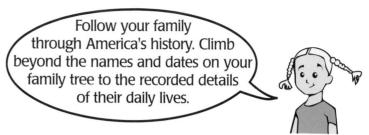

Follow your family through America's history. Climb beyond the names and dates on your family tree to the recorded details of their daily lives.

your ancestors with unlimited access to: Over 1 billion names, more than 4,300 newspapers from all 50 States from 1690 to today, over 130 million obituaries and death records appearing in American newspapers that document and give the details of our ancestor's lives.

More Newspapers

It contains more newspapers from across the US than any other site. More Colonial pre-1860 newspapers, more Hispanic newspapers (over 360), and more African American newspapers (over 280) than any other site. You will find firsthand perspectives on notable African

Americans from Frederick Douglass to Martin Luther King, Jr., as well as obituaries, advertisements, editorials and illustrations.

Newspapers are published every day, and give a host of family history records. You can also learn about the triumphs, troubles and everyday experiences of your American ancestors. The unique primary documents go beyond just names and dates. They provide first-hand accounts that simply aren't available from the census or vital records alone. Newspapers often add crucial details that tell the rest of the story, the actual images of our ancestors, and the homes where they lived. Who knew it would be this easy to find them after all these years.

Books, Documents, & More

A unique source that provides you with complete text of over 286,000 historical books and documents, including: U.S. genealogies, biographies, funeral sermons, local histories, cards, charts, and more published 1800-1980. Find military records, casualty lists, Revolutionary and Civil War pension requests, widow's claims, orphan petitions, land grants and much more, including all of the American State Papers (1789-1980), and all genealogical content carefully selected from the U.S. Serial Set (1817-1980). It contains the most comprehensive SSDI (Social Security Death Index) available. It's the only site updated weekly, and it's free to search.

Contains full text and digital images of: Senate Journal; House Journal; War of the Rebellion Record; DAR Reports: Graves of Soldiers of the Revolution; Army Register, Navy Register, Air Force Register and much more. These annual service registers give genealogical information about military personnel. The format and specific information has varied over the years, but generally the entries include the person's name, rank, birth date/place; death date/place and details of their military service.

New content added daily. You can search for free, but you need to subscribe to view the details. $9.95/30 day trial. $19.95/month, $69.95/year.

7. U.S.GenWeb.org FREE

www.usgenweb.org

This free, sprawling, all-volunteer site is packed with how-to tips, queries and records such as censuses, tombstones, family group sheets, cemetery surveys and marriage indexes for every U.S. state and virtually every county. Organization is by county and state, so they provide links to all the state genealogy websites (which includes historical information on the county and geographical boundaries) which, in turn, provide gateways to the counties. They often provide abstracts of actual records on file (such as cemetery, marriage, birth, death, census, tax, probate, or military records). They also sponsor important special projects at the national level and links to all those pages, as well.

8. U.S. National Archives

www.archives.gov FREE

The National Archives and Records Administration is the nation's record keeper. It's a treasure trove of records and documents to trace your family roots. This site increasingly lets you tap its treasures from home, e.g. see Footnote. Access to Archival Databases encompasses more than 85 million historical records, including extracts from WWII Army enlistment papers and 19th-century arrivals of German, Italian, Irish and Russian immigrants. For historical photos and maps and American Indian records, try the *Archival Research Catalog.* The records that are most commonly used by genealogists include:. The actual census, military, immigration (Ship Passenger Lists), naturalization, and land records are not online, but there are finding aids, such as microfilm indexes, and information on how to conduct research in the different types of records.

9. Godfrey $ Memorial Library

www.godfrey.org

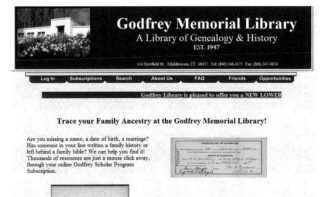

The Godfrey Memorial Library has long been a valuable resource for genealogists. This private library houses over 200,000 books and periodicals in its collection including: state and local histories, international resources, family histories, biographies, records by religious organizations, church records, funeral records, cemetery records, military records, maps, and collection of hand-written material, much of which is not available elsewhere. In addition, the Godfrey Library produces the *American Genealogical-Biographical Index,* which is the equivalent of more than 200 printed volumes. This index contains millions of records of people whose names have appeared in printed genealogical records and family histories. It's an especially good resource for historic newspapers, including the London Times, 19th century U.S. newspapers, and early American newspapers. $45/year (without the newspaper databases)

10. FamilyTree Connection.com $

www.familytreeconnection.com

A growing collection of unique data indexed from a variety of secondary sources such as high school and college yearbooks, Masonic rosters, club and society member lists, insurance claims data, church directories, orphanage and soldiers' home residents, prisoner logs and much, much more. This data is very useful for connecting with your ancestors, and isn't available elsewhere. The records are compiled from rare documents, pamphlets and unique out-of-print books that contain genealogical tidbits about people from around the world. The database resides at Genealogy Today and is integrated into the search engine on that site. $29.95/year.

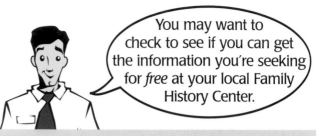

You may want to check to see if you can get the information you're seeking for *free* at your local Family History Center.

Family History Centers offer HeritageQuest Online, Godfrey Memorial Library, WorldVitalRecords.com, Footnote.com, MyTrees.com, and Ancestry.com for free.

More 'Best of the Internet'

A lot of people ask the question *"which family history web sites are the best?"* And the best answer is *"The ones that have the records you need to trace your ancestors."* Plus, since you'll probably also want to access 'how to' sites for guidance and tips, they are also the best for you.

First, you may want to see if someone has already found info on your ancestors by searching online family trees and published family histories. Then the US census, immigration, and military records are always helpful. For example, WWI draft cards are useful, since virtually every man born from 1872 to 1900 (and living in the US in 1917 and 1918) registered. You can discover the place your ancestors called home by conducting a "place search" in the Family History Library, by searching international web sites, and by utilizing maps. And historical newspapers and city directories can open windows to the past about the lives of your ancestors, and fill gaps between censuses.

National Archive Databases - FREE

http://aad.archives.gov/aad

Access to hundreds of databases; browse by subject or category which includes: Military, Passenger Lists, Photographs, Places, Wars, Time Spans, etc.

NewEnglandAncestors.org -
www.newenglandancestors.org

The New England Historical Genealogical Society research library provides access to some of the most important and valuable genealogical resources available anywhere in the world that are not available anywhere else. It is home to more than 2,400 searchable databases containing over 110 million names, over 12 million original documents, artifacts, records, manuscripts, books, family papers, bibles, and photographs dating back more than four centuries. And every week, they add at least one new database on-line. Although their name says New England, they also offer an extensive collection of resources for New York, Canada and Europe as well. $75.00/year

Tribal Pages.com - www.tribalpages.com

This innovative collaboration site hosts more than 175,000 pedigree files, a database of more than 80 million names and 2 million photos. Plus, you can store your own family tree data here and generate charts and reports right from the site.

HeritageQuest Online.com - (FREE)
www.heritagequestonline.com

You can't subscribe to this website yourself, but your local library can. If your library subscribes, you can use your library card at home to access the complete U.S. Census (1790-1930), over 24,000 family and local histories, Revolutionary War Pension and Bounty-Land Applications, Freedman's Bank records index (1865-1874), the PERSI index to 2.1 million genealogy articles, and part of the U.S. Serial Set of Memorials, Petitions and Private Relief Actions of Congress.

New England Early Connections - (\$)
www.genealogyne.com

A 73,000+ name database containing connected names for those searching for ancestors from the early New England period of 1600-1700+/-. No individual name is included unless it has at least one connection to another, through father, mother, son, daughter, spouse, sister, brother with accompanying basic data when available: birth, death, marriage dates, towns of residence, citations documenting sources. An annual subscription is required for full access. $34.95/year.

FamilyHistory Online.net – (FREE) (\$)
www.familyhistoryonline.net

The Federation of Family History Societies publishes records compiled by over 210 family history societies – quality data from experienced researchers with local knowledge providing more accurate details. You can now search over 67 million records including parish registers, memorial inscriptions, censuses, poor law documents and others. Search the name index for free, and pay a small fee to view the details if desired.

American Memory Library - (FREE)
www.memory.loc.gov

The Library of Congress' friendly web site to a wealth of digitized historical documents and photos – more than 9 million items in all, organized into more than 100 thematic collections. The library's regular catalog is also an excellent place to look up pretty much any book in existence.

Canadian Genealogy Centre - FREE
www.collectionscanada.gc.ca/genealogy

Library and Archives Canada collects and preserves Canada's documentary heritage including publications, archival records, sound and audio-visual materials, photographs, artworks, and electronic documents such as websites. It offers genealogical content, services, advice, research tools and searchable databases for vital, census, immigration and naturalization, military, land and people records, all in both official languages.

UK NationalArchives - FREE
www.nationalarchives.gov.uk

The official archive for England, Wales and the central UK government, containing 1,000 years of history. Provides searchable databases for vital, census, passenger lists, military, citizenship and naturalization, wills records, and more.

WorldCat - www.oclc.org > FREE
US English Site > *WorldCat*

Tap into the treasures of more than 69,000 libraries worldwide with this one-click search of more than 1.3 billion holdings in 112 countries.

FindMyPast.com - www.findmypast.com

A family history website based in London containing over 550 million family history records, with more being added all the time. The only website that has the complete collection of England and Wales census records 1841-1911. You will find links to many resources as well as useful tips and advice on researching your family tree. It helps you organize and illustrate your family tree, adding pictures, stories, dates and events. You can also communicate with other members who are researching their family trees. Searching and building an online family tree with the innovative *Family Tree Explorer* software is free. However, to view records you will need to purchase credits, either by buying pay-per-view units or one of three subscription options. 14 day free trial. £94.90/6 months (about $144).

Genealogy.com Library -
www.genealogy.com/cgibin/
odl_browse.cgi?SUBDB=GLC

One of the largest online genealogy collections in the world with over 100 million records spanning five centuries. Requires subscription. $9.99/ month $49.99/year

WorldGenWeb.org - www.worldgenweb.org FREE

This is the global counterpart of US GenWeb dedicated to providing family history and historical

records and resources for world-wide access. Most countries have their own sites and many, especially for European ancestries, are packed with advice for beginners.

SearchSystems.net -
www.searchsystems.net

A directory of public records and a resource for background checks and criminal records on the Internet. A good resource of business information, corporate filings, property records, deeds, mortgages, criminal and civil court filings, inmates, offenders, births, deaths, marriages, unclaimed property, professional licenses, and much more. Offers a database of over 300 million state, national, and international criminal records, and a database of over 100 million bankruptcies, judgments, and tax liens. Easy access to billions of records. $9.95/month $29.95/year

Genealogy Today.com - *FREE*
www.genealogytoday.com

They track new and exciting resources for family historians, and host some features and unique databases themselves. It utilizes *Genealogist's Index to the World Wide Web* which is a combined index for family history research that contains over 10 million names across 5,000 sites. You'll find hundreds of articles on a variety of family history topics, a community of amateur and professional genealogists, plus a store filled with unique items.

FamilyRelatives.com -
www.familyrelatives.com

This UK/Ireland site has Irish records, British military records, British parish records, Pigot's trade directories and more − organized by country and record type. Pay-as-you-go credits / about $9 for 90 units, or about $50 per year.

Many web sites are directories of where you can go to try and locate more information. They do not contain actual records, but direct you where to find them.

Best Web Directories/Portals

AcademicGenealogy.com - *FREE*
www.academic-genealogy.com

A mega portal of key worldwide educational genealogical databases and resources. Professional, worldwide humanities and social sciences mega portal, connected directly to numerously related sub-sets, with billions of primary or secondary database family history and genealogy records.

Cyndi's List.com - www.cyndislist.com *FREE*

Perhaps the best known of the comprehensive web directories that serve as a list or catalog to the entire Internet to help you find other family history web sites. It contains a categorized and cross-referenced index of over 265,000 genealogical online resources; a list of links listed in over 180 different categories that point you to genealogical research sites. It receives more than 3 million visits each month.

Linkpendium.com - www.linkpendium.com *FREE*

A huge directory of over 7 million genealogy web links categorized by U.S. localities and worldwide surnames.

5 Best of the Internet

GenealogyToolbox.com - FREE
www.genealogytoolbox.com

A searchable, categorized (by people, places, and topics) collection of tools to help you research your genealogy or family history. Provides links to hundreds of thousands of family history Web sites, as well as linking to content and digitized images of original documents.

GenealogySleuth -
www.progenealogists.com/genealogysleuthb.htm

A list of web sites FREE that professional genealogists use daily when conducting U.S. genealogy research. You can also link to the International Genealogy Sleuth.

AccessGenealogy - www.accessgenealogy.com

A free search center that offers links for searching many FREE different types of records, such as census reports, newspapers, periodicals, emigration and immigration forms, vital records, voting records, military records, library archives, cemeteries, churches, and courts; plus Native American and African American essentials. It includes tons of links to other web sites.

GenealogyHomePage.com - FREE
www.genhomepage.com

Links to genealogy tutorials, resources, newsgroups, online resources, maps and software.

RootsSearch.net - www.rootssearch.net FREE

A genealogy portal where you can post queries, download software, find websites by surname and more.

AncestorHunt.com - www.ancestorhunt.com FREE

Convenient genealogy search engines for Ellis Island, Census online, RootsWeb, Social Security Death Index, LDS Church records, Ancestry.com, United Kingdom Records, CensusDiggins, Genealogy.com and more.

OliveTreeGenealogy.com - FREE
www.olivetreegenealogy.com

Here you will find links to obscure genealogy databases, genealogy resources you can use offline to find ancestors, nuggets of information about a variety of subjects, explanations of genealogical terms, genealogy repositories, address and phone numbers of places and organizations you will need in your family tree search, and much more.

FamilyHistory101.com - FREE
http://familyhistory101.com

This site is an introduction to the wide and rich variety of materials that you can use to build a bridge for your personal journey back in time. Contains numerous web links to database records.

Best International Web Sites

Searchable online databases or informative tools

Most everyone wants to find out where their ancestors came from, and search for their roots in the *'old country'*. More than 60% of Americans today claim ancestry from the 23 largest European heritage groups. The most common European ancestries are: German (50.8 million), Irish (36.5 million), English (28.2 million), Italian (17.8 million), Polish (10 million), French (9.6 million), Scottish (6 million), Scotch-Irish (5.3 million), Dutch (5.1 million), Norwegian (4.7 million), Swedish (4.3 million), and Russian (3.2 million). Other common ethnic groups include: African (2.7 million), West Indian (2.5 million), and French Canadian (2.2 million). You might think that unfamiliar records and language barriers could thwart your search for your family roots, but they don't have to. Here are the best tools and online resources to help you trace your ancestors in North America, British Isles, Europe, and beyond.

Many web sites are directories or portals containing numerous links to international web sites. See the *Best Web Directories/Portals* section on page 173 for a list of directories to guide you to additional sites.

Australian Family History Compendium -

www.cohsoft.com.au/afhc **FREE**

A free Internet resource for researching your Australian family tree; contains information on a wide variety of categories related to genealogy.

Australia FamilySearch -

https://wiki.familysearch.org/en/Australia **FREE**

A community website to help you learn how to find your Australian ancestors with extensive articles, information and links to key web sites.

Canadian Genealogy Centre -

www.genealogy.gc.ca **FREE**

This Web site facilitates the discovery of your Canadian heritage roots and family histories. Collections include published histories of Canadian families and communities, transcriptions and indexes of parish registers, census, cemetery, immigration, military and land records, newspapers and directories, journals of Canadian genealogical and historical societies, genealogical reference tools, government publications including genealogical data, and much more.

Canada - Library and Archives - **FREE**

www.collectionscanada.gc.ca/

Canada's national collection of books, historical documents, government records, photos, films, maps, music...and more. This heritage includes publications, archival records, sound and audio-visual materials, photographs, artworks, and electronic documents such as websites.

Canada FamilySearch - **FREE**

https://wiki.family-search.org/en/Canada

A community website to help you learn how to find your Canadian ancestors with extensive articles, information and links to key web sites.

5 Best of the Internet

> One of the most important things to discovering your European heritage – besides your ancestors' names – is the precise place your family came from. You need more than just a country; you need the specific locale, district or village that they came from.

Tips to Help Search the 'Old Country'

Language Barrier

You can find free help deciphering the foreign words in your family's old documents and microfilmed records in the genealogical word lists online at www.FamilySearch.org > *Search > Research Helps > Sorted by Document Type*. Other free translation tools can be found online at www.Babelfish.altavista.com and www.FreeTranslation.com. **FREE**

Records in Your Back Yard

Start by tapping into the Family History Libraries' millions of microfilm rolls by searching its online catalog for free at www.FamilySearch.org > *Search > Family History Library Catalog > Place Search*. Enter as much information as you know about your ancestral village.

How About a Map

Good maps and a gazetteer are essentials. Check these free map sources out:

Perry-Castaiieda Library Map Collection - **FREE**
www.lib.utexas.edu/maps

Global Gazetteer - www.fallingrain.com **FREE**

Research Outlines

FamilySearch also has *Research Outlines* on quite a few countries and ethnicity, from Australia to Wales. Research outlines describe the records and strategies that can be used to pursue family history research in a specific geographic location or particular type of record.

Huge Benefits of Ancient Records

Much of the record-keeping in Europe was done by the church. Vital records and some types of censuses were the domain of the church for centuries. Fortunately for us, the Family History Library has photographed and microfilmed tons of these church records from one end of Europe to the other for over a century. You access these records using the library catalog at the same home page at FamilySearch as provided above.

And FamilySearch is currently in the process of digitizing and indexing the billions of records on microfilm and making them available for free on their web site as they become available. You can access the newly digitized and indexed records at **FREE** www.familysearch.org > *Search Records > Record Search pilot*. And you can volunteer to help index these billions of records and make them available to everyone for free. Go to http://indexing.familysearch.org for more information. Join thousands of others, and index records from home at your leisure.

Canada Places -
www.johncardinal.com/ca **FREE**

This site includes place information and mapping resources for 28,898 places in Canada. You can review a list of place names by province or territory. From there, you can navigate to a link to locate a place using Google Maps, Live Local, MapQuest, or Yahoo! Maps.

Canada - GenWeb.org - **FREE**
www.canadagenweb.org

This is the gateway to free Canadian genealogy organized into regional sites for each of the provinces and territories. From these sites you can get closer to your area of research. Contains resources and read/post queries

Canada - ProGenealogists - *FREE*

www.progenealogists.com/canada

This web site's aim is to educate and inform about the crucial resources that exist in Canada. They have province-specific pages that outline resources specific to those locations. You may wish to peruse their *Canadian Sleuth* page that contains links to hundreds of resources.

Canada - Cyndi'sList - *FREE*

www.cyndislist.com/canada.htm

Provides links to sites for provinces and territories; military, census, cemeteries, land, obituaries, and vital records, general resource sites, government and cities, history and culture, libraries, archives and museums; mailing lists and newsgroups; maps, gazetteers and geographical information; newspapers; and queries, message boards and surname lists.

Canada - Geographical Names - *FREE*

http://geonames.nrcan.gc.ca/index_e.php

Toponyms, or geographical names, are used by us all every day to describe our surroundings and to tell others where we have been or where we plan to go. When we use maps we expect the names to help us identify features of the landscape, and perhaps even to throw light on the local history of an area. This site is the national data base to provide official names of mapping and charting, gazetteer production, and World Wide Web reference, and other geo-referenced digital systems.

Canada - Quebec Family History Society - *FREE*

www.qfhs.ca

A Canadian non-profit organization to foster the study of genealogy among the English speaking peoples of Quebec.

Canadian-French Article - *FREE*

www.ancestry.com/learn/library/article.aspx?article=6830 —*or you can Google "david ouimette tracing french canadian article".*

An excellent article titled *Tracing Your French-Canadian Ancestry* by David Ouimette, a genealogy researcher, writer, and lecturer with over twenty years experience in French-Canadian research. He currently is the manager for collections at FamilySearch.org.

Denmark FamilySearch - *FREE*

https://wiki.familysearch.org/en/Denmark

A community website to help you learn how to find your Danish ancestors with extensive articles, information and links to key web sites.

Danish Demographic Database - *FREE*

www.ddd.dda.dk/ddd_en.htm

Created by the Danish State Archives, it is designed to be an every name index for searching the Danish censuses. It is not linked to the original census images. Although the census database does not include all parishes for every year of national census yet, the 1801, 1834, 1840,and 1845 are complete for the entire kingdom. The next year to be complete for the entire kingdom is the 1880 census.

Danish Data Archive - *FREE*

http://samfund.dda.dk/default-en.asp

The DDA is the national social science data archive used by researchers wanting access to data materials created by Danish researchers or about Denmark.

Danish Emigration Archives - *FREE*

www.emiarch.dk

The archive has an extensive database where relevant emigration information can be searched. Holds a large collection of private letters, manuscripts, diaries, biographies, newspaper clippings, photographs, portraits, etc.

Denmark - Distant Cousin.com - *FREE*

www.distantcousin.com/Links/Ethnic/Danish.html

A directory of links to Danish genealogy.

Denmark - Cyndi'sList - *FREE*

www.cyndislist.com/denmark.htm

Provides links to sites for General Resources, Government & Cities, History & Culture, How To, Language & Names, Libraries, Archives & Museums, Locality Specific, Mailing Lists, Newsgroups & Chat, Maps, Gazetteers & Geographical Information, Military, Newspapers, People & Families, Volunteers & Other Research Services, Publications, Software & Supplies, Queries, Message Boards & Surname Lists, Records (Census, Cemeteries, Land, Obituaries, Personal, Taxes and

Vital), and Religion and Churches.

Danish-American Genealogical Society -

www.danishgenealogy.org *FREE*

Danish immigration, genealogy books, photography, history, etc; a branch of the Minnesota Genealogical Society.

Dutch FamilySearch - *FREE*

https://wiki.familysearch.org/en/The_Netherlands

A community website to help you learn how to find your Dutch ancestors with extensive articles, information and links to key web sites.

Dutch Genealogy Links - *FREE*

www.euronet.nl/users/mnykerk/genealog.htm

Links to the best of what is available in the Netherlands.

DutchGenWeb - *FREE*

wwww.rootsweb.ancestry.com/~nldwgw

Some of the best resources for research in The Netherlands.

Dutch (Netherlands) Genealogy - *FREE*

www.dutchgenealogy.nl

This site helps people of Dutch descent research their Dutch ancestors. Many articles explain the research opportunities, give background information about Dutch history in general and emigration in particular. Also, some primary sources you can use for your research are provided.

DutchGenealogy.com - $

www.dutchgenealogy.com

CD products for sell which provide useful information and resources for your family history search in the Netherlands; includes names and data from court records, notary archives, church records, etc. Over one million names to help connect you with information and help. $59.95

England/Wales/Scotland - FamilyRelatives.com - $

www.familyrelatives.com

An award-winning UK-based site that offers access to over 600 million records (400 million fully indexed), and growing. They recently added more than 250,000 new Victorian Scottish Trade Directory records online. It's unique in a number of ways: it has more than 150 million indexed records from the General Register Office (GRO) Civil Registrations Indexes for Births, Marriages and Deaths for England and Wales (1866-1920 and 1984-2005) which is more than any other existing website. There are 150 million records which are also searchable on surname and forename (1837-1865 and 1921-1983). Military and Parish records are also fully indexed. You can connect with fellow researchers and upload your own data. £30/year (about $49), Pay Per View £6/60 units (about $9).

England - FindMyPast - $

www.findmypast.co.uk

The addition of more than 22.4 million pre-1837 baptism, marriage and burial parish records makes this one of the most wide-ranging collections of UK data— more than 500 million records. Databases include censuses (1841, 1851, 1861, 1871, 1881, 1891, 1901), 38 military datasets, migration and passport records, and government birth, marriage and

---

> FamilySearch has a variety of free vital records databases for Scandinavia and Mexico.

death indexes (1837 to 2006). It now holds most of the on-line records compiled by Family History Societies that were available from FamilyHistoryOnline.net. Some records can be searched for free, but you'll need to pay for full access. Pay-as-you-go £6.95/60 credits (about $11), £54.95/6 months (about $86)

England/Ireland/Scotland - Origins.net - $

www.origins.net

Genealogy search for English, Irish, and Scots origins. A rich source of British genealogy online, featuring marriages, censuses, wills, and many more record collections, most not available anywhere else in digital form. £7.50/ 72 hours (about $12), £10.50/ month (about $16).

England FamilySearch -

https://wiki.familysearch.org/en/England **FREE**

A community website to help you learn how to find your English ancestors with extensive articles, information and links to key web sites.

England - UK and Ireland -

www.genuki.org.uk **FREE**

Free resources for the UK (England, Scotland, Wales, Channel Islands and the Isle of Man) and Ireland. It serves as a "virtual reference library" of genealogical information provided by volunteers in cooperation with the Federation of Family History Societies. In the main, the information relates to primary historical material, rather than material resulting from genealogists' ongoing research, such as GEDCOM files.

England/Wales Census -

www.nationalarchives.gov.uk/

Provides links to census records for England and Wales from 1841 to 1911, military records, and much more. The work of putting these records online was done by their commercial partners. It is free to search their websites, but there may be a charge to view and download documents.

England/Wales - Free BMD - *FREE*

www.freebmd.org.uk

An ongoing project by dedicated volunteers to transcribe the Civil Registration index of births, marriages and deaths for England and Wales from 1837 to date, and to provide free Internet access to the transcribed records. In recent times, it has also expanded into census and Parish Register transcriptions. As of February 2010, they have transcribed over 180 million records, which represents the overwhelming majority of Births, Marriages and Deaths registered from 1837 to 1931. Contains over 230 million total records.

British Isles Family History Society - $

www.rootsweb.ancestry.com/~bifhsusa

If your ancestors came from the British Isles this US society offers to help you in your quest; featuring a "guide to research". $35/year membership.

UK Ancestry - www.ancestry.co.uk

This site maintains an extensive archive of 820 million searchable records from England, Ireland, Scotland and Wales, including England, Wales and Scotland Censuses, exclusive online access to UK birth, marriage and death records, plus a comprehensive selection of WW1 military, immigration and parish records.

European Family History -

http://feefhs.org

The Federation of East European Family History Societies is a very large collection of materials for people with ancestry in Eastern Europe. Contains links to: Albania, Armenia, Austria, Banat, Belarus, Bosnia, Bukovina, Carpatho-Rusyn, Croatia, Czech Republic, Denmark, Estonia, Finland, Galicia, Germans/Russia, Germany, Hungary, Jewish, Latvia, Lithuania, Poland, Romania, Russia, Slovakia, Slovenia, and Ukraine, among others.

European History - *FREE*

http://eudocs.lib.byu.edu/index.php/Main_Page

These free links from BYU library connect to European primary historical documents—ancient, medieval, renaissance, and modern times—that shed light on *key historical happenings* within the respective countries and within the broadest sense of political, economic, social and cultural history.

EuroGenWeb - *FREE*

wwww.rootsweb.ancestry.com/~ceneurgw

Links to European countries websites.

French Family History: About.com -

http://genealogy.about.com/od/france/French_Genealogy_Family_History.htm

Search for your French and French-Canadian ancestors in this excellent collection (with links) of family history databases and resources for France. Includes tutorials for researching French ancestors, suggestions for writing to France and translating French records, and information on civil records, parish registers and other French genealogical records.

France FamilySearch - FREE

https://wiki.familysearch.org/en/France

A community website to help you learn how to find your French ancestors with extensive articles, information and links to key web sites.

France GenWeb - FREE

www.francegenweb.org

Excellent guide to French family history research includes sections for each department and region. Some information available in English

France - Geneactes.org - FREE

www.geneactes.org/index-en.html

Web databases of French civil records, including marriage records that are searchable by keyword, name or place.

French-Canadian Research - FREE

www.afgs.org

The American-French Genealogical Society is an organization for French-Canadian research.

Germany FamilySearch -

FREE

https://wiki.familysearch.org/en/Germany

A community website to help you learn how to find your German ancestors with extensive articles, information and links to key web sites.

Germany - Genealogy.net - FREE

www.genealogienetz.de/genealogy.htm

The German genealogy Internet portal, including: links to local German genealogical societies, a GEDCOM based database (German language only), a Place gazetter (Austria, Swiss and Germany), newspapers, books, passenger lists, etc.

German Research Team - FREE

www.scgsgenealogy.com/Germansig.htm

The German Research Team at SCGS can help you navigate the unique challenges of researching your German ancestors. The specialized German Collection of the Southern California Genealogical Society and Family Research Library includes over 3,000 books, CDs, maps, manuscripts, and databases.

German Family History - FREE

http://feefhs.org > Germany

The Federation of East European Family History Societies is a very large collection of materials for people with ancestry in Eastern Europe, including Austria, Germans/Russia, Germany, and Hungary, among others.

German Genealogy Eastern Europe - FREE

www.sggee.org

Focuses on the genealogy of Germans from Russian Poland and Volhynia and related regions.

German Genealogy - FREE

www.daddezio.com/germgen.html

Provides original articles and valuable links to other inform-ation on the Internet; information on Germany, Italy and Greece.

German Roots.com - FREE

www.germanroots.com

Resources and guides for German genealogy.

Germany GenWeb -

www.rootsweb.ancestry.com/~wggerman FREE

Provides databases, resources, maps, ship lists, etc. as part of World GenWeb.

German Genealogical Society - FREE

www.palam.org

An American German genealogy society dedicated to the study of ancestors from all German speaking lands. Membership required $35/year.

Germanic Ancestors Book -

www.amazon.com/gp/product/1558705201 $

A Genealogist's Guide to Discovering Your Germanic Ancestors by Chris Anderson and Ernest Thode (Betterway Books). This hands-on guide addresses virtually every aspect of tracing Germanic lineage. Written for beginners, it covers the basics of genealogy, clearly explaining how to plan, organize and begin searching. $38. (used)

Italian FamilySearch - FREE

https://wiki.familysearch.org/en/Italy

Getting started with Italian research. Learn how to find, use, and analyze Italian records of genealogical value. Learn what Italian records are available through FamilySearch, and a directory of Italy websites with links.

Italian Emigration -

https://wiki.familysearch.org/en/ Italy_Emigration_and_Immigration

Article about Italian emigration and immigration. Records were created when individuals emigrated from or immigrated into Italy. Separate records document an ancestor's arrival in his destination country.

Italy GenWeb -

www.italywgw.org

A self-help resource to assist you in finding your Italian ancestors in your genealogical research of Italy.

Italian Heritage -

www.theitalianheritage.it/?&lang=english

Provides useful information on emigrants from Italy.

Best Irish Web Sites

Irish Web Directories/Portals

Ireland FamilySearch - *FREE*
https://wiki.familysearch.org/en/Ireland

A community website to help you learn how to find your Irish ancestors with extensive articles, information and links to key web sites.

GENUIKI.org (UK and Ireland Genealogy) -
www.genuki.org.uk/big/irl *FREE*

IrelandGenWeb.com - *FREE*
www.irelandgenweb.com

Irish Family History Foundation - *FREE* $
www.ifhf.brsgenealogy.com
View records £5.00/record (about $7)

FamilySearch.org - *FREE*
www.familysearch.org

Irish Genealogy - *FREE*
www.irishgenealogy.ie

Cyndi's List.com - *FREE*
www.cyndislist.com/ireland.htm

Ancestry.com - $
www.ancestry.com

Irish Libraries, Archives and Records Offices

Contains parish records, censuses, wills, military records, and detailed maps from the 1800s.

National Archives of Ireland - *FREE*
www.nationalarchives.ie

National Library of Ireland - *FREE*
www.nli.ie

National Archives (UK) - *FREE*
www.nationalarchives.gov.uk

Public Records Office of Northern Ireland -
www.proni.gov.uk *FREE*

General Register Office for Northern Ireland -
www.groni.gov.uk *FREE*

General Register Office - *FREE*
www.groireland.ie

Historical Mapping Archive - *FREE*
www.irishhistoricmaps.ie/historic

Irish Family History - More Great Web Sites

Eneclann - www.eneclann.ie *FREE*
A Dublin college campus company providing professional services in historical, heritage, archive and records management.

Irish Ancestors - $
www.ireland.com/ancestor

Contains civil registration, parish, and census records, maps, etc. Pay-per-view £50/30 units (about $67)

Irish Origins - www.irishorigins.com $
Contains Griffith's Primary Valuation of Ireland records and maps (1847-1864), the most important Irish genealogy research source prior to the 20th century, Irish Wills Index (1484-1858), 1851 Dublin City Census, Irish Royal Garrison Artillery Records, rare and vintage photos, maps and books. £7.50/3 days (about $11)

Irish Roots Cafe -
www.irishroots.com/podcast.php $

Free Podcasts, but must be a member to access the newsletter, journal of Irish families, etc. $12.50/3 months.

Ulster Historical Foundation - $
www.ancestryireland.com

Online databases of over 2 million records, genealogy and history books, and personal ancestral research. Pay-per-view £2/2 credits

IreAtlas Townland - *FREE*
www.seanruad.com

By entering a Townland and a County, it will return all lines that contain the requested Townland and County.

Continued on next page

Irish Family History Foundation - $

www.irish-roots.ie

A network of county genealogical research centers on the island of Ireland. These centers have computerized millions of records, including church records (mostly 1864-1900 to date), census returns (1901 and 1911) and gravestone inscriptions. Searching is free; to view each record will cost you about $6.50.

Irish Townland Maps - $

www.pasthomes.com

Obtain a historical map of any Irish townland or property; surveyed between 1829 and 1843. Subscription to browse $25/year, fee to download a map

Italian Genealogy Homepage - FREE

www.italgen.com

Information that explains the research process and conditions in Italy. Also includes resources to locate other researchers who may be researching your places or surnames of interest.

Italia Mia - FREE

www.italiamia.com/gene.html

Selected Italian genealogical links. Name search. A guide on how to search for your Italian ancestors.

Italian Genealogy - www.daddezio.com FREE

Resource for Italian genealogical research provides articles, research services, passenger lists and

information on archives in Italy.

ItalyLink.com - FREE

www.italylink.com/genealogy.html

A list of Italian genealogy related links. Check out the forum, person locator.

Italy World Club - FREE

www.italyworldclub.com/genealogy

Resources and professional services for genealogical research in Italy. Includes surname lists and place-names.

Italian Genealogy - FREE

http://members.tripod.com/pippee/alizadecredico.html

How to locate relatives in Italy and Liza's list of links for Italian genealogy.

Italian Genealogy Web Pages - FREE

www.deborahmillemaci.com

A list of links to Italian-related genealogy.

Italian Emigrants to US -

http://213.212.128.168/radici/ie/defaultie_e.htm FREE

Contains databases of Italian immigrants to Argentina, Brazil and the United States 1858-1920; requires free registration.

Italian Ancestry.com - FREE

www.ItalianAncestry.com

A good portal or jumpsite for all things Italian.

Italian Genealogical Society of America - $

www.italianroots.org

A non-profit educational organization to promote Italian genealogy. Membership $15/year

Italy - American Italian Heritage Assoc. - $

www.aiha-albany.org

Committed to Italian heritage, history and culture. Membership $22/year

Norway FamilySearch - FREE

https://wiki.familysearch.org/en/Norway

A community website to help you learn how to find your Norwegian ancestors with extensive articles, information and links to key web sites.

Norway DigitalArkivet - FREE

www.digitalarkivet.uib.no

The National Archives of Norway offers 1801, 1865, 1875 and 1900 Norwegian censuses, images, transcribed texts, 1.85 million pages of parish registers, and real-estate registers. The parish images are indexed at page level, meaning that you can easily find the first page of a register, as well as the start of a list of records, or the start of each year in this list allowing you to browse through the pages in the register or through a list of records. You cannot search for single records and names.

Norway Ancestors - FREE

www.rootsweb.ancestry.com/~wgnorway

Through this web site you will find links to Norwegian bygdeboker, census, emigration, farm and parish listings, history, lookup volunteers, message (query) boards, and a variety of other useful links.

Norwegian Emigration Center - $

www.utvandrersenteret.no

Assists people with Norwegian ancestry in tracing their roots. $100/3 hours

Norwegian-American Genealogical Center - FREE

www.nagcnl.org/links.php

Links to Norwegian resources.

Poland FamilySearch - FREE

https://wiki.familysearch.org/en/Portal:Poland

A community website to help you learn how to find your Polish ancestors with extensive articles, information and links to key web sites.

Polish Genealogy - www.polishroots.com FREE

Covers all areas that were historically part of the Polish Commonwealth.

Poland GenWeb - FREE

www.rootsweb.ancestry.com/~polwgw/polandgen.html

A self-help resource to assist you in finding your Polish ancestors.

Polish Genealogical Society of America - $

www.pgsa.org

Produces a quarterly publication which provides helpful information $25/year.

Romania FamilySearch - FREE

https://wiki.familysearch.org/en/Portal:Romania

A community website to help you learn how to find your Romanian ancestors with extensive articles, information and links to key web sites.

Romania GenWeb -

wwww.rootsweb.ancestry.com/~romwgw FREE

A self-help resource to assist you in finding your Romanian ancestors through maps, surnames, queries, etc.

Romanian Resources - FREE

www.feefhs.org/links/romania.html

Links to web site resources.

Russia FamilySearch - FREE

https://wiki.familysearch.org/en/Portal:Russia

A community website to help you learn how to find your Russian ancestors with extensive articles, information and links to key web sites.

Russia Archives: ArcheoBiblioBase - FREE

www.iisg.nl/abb

The Russian Federal Archives and major federal agencies, universities and libraries.

RussianArchives Online.com - FREE

www.russianarchives.com

Collections of Russian archival collections of photographs and films, audio, clips and transcripts from the 15

republics of the former Soviet Union, including Russia, Ukraine, Georgia and many more.

Scotland FamilySearch - FREE

https://wiki.familysearch.org/en/Scotland

A community website to help you learn how to find your Scottish ancestors with extensive articles, information and links to key web sites.

Scotlands People - FREE

www.scotlandspeople.gov.uk

The official online source of parish register, civil registration, census and wills & testaments records for Scotland. Containing over 50 million records providing a fully searchable index of Scottish births (1553-2006), marriages (1553-2006) and deaths (1855-2006). In addition, indexed census data (1841-1901) as well as Scottish Wills & Testaments (1513-1901) and Coats of Arms records (1672-1907). To respect privacy of living people, internet access has been limited to birth records over 100 years old, marriage records over 75 years, and death records over 50 years. You may view, save and print images of many of the original documents, and order extracts of any register entries by mail.

Scottish Archive Network - FREE

www.scan.org.uk

History of Scotland in more than 20,000 collections of historical records held by 52 Scottish archives.

ScottishDocuments.com - FREE

www.scottishdocuments.com

Scottish historical records, including wills and testaments (from 1500 to 1901), kirk sessions, presbyteries, synods and the General Assembly of the Church of Scotland.

Scotland GenWeb - FREE

www.scotlandgenweb.org

A self-help resource to assist you in finding your Scottish ancestors.

Scottish Census Records - FREE

www.ukbmd.org.uk/index.php?form_action=census

Links to Births, Marriages, Deaths Indexes and Census Transcriptions.

Sweden - Demographic Data Base - FREE

www.ddb.umu.se/ddb-english/?languageId=1

The statistical study of the population, its size, distribution and change.

Sweden FamilySearch - FREE

https://wiki.familysearch.org/en/Portal:Sweden

A community website to help you learn how to find your Swedish ancestors.

Swedish National Archives - FREE $

www.riksarkivet.se > *English*

All public records of the agencies of the central government, including regional archives, census records, and military records. There are some databases and images that require a subscription. 50 krona/3 hours (about $7).

Swedish Church Records - $

www.genline.com

This site offers more than 17 million Swedish Church Records from

The Scottish Church Records database is available in Family History Centers around the world and online.

Scotland National Archives - FREE

www.nas.gov.uk/recordkeeping/churchrecords.asp

The *Scottish Church Records* database is an index of approximately 10,000,000 names extracted from records of the Church of Scotland. Most records come from the late 1500s to 1854. Birth, christening, and marriage information is included and can be searched by looking for an individual, a marriage record, or parents of an individual. They also hold some records of other Protestant denominations (Methodist, Congregational/United Reformed and Scottish Episcopal churches, the Unitarian Church and the Quakers). Records of the Roman Catholic Church in Scotland are held by the Scottish Catholic Archive and the Roman Catholic Archdiocese of Glasgow Archive.

1500-1860. They offer photographic quality images scanned from microfilm of the original church records. The archive records consist of birth/baptismal, confirmation, marriage, death/burial, church ledgers and household examination rolls. About $21 for 20 days, $85/quarter.

Swedish Emigration - FREE

www.americanwest.com/swedemigr/pages/emigra.htm

An article about mass emigration from Sweden and a list of links for emigration from other countries.

Swedish Ancestry Research Assoc. - $

http://sarassociation.tripod.com

A place to meet and share ideas with others who have similar interests. Membership $15/year.

Swedish Immigration Research Center - FREE

www.augustana.edu/x13856.xml

The Swenson Center at Augustana College in Illinois is a national archives and research institute providing resources for the study of Swedish immigration to North America.

Wales Cyndi's List - FREE

www.cyndislist.com/wales.htm

A range of information and links.

Wales FamilySearch - FREE

https://wiki.familysearch.org/en/Wales

Extensive information and links to doing Welsh genealogy.

Welsh Genealogy - http://ellyn.francis.tripod.com

Family histories, records, pictures, maps and interesting stories. Research assistance available and all questions answered.

Wales GENUKI - FREE

www.genuki.org.uk/big/wal

Directory provides links to individual county family history resources, including surname lists, official archives, maps, and history profiles.

Wales Genealogical Research - FREE

www.cefnpennar.com

Searchable genealogical database for South Wales.

Wales History BBC - FREE

www.bbc.co.uk/wales/history

Articles and links to Welsh family history.

Wales National Gazetteer - FREE

http://homepage.ntlworld.com/geogdata/ngw/home.htm

Comprehensive index and maps of Wales.

WorldGenWeb.org - FREE

www.worldgenweb.org

A non-profit, volunteer based organization dedicated to providing genealogical and historical records and resources for world-wide access. Regional, country and ethnic sites here span the globe.

Family History Library Favorite Websites -

www.fhlfavorites.info

A website using the bookmarks from the Family History Library for the best websites for each country. Other genealogy and family history links have been added to the site.

Best Tools to Make It Easier

About Family History.com -
http://familyhistory.about.com -and- FREE
http://genealogy.about.com

The "About" network consists of an online neighborhood of hundreds of helpful experts, eager to share their wealth of knowledge with you. It's

FamilySearch Wiki Portals are useful entry points into content for a major area or region (countries, provinces, and states), or to a major area of research. At present, here are links to the additional international portals that are available.

Other International FamilySearch Portals

Albania - https://wiki.familysearch.org/en/Albania

Algeria - https://wiki.familysearch.org/en/Algeria

Argentina - https://wiki.familysearch.org/en/Argentina

Armenia - https://wiki.familysearch.org/en/Armenia

Austria - https://wiki.familysearch.org/en/Austria

Bangladesh - https://wiki.familysearch.org/en/Bangladesh

Belarus - https://wiki.familysearch.org/en/Belarus

Belgium - https://wiki.familysearch.org/en/Belgium

Brazil - https://wiki.familysearch.org/en/Brazil

Bulgaria - https://wiki.familysearch.org/en/Bulgaria

Croatia - https://wiki.familysearch.org/en/Croatia

Czech Republic - https://wiki.familysearch.org/en/Czech_Republic

Fiji - https://wiki.familysearch.org/en/Fiji

Finland - https://wiki.familysearch.org/en/Finland

Hispanic Countries - https://wiki.familysearch.org/en/Portal:-_Hispanic_Family_History_Resources

Hungary - https://wiki.familysearch.org/en/Hungary

Iceland - https://wiki.familysearch.org/en/Iceland

Indonesia - https://wiki.familysearch.org/en/Indonesia

Lithuania - https://wiki.familysearch.org/en/Lithuania

New Zealand - https://wiki.familysearch.org/en/New_Zealand

Japan - https://wiki.familysearch.org/en/Japan

Slovenia - https://wiki.familysearch.org/en/Slovenia_Emigration_and_Immigration

South Korea - https://wiki.familysearch.org/en/South_Korea

Spain - https://wiki.familysearch.org/en/Portal:Spain/Research_Tools

organized into categories that cover more than 50,000 subjects with over 1 million links to the best resources on the Net. Each category includes the best new content, relevant links, How-To's, Forums, and answers to just about any question. The family history pages–hosted by Kimberly Powell, a professional genealogist, Web developer, author of *Everything Family Tree, 2nd Edition by Adams Media* (2006), and Webmaster for the Western Pennsylvania Genealogical Society– authentically covers many subjects, such as: Ways to celebrate your family heritage, family history projects, find your family history, American family immigration center, genealogy databases, coat of arms, family history resources on the internet, family history software, and much more. Every month, over 60 million people visit this site for help. It offers solutions with over 2 million original articles, product reviews, videos, tutorials and more.

Roots Television.com - http://rootstelevision.com

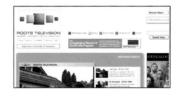

A new kind of web site that features Internet TV (or short videos) for all family history lovers available at any time you wish to view it. They even have some training programs to teach you how to do better Family History research. And now you can view the numerous videos on your TV and other devices. They're working hard to find those hidden gems that are scattered everywhere and bring them under one umbrella so you can find everything roots-related you could possibly imagine–all in one place. You can also access links to family history blogs, vlogs (video blogs), and online shopping.

One-Step Search Tools – www.stevemorse.org

 **FREE** Offers dozens of unique software tools for searching passenger records, census and vital records, and naturalization records. There are tools for DNA genealogy, relationship calculator, calendar, zip codes, characters in foreign alphabets, and more.

Shared Tree.com - www.sharedtree.com **FREE**

 A free online family history and genealogy application. There's nothing to download, it's GEDCOM compatible, files have no size limit, and you can collaborate with family and friends instantly.

WeRelate.org - www.werelate.org **FREE**

 A free genealogy wiki where users generate and update the content; sponsored by the Foundation for On-Line Genealogy in partnership with the Allen County Public Library with pages for over 2,000,000 people and families and growing. You can upload GEDCOM files, your documents and photos, share family stories and biographies, and generate maps of ancestors' life events.

Random Acts of Genealogical Kindness - **FREE**
http://raogk.org

 A global volunteer organization with over 4000 volunteers in every U.S. state and many international locations have helped thousands of researchers. Their volunteers take time to do everything from looking up courthouse records to taking pictures of tombstones. All they ask in return is reimbursement for their expenses (never their time) and a thank you.

U.S. Government Made Easy - **FREE**
www.usa.gov/Citizen/Topics/History_Family.shtml

 Official information and services from the U.S. government

for genealogists and family historians: Learn how you and your ancestors interacted with the government.

Bible Records.com - www.biblerecords.com **FREE**

 Home to over 1100 Bibles online representing about 3,400 surnames. You can search the collection or browse by Bible or by surname.

Generation Maps.com -
www.generationmaps.com

 An easy to use, very affordable, genealogy chart design and printing service. They offer personalized working charts, beautiful decorative charts, custom heirloom charts, and a printing service for charts you've created. Now you don't have to fill in a chart yourself – just send your genealogy computer file and/or your digital photos, tell them how you want it to look, and it arrives on your doorstep for a very reasonable price. They can help you get your research out where you can see it and surround your family with a sense of their heritage. It's also a wonderful, easy way to explain to your family members the research that has been accomplished.

How to Obtain Birth, Death, Marriage, **FREE**
and Divorce Certificates - www.cdc.gov/
nchswww/howto/w2w/w2welcom.htm

Where to write for vital records from the National Center for Health Statistics.

Geneabios.com - www.geneabios.com **FREE**

Free genealogy database of biographies, and a portal to 1,000's of biography sites. Search for ancestors by entering a name or location, or see a list of all genealogy biographies in the database.

Genealogy Search Advice -
www.genealogy-search-advice.com **FREE**

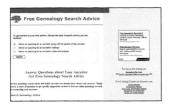

Get free genealogy search advice that builds on what you already know about your ancestry. Simply answer a series of questions to get specific suggestions on how to best use online genealogy records for researching your ancestors.

FamilyForest.com - www.familyforest.com **$**

A fully sourced lineage-linked database that digitally connects people with each other and with the history they created. Search, browse and print family group sheets, kinship charts, ancestor charts, fan charts, ahnentafel charts, and descendant charts.

Cousin Calculator - www.iroots.net/tools/cusncalc

Calculates the **FREE** relationship between two people.

This Day in History -
www.progenealogists.com/dayinhistory.asp **FREE**

Find out what happened on the day that you or your ancestor was born.

Internet Archive - www.archive.org **FREE**

A non-profit digital library of Internet sites and other cultural artifacts in digital form: music, movies, audio records, text, software, and web pages. You can search their database and download certain documents.

Current Value of Old Money - **FREE**
http://projects.exeter.ac.uk/RDavies/arian/current/howmuch.html

How much would a specified amount of money at a certain period of time be worth today?

Inflation Calculator - www.westegg.com/inflation

Adjusts any given **FREE** amount of money for inflation, according to the Consumer Price Index, from 1800 to 2007.

Google Genealogy - **FREE**
www.google.com/Top/Society/Genealogy

A directory of genealogy links by category from Google.

Diigo.com - www.diigo.com **FREE**

Best described as collaborative online sticky notes, Diigo (an abbreviation for "Digest of Internet Information, Groups and Other stuff) isn't specifically for genealogists, but it's a nifty free tool for bookmarking and annotating sites, for yourself or to share with other researchers. If you browse or read a lot on the web, you may find Diigo indispensable. It's two services in one – a research and collaborative research tool on the one hand, and a knowledge-sharing community and social content site on the other.

Family Tree DNA - FREE

www.ysearch.org and www.mitosearch.org

Search and compare your DNA profile side-by-side with others, even if you tested with a different company. The Ysearch tool covers over 61,000 surnames in over 82,000 DNA records.

Suite 101 - http://genealogy.suite101.com/ FREE

Weekly articles on topics relating to genealogy, including lots of how-to columns for beginners. They offer authoritative articles, reviews, and expert commentary written by professional writers.

Best Sites for Vital Records

Records of births, marriages, deaths, divorces and adoptions kept by most countries are one of the best resources for helping you build your family tree. The official governmental records of births, marriages, and deaths in the US and every Canadian province except Québec are called *vital records*. In other countries and Québec, official government records are called *civil registration*.

About.com - http://genealogy.about.com/od/ FREE
vital_records/a/research.htm

Introduction to vital records.

Cyndi'sList - www.cyndislist.com FREE

Hotlinks for general resource web sites and by state.

National Center for Health Statistics - FREE

www.cdc.gov/nchs/howto/w2w.htm

Where to write for vital records.

Vital Records Assistant - www.vitalrec.com FREE

A comprehensive resource for locating vital records: U.S. birth certificates, death records and marriage licenses.

WorldVitalRecords - www.worldvitalrecords.com $
> *Record Types* > *Birth & Marriage Records*

Browse all birth, marriage and death records databases.

BirthDatabase.com - www.birthdatabase.com

A database of 120 million names and birth dates. FREE

Social Security Death Index - FREE

http://ssdi.rootsweb.ancestry.com/
cgi-bin/ssdi.cgi -and- www.geneologybank.com

Over 85 million records.

Bible Records Online - www.biblerecords.com

A site dedicated FREE to transcribing and digitizing the contents of family records that were written inside family Bibles and in other important documents from as early as the 1500s through today. Often, these were the only written records of births, marriages and deaths of a family and these remain solid components to proving a family genealogy.

Western States Marriages Index -

http://abish.byui.edu/specialCollections/ westernStates/search.cfm

 Over 700,000 early marriage records from counties in the western part of the United States. It is not comprehensive for the time period and/or localities described. However, their goal for is to have marriages from all 12 western states.

Death Indexes.com - www.deathindexes.com *FREE*

 A directory of links to websites with online death indexes, listed by state and county.

Funeral Cards - www.genealogytoday.com/ *FREE* guide/funeral_cards-a.html

 While not a traditional "vital record", they often provide great clues like death and birth dates, name of the cemetery where the deceased was interred, name of the funeral home, and sometimes even a photo of the ancestor.

GenealogySleuth - www.progenealogists.com > *Genealogy Sleuth*

Links to vital records for each state.

 FREE

USGenWeb Archives - www.usgwarchives.net *FREE*

 The USGenWeb Digital Library offers actual transcriptions of public domain records on the Internet. A cooperative effort of volunteers containing electronically formatted files on census records, marriage bonds, wills, and other public documents.

American History & Genealogy Project - *FREE*

 www.ahgp.org

A not-for-profit network of independent sites devoted to history and genealogy, and covering North American countries and territories.

State and County QuickFacts - *FREE*

http://quickfacts.census.gov/qfd

 The U.S. Census Bureau's quick, easy access to facts about people, business, and geography.

FamilySearch Vital Records Index -

www.familysearch.org > *Search Records* > *FREE*
Advanced Search > Vital Records Index

Collections of official birth, marriage, and death records from Mexico and Scandinavia. You can also go to > *Search Records > Records Search pilot*, then click on *Browse Record Collections* to search numerous additional new vital records databases from the US and many parts of the world. These databases will eventually be added to an updated FamilySearch home page.

Best Sites for "What's New?"

Keep Up-to-Date on the Latest Technology

Ancestry Insider -

http://ancestryinsider.blogspot.com **FREE**

The unofficial, unauthorized view of Ancestry.com and FamilySearch.org; reports on, defends, and constructively criticizes these two websites and associated topics. The anonymous blogger attempts to fairly and evenly support both, and is often the first to note what's new with these genealogy giants.

Eastman's Genealogy Newsletter - **FREE** **$**

www.eogn.com

The daily newsletter for genealogy consumers, packed with straight talk on all kinds of family history topics by longtime genealogy tech watcher Dick Eastman. Standard Edition is free; $19.95/year for the PLUS Edition gets you access to articles from industry experts.

GenealogyGems.TV - www.genealogygems.tv **$**

A genealogy radio show and TV channel by Lisa Louise Cooke available online, all the time. Listen from your computer or mp3 player. You'll hear research strategies, the latest Internet search techniques and advice from the top genealogy experts. Enjoy video series that explore online research techniques, heritage crafts, and everything family history. Plus a message board forum and polls, complete access to newsletter back issues, behind the scenes with Lisa, and crossword puzzles. $29.95/year

Dear MYRTLE.com - www.dearmyrtle.com **FREE**

Pat Richley's *Dear Myrtle* free website, your friend in genealogy, is a fun, helpful family history site with a blog of genealogy news and tips, beginning

online lessons, and information about getting organized, family history for kids, using Family History Centers, and writing your personal history. She is the author of *Joy of Genealogy,* and you can also listen to her Family History Hour podcast via your computer or transferred to any .mp3 player.

GenealogyGuys.com - www.genealogyguys.com **FREE**

This is the oldest genealogy podcast site which offers programs featuring the latest news and technology from the movers and shakers and top experts in the field. You can access their videos and podcasts at http://genealogyguys.blip.tv

Roots Television.com - http://rootstelevision.com **FREE**

A new kind of web site that features Internet TV (or short videos) for all family history lovers available at any time you wish to view it. They even have some training programs to teach you how to do better Family History research. And now you can view the numerous videos on your TV and other devices. They're working hard to find those hidden gems that are scattered everywhere and bring them under one umbrella so you can find everything roots-related you could possibly imagine–all in one place. You can also access links to family history blogs, vlogs (video blogs), and online shopping.

LiveRoots.com - www.liveroots.com **FREE** **$**

An information resource with an innovative approach to genealogy metasearch that scours hundreds of different sites, including libraries and data providers, by keyword, surname, title, or web address. You can also discover the latest resource releases (updated daily), navigate around the planet for resources, and manage your genealogical research projects. Some hits require a $32.95/year subscription package, while others include the option of getting live assistance for a nominal fee.

CHAPTER 6

Organizing and Archiving Your Information

To succeed in family history, you need a simple, user-friendly system for organizing documents, notes, research aids, photographs, copies of family group records, pedigree charts, research logs, etc. And it needs to be in a readily-accessible form without digging through piles of papers. Staying organized makes your information more valuable to you, and allows you to use your limited family history time more efficiently.

You also need to learn about how to digitize and archive your precious photographs and documents to preserve them for posterity and share them with other family members. New technology can assist you and make it easier. This chapter provides tips and tools to help you get organized and archive your family treasures.

INSIDE THIS CHAPTER:

6 Organize

Family History Insights - 6

Simone Weil

Finding Your Roots

"To be rooted is perhaps the most important and least recognized need of the human soul."
– Simone Weil (1909-1943), Philosopher

Consider the Past

"Consider the past and you shall know the future." – Chinese Proverb

Harold B. Lee
© by Intellectual Reserve, Inc.

Forces Working With Us

"I have a conviction born of a little experience...that there are forces beyond this life that are working with us. ... I have the simple faith that when you do everything you can, researching to the last of your opportunity, the Lord will help you to open doors to go further with your genealogies, and heaven will cooperate, I am sure." Harold B. Lee

Ezra Taft Benson
© by Intellectual Reserve, Inc.

Our Noble Heritage

Fifty-six men signed the [Declaration of Independence] on August 2, 1776, or, in the case of some, shortly thereafter. They pledged their lives!—and at least nine of them died as a result of the war. If the Revolution had failed, if their fight had come to naught, they would have been hanged as traitors. They pledged their fortunes!—and at least fifteen fulfilled that pledge to support the war effort. They pledged their sacred honor!—best expressed by the noble statement of John Adams. He said: "All that I have, and all that I am, and all that I hope, in this life, I am now ready here to stake upon it; and I leave off as I begun, that live or die, survive or perish, I am for the Declaration. It is my living sentiment, and by the blessing of God it shall be my dying sentiment, Independence, now, and INDEPEND-ENCE FOR EVER." (Works of Daniel Webster, Boston: Little, Brown & Co., 1877, 17th ed., 1:135.)

How fitting it is that we sing: O beautiful for heroes proved, In liberating strife, Who more than self their country loved, And mercy more than life!

("America the Beautiful" Hymn)

...[Our forefathers] came—with indomitable faith and courage, following incredible suffering and adversity. They came—with stamina, with inspired confidence for better days. We live amid unbounded prosperity—this because of the heritage bequeathed to us by our forebears, a heritage of self-reliance, initiative, personal industry, and faith in God, all in an atmosphere of freedom. Though they did not possess our physical comforts, they left their posterity a legacy of something more enduring—a hearthside where parents were close by their children, where daily devotions, family prayer, scripture reading, and the singing of hymns was commonplace. Families worked, worshipped, played, and prayed together. ...

There should be no doubt what our task is today. If we truly cherish the heritage we have received, we must maintain the same virtues and the same character of our stalwart forebears—faith in God, courage, industry, frugality, self-reliance, and integrity. We have the obligation to maintain what those who pledged their lives, their fortunes, and sacred honor gave to future generations. Our opportunity and obligation for doing so is clearly upon us. As one with you, charged with the responsibility of protecting and perpetuating this noble heritage, I stand today with bowed head and heart overflowing with gratitude. May we begin to repay this debt by preserving and strengthening this heritage in our own lives, in the lives of our children, their children, and generations yet unborn." Ezra Taft Benson

Thich Nhat Hanh

Continuation of Your Ancestors

"If you look deeply into the palm of your hand, you will see your parents and all generations of your ancestors. All of them are alive in this moment. Each is present in your body. You are the continuation of each of these people." Thich Nhat Hanh, Vietnamese Zen Buddhist monk, teacher, author, poet and peace activist. *A Lifetime of Peace,* 2003, 141

6 Organize

Organizing Your Information

Computers work the best to help you organize your information into family group records and pedigree charts which can be searched by name, date, place, or relationship. They'll help keep tract of your ancestors and descendants. Computers offer an important advantage because you only have to type the information once, then you can use it repeatedly in many different charts and forms, and easily share the information with others. Family histories and correspondence can be written and then edited easily. Photographs and documents can be scanned and archived for safe-keeping, easy retrieval, and sharing with others.

 Computers are wonderful to help you organize your information and save lots of time, but you may still want to print out some family group sheets and pedigree charts and keep them in folders. Try to keep yourself organized and your information readily accessible as your family tree grows.

It's usually better to choose a combination of computer files, filing cabinet folders and 3-ring binders.

Getting Started

For organizing paper copies of family records, first make sure you have the organizational supplies you will need, such as: file cabinet or boxes to store files in, file folders and index tabs, manila folders with assorted tabs, pre-printed forms to record data (you can print free forms from your computer family history program), and 3-ring binders with index dividers. Your investment in a good file cabinet will reap many rewards over the years in well-organized and preserved documents, and it's the easiest way to keep track of your family history papers.

Consider setting up an organizational system as early in your research as possible. If you stay on top of filing your documents as you receive them, it's much easier and less time consuming than if you have to go back through over-flowing files.

File Your Papers.com - *FREE*
www.fileyourpapers.com

 It doesn't take long once you have started your genealogy adventure to collect so much

information that it seems hard to handle. Dealing with information overload is handled by systematic organization of materials. If the organization of materials can be easily, quickly, and cheaply organized, and cross-referenced to other aspects of your files, it will free your mind. This will allow you much more time to devote your energy to the research itself and time to analyze your information more effectively. This website offers free online lessons for getting organized using different software programs: Ancestral Quest, Legacy Family Tree, My Trees online, and Personal Ancestral File. Sponsored by Genealogy Research Associates.

Organizing Your Family Records -
www.arkansasresearch.com > *Guide to Research*

 Article describes **FREE** a system to keep organized including family group sheets, family folders, pedigree charts, research notes, correspondence, and photographs.

Time For It Now -
http://timeforitnow.knotsindeed.com **FREE**

 Contains a guide entitled: *In a Pile or a File* by Rita Bartholomew to organizing your search and records, including a research folder, research log, and research and correspondence indexes.

Ancestry.com Learning Center - **FREE**
www.ancestry.com/learn/start/surveying.htm

A series of articles on organizing your data.

Organizing Your Genealogy - **FREE**
www.familysearch.org > *Search* > *Research Helps*

 Excellent articles entitled: *Organizing Your Genealogy Using Computers* and *Organizing your Paper Files.* Click on *Search* > *Research Helps* > *Sorted by Title* > *"O"*.

Clooz.com Filing Cabinet - www.clooz.com

Clooz is a database for systematically organizing and storing all of the clues to your ancestry that you have been collecting over the years. It's an electronic filing cabinet that assists you with search and retrieval of important facts you have found during your ancestor hunt, showing you a complete picture of what you have and what you lack. Once you import your information, you can assign documents to each person. Then, a report will show you all the birth and death certificates, wills, deeds, diary entries, or other documents that pertain to each individual. $39.95

Organize Folders First by Surname

Start by grouping what information you have by **family surname** (last name). Start a separate index folder for each family. Print out family group sheets from your family history computer program. Print a complete set of your 5-generation family group sheets, or write the names of the parents of each family at the top (using the maiden name for women).

> Create a file folder for each family group using the last name on the label.

Start with yourself and your spouse, and work backward in time, generation by generation, putting the names of each married couple at the top of a page. As you record each piece of information about each of your ancestors, document the sources of the information using your computer family history program in the *Notes or Citations* section. Use index tabs to divide your folders into sections, with a separate section for each surname.

To start, label one section with your father's last name, one with your mother's maiden name, one for your father's mother's maiden name, and one for your mother's mother's maiden name. As you progress in your research, add more index tabs with new surnames you have found.

Color Code Your Files

Color coding can be helpful in separating the lines of your 4 grandparents and keeping the lines straight. For example, *blue* for all ancestors of your father's father, *green* for all ancestors of your father's mother, *red* for all ancestors of your mother's father, and *yellow* for your mother's mother line. There will be 16 hanging file folders, 4 of each color, for your 16 great great grandparents.

If you want, you can also mark the families on your 5-generation pedigree chart using matching colored highlight pens to use as a map. You can even color coordinate each family group sheet by marking the color on the top of each sheet, and manila folders by putting a colored mark on the tab, if you wish.

> Another idea is to use a particular color for direct line ancestors, and other colors for collateral lines.

Filing Your Documents

After creating hanging file folders by surname and manila folders for each family, you can file all of your documents in the appropriate folder for the family to which it belongs. For example, file your birth certificate in the folder labeled with your and your spouse's names, and your parent's marriage certificate in the folder labeled with your mother and father's names.

Add the following items to each family folder as you need:

- *Pedigree Chart*
- *Family Group Sheets* - including the families of children who are not the direct-line child
- *Research Log* - to keep a record of your research so you don't waste time
- *Research Notes*
- *To-Do-List* - questions about this family and things to do
- *Timeline* - a chronology of this family's life events
- *Maps* - showing where this family lived
- *New Documents*

Later you can set up useful *holding files* right behind the surname hanging files for storing additional information which pertains to a family, including: photographs, maps, notes, letters, e-mails, documents, abstracts of censuses, deeds, wills, etc.

Using 3-Ring Binders

After organizing your basic file cabinet system with hanging folders, an excellent additional method of organizing is to supplement your system with 3-ring binders for various special needs, such as:

- *Working files:* copies of pedigree charts, family group sheets
- *Other documents* and quick-reference aids
- *To do list*

You can then carry these binders easily with you to the library or family history center for doing research as needed. Once your research is completed, you can enter the information into your computer family history database, document your findings in the *Sources* section, and make necessary explanations in the *Notes* section.

> When writing for information, you should enclose a self-addressed, stamped envelope.

> Always keep your originals safe and protected.

You can keep valuable original documents, family histories, and photographs stored in archival quality sheet protectors in binders filed in folders in your file cabinet.

Research Notes

> As you do research, keep notes about each family (or surname).

Record the new information on your family group sheets and pedigree charts in your computer database, and record the source for all new information. File each document and all of your notes in the appropriate file folders. *(See documenting your information on page 31.)*

Organizing Your e-Mails and Letters

> Family history is a collaborative effort. You often write many emails or letters.

Keep copies of all your letters and emails in a letter file folder or organized on your computer, and when you receive an answer to a letter, pull your original letter from the file, attach it to the reply, and file both in the appropriate family file folder. Or you can keep your inquiry in the document folder of that particular family where you can refer to it as you are researching that family.

Organizing Your Personal Computer Library and Files

In today's world, Internet sites are probably the fastest, easiest-accessible, and most-used reference sources by most people who use the Internet. Your favorite places on the internet really become your own self-made personal Internet library.

If you are a user of Microsoft's *Internet Explorer*™ browser, you mark your sites as "favorite places". (A Web browser is a software application which enables you to display

and interact with text, images, videos, music, games and other information typically located on a Web site.) In the *Firefox, Google Chrome,* and *Safari* browsers, you are familiar with the term "bookmark."

Firefox features one-click bookmarking to bookmark, search and organize Web sites quickly and easily.

Google Chrome, the new web browser developed by Google, claims to make the web faster, safer, and easier with sophisticated technology.

They both allow you to bookmark a web page by just clicking the star icon at the left edge of the address bar and you're done.

Apple's *Safari* claims to be the fastest and easiest-to-use web browser. One click opens the single-window interface, where you can browse, search, and organize bookmarks.

The bookmarked collections of Web sites that you have compiled provide you with personal resources and can be organized into categories to fit your needs. Organize your internet library into major subject areas with sub-categories. Major categories might include: art, church, family history, health, investments, music, news, travel, etc., any subject you want for which you create a folder in your bookmark file. Then you can create sub-folders under the main folders if you wish. It's easy to do. Refer to your browser's *Help* file for details of how to do this if you need.

Is your collection of printed books starting to take over your home? If desired, create a database or document detailing your collection of books that helps you organize them. A couple of web sites − www.library thing.com and www.goodreads.com − allows you to

maintain a database of your own book collection, enables you to share your collection electronically on a personal website, and connects you with people who read the same things.

FileSync -

www.fileware.com > *Download* **FREE**

A good free file/folder synchronisation utility for keeping files up to date between your laptop and desktop computers, or your desktop and backup hard drive, etc. By simply specifying source and target folder paths and the file types that you require, it will produce a comparison list of the relevant files showing which need to be copied and in which direction. You then have the option to filter the list, examine specific files for differences and change copy directions before going ahead with the synchronisation process.

Free Home Library Software - FREE
www.pilibrary.com

This software allows you to create as many libraries as you need: Books, journals, magazines, CDs, videos, photographs, digital graphic files (JPGs, GIFs, etc.), audio files (Podcasts, Music), HTML (Internet information), PDF/Textual documents, web sites, etc.

What Are Your Memories Worth?

Your life is full of memories that are precious to you and your family. For example, your love story. Before the house. Before the kids. Before the toothpaste started disappearing twice as fast as it used to...there were two people who fell in love. How did it all start? Where is that bundle of love letters you wrote to each other when you were young? Are all your cherished family photos in a box or a dusty photo album?

It's your life and your story and they should live *happily ever after*! If your memories are worth so much to you, shouldn't they be preserved to last for many future generations? Aren't they worth keeping safe and secure for many years to come so they can be shared and enjoyed by everyone who touches your life? How do you preserve your stories, photos, documents, images, mementos, home movies, digital files, etc?

Create Your Own Family Archive

Creating a family archive is one of the most rewarding projects you and your family can undertake. In fact, an archiving project can be very enjoyable and brings family members together. Most importantly it is a rare opportunity to preserve your cherished family memories and guarantee that future generations of your family will have access to the memories that make your family special.

Family history and a family archive are a great combination. As you trace your family roots and collect research, you will probably discover important new photographs and documents that you want to preserve. By creating your own family archive, you can not only archive your cherished family memories, but also the new documents and photos you collect as part of your research.

Scrapbooking is a great way to have fun and remember important events in your life. But if you preserve your original photos and mementos in a family archive and then use color photocopies or high-quality digital scans in your scrapbook, your memories will last for generations to come, instead of letting them yellow or deteriorate.

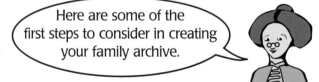

Here are some of the first steps to consider in creating your family archive.

First Steps to Creating Your Family Archive

Goals - Set some goals for your family archive that will help make the decisions about your archive much easier. Your goals might be to organize your family materials so they're accessible and easy to enjoy, create a collection of photographs and mementos that illustrates and complements your family history research or writing project, or to share your archive with other family members.

Decide What to Keep and What NOT to Keep - Once your project goals are clear, review all the materials you have in your home. Make a detailed inventory of everything you might include in your archive. Then go over your inventory and decide what to keep and what not to keep. Don't forget to include items that are out of sight, like materials in boxes, cupboards, dressers and other storage areas.

Reach Out to Others - You may want to talk to family members or friends to augment your family archive. Ask family members for photos of a particular person or event. Take digital photographs, make digital scans to add to your archive. You can also develop an inventory of items that are currently not in your possession so that a record of these items exists. Libraries, archives and historical societies often have materials relevant to your family archive.

6 Organize

Organizing & Maintaining Your Family Archive

You may want to establish guidelines for what you want to add to your archive in the future, and to keep it up-to-date. It's important to organize your documents, photos and other objects into an accessible and usable archive that can grow and adapt with your archive over time.

Here's some organizational category considerations for your family archive.

Each person

Eras (1940s, 1950s, 1960s, etc.)

Events (vacations, birthdays, graduations)

Activities (schools, jobs, organizations)

Collectibles (artworks, stamps, baseball cards)

Financial documents (mortgage, investment and retirement documents, insurance policies, bills or financial documents)

Personal documents (birth certificates, marriage certificates, passport and/or immigration documents, medical information, wills and other legal documents)

There are a lot of ways to arrange your family archive. The best way to get started is to look over the inventory of materials you've decided to keep and see where the natural groupings occur. Then, map out how things should be organized by setting a few high level categories and filling in the rest.

After your family archive is organized and safely stored, you can think about what to add to your family archive in the future. Soon you may collect new photographs, mementos, documents and digital files. You can establish collection priorities to determine what kind of items you want to add to your archive in the future and what kinds of items you don't want.

Save Your Stuff -
www.saveyourstuff.com

Scott Haskins is *the* expert, providing essential information for preserving: family history, scrapbooking, collectibles, old letters, memorabilia, photos, books, etc. that have been afflicted with mold, dirt, smoke, tears and water damage caused by fires, earthquakes, floods, Father Time…or even grandchildren! He works with historical societies, museums, private collectors, art galleries, and governments and has helped tens of thousands of people save their "stuff." His website offers free articles (which are available for free redistribution on your newsletter and blog), and an e-book which is available by chapter or complete book. $19.95

Archival Tools

To protect your family archive, you may want to purchase boxes, folders, paper, etc. that are *acid-free* and *lignin-free*. Most archival materials will also have a neutral pH; meaning they don't contain acid or other chemicals that will cause harm or deterioration of your materials. You'll also need to know a few basic techniques for handling delicate archival materials. Keep in mind that the most important archival materials are those that touch the photos and documents in your archive every day and those that protect your archive from dust and moisture from the outside. Regular cardboard boxes and paper contain acid, which can lead to further deterioration and cause irreparable damage to your precious memories.

Archival Paper

Standard paper is made from wood-based pulp that has not had its lignin removed. It turns yellow and deteriorates over time, and can break down even faster if exposed to light and/or heat. Keep your materials away from outside influences, such as heat and humidity, which can cause changes and damage. The best archival paper has a life expectancy of over 1,000 years. Use only paper that is labeled "acid-free" and "buffered." Acid and other chemicals in paper, and other types of storage sleeves, folders and containers, can speed up the deterioration process.

6 Organize

Here are some basic instructions for handling archival materials.

Archival Techniques

Your hands should be free of dirt, oil or lotion. Thoroughly wash and dry your hands prior to handling or working with any family mementos. Use cotton gloves to handle documents and photographs, especially those that are particularly old or fragile. Be careful when handling glass or ceramic materials as its easy to lose your grip. If you don't have cotton gloves, handle materials by their edges. Handle items carefully, with both hands if necessary, providing stability for the entire item. Do not bend or fold materials. When examining an item, leave it flat on the table. Work on a clean surface. Avoid working in or leaving items in direct sunlight. And avoid leaving items directly in artificial light for extended periods.

Regular plastic sleeves are not recommended for use in a family archive.

Protective Sleeves

Storing materials in sleeves can also be an economical first step in the preservation process. Your materials will be protected from dust, dirt and oils, damage from handling, as well as other contaminants, and you will be able to view both sides of the object. It's critical that you store documents, photographs and other types of paper-based materials in Mylar® (polyester) or polypropylene sleeves because they do not contain harmful chemicals.

Brushes

When cleaning documents and photographs, soft-bristled brushes can be used to gently clear away dust, dirt, debris or particles. Keep brushes clean by washing them with soap and water. Make sure they are thoroughly rinsed and dried before using them again.

Cotton Gloves

Cotton archival gloves should be worn when working with photographic materials, including prints, negatives or slides, as well as dirty or dusty documents and other materials. They should be regularly washed when dirty.

Archival Pencils / Pens

When working with your precious materials, it is preferable to use only pencils. Markers and pens can easily transfer ink onto your materials and cause damage. Archival pencils called "All-Stabilo" pencils are available in black or white water-soluble lead which can be wiped or erased from surfaces easily. If you are seeking to permanently label folders, boxes, CDs, DVDs or other items, use only pens or markers that are waterproof.

Archiving Your Digital Files

The digital revolution has dramatically changed how we communicate, entertain, work and live. We take digital photos, listen to digitized music, and capture and watch digital video and audio. We may send e-mail instead of letters, and stay-in-touch through social networking sites, such as Facebook, FamilyLink, or MyFamily. Now we keep our memories safe and easily share them by creating digital copies of all of our photos and documents, plus backups to protect them.

Over the last decade, many of us have amassed gigabytes of digital files. And just like our physical mementos, these files need to be properly archived to preserve them. If you think that archiving your digital files is a daunting

If there are some items in your family archive that you like to look at regularly or use for reference while doing research, make photocopies or high quality scans that you can use every day. Keep the originals protected from heavy use in your archive.

Archival Suppliers

FamilyArchives.com -
www.familyarchives.com

A web site to help you capture, preserve, organize and enjoy your family's most valuable memories using archival best practices and supplies employed by professional archivists and museum experts. All of the advice is free to use. You can download a free Guide to Creating Your Own Family Archive which is a checklist to identify items to include in your family archive. You can also purchase all the archival supplies you'll need.

Hollinger -
www.hollingermetaledge.com

A leading supplier of archival storage products for government and institutional archives, historical societies, museums,

libraries, universities, galleries and private collectors for over 60 years. They helped develop acid free papers, storage boxes and envelopes for the proper preservation of valuable documents and photographs.

Light Impressions -
http://lightimpressionsdirect.com

Offers a large variety of fine archival storage, display and presentation materials for negatives, transparencies, CDs, photographs, artwork and documents.

University Products -
www.universityproducts.com

Whether you need library supplies, storage boxes, tools and equipment, or preservation framing products, you'll find all the conservation, preservation, restoration and exhibition materials you need.

You should plan now to protect your photographs and documents; don't wait until a disaster happens to them.

Safeguard your digital files. Using today's technology you can readily archive all of your heirloom photos, slides, negatives, home movies, letters, journals, maps, newspaper articles, etc. But you need to have a computer, a scanner, and graphics software.

 Digitizing or scanning your photographs and documents converts them to a more permanent and usable format in today's world and makes them easier to share with other family members and preserve them for posterity. You can then add your cherished photos to your family history software program, a family Web page, blog, or an online photo album you've created, or just e-mail the pictures to others.

When taking new pictures with your digital camera, pay attention to the setting for image resolution. If you take a digital picture on a low resolution setting, there is no way to make the original picture high resolution.

task, you're not alone. Institutions like libraries, museums and archives are always searching for the best ways to archive their digital libraries.

Remember your digital assets are going to continue to grow, almost exponentially, so establishing a system now is only going to benefit you and your family for generations to come. Remember that some image and video files can be very large. You may need to prepare a space on your computer hard drive, purchase an external hard drive, use a storage medium like an online backup service, or copy them onto archival-quality DVDs.

You should be aware of *Lossy* and *Lossless* compressions when saving your digital files.

Information loss

Lossy vs *Lossless*

Lossy compression formats suffer from *generation* loss: repeatedly compressing and decompressing the file will cause it to progressively lose quality. This is in contrast with *lossless* data compression. The advantage of lossy methods is that in some cases it can produce a much smaller compressed file, while still meeting the requirements of the application. For example, to reduce download time. When you acquire a lossily compressed file, the retrieved file can be quite different from the original at the *bit* level while being indistinguishable to the human ear or eye for most practical purposes.

Lossy methods are most often used for compressing sound, images or videos. This is because these types of data are intended for human interpretation where the mind can easily "fill in the blanks" or see past very minor errors or inconsistencies – ideally lossy compression is imperceptible.

Lossless compression is used when it is important that the original and the decompressed data be identical, e.g. to archive your precious photos. Lossless data compression is also used in other applications. For example, it is used in the popular ZIP file format.

Understanding File Formats

You will undoubtedly encounter many different types of electronic file formats today. Most files will be either text, graphic, photo, audio or video files. The way to identify the file type is by looking at its extension, typically expressed as a *dot* followed by 2 to 4 letters, e.g. (.jpg). Why should you care? You need to decide how to best archive your photos and documents,

Image File Formats

Whether you're downloading a picture from the Internet or scanning in a family photograph, the graphic file format you use will determine how good or poor the final result is. There are many different graphic file formats to choose from. Each format has its own unique advantages, disadvantages, and quirks. Here's a brief summary of the different key formats:

TIF - (.tif) *Tagged Image File Format* is widely used for **MASTER COPIES** of scanned data. As images are scanned in they are saved in .tif format, then manipulated and saved in other formats for different purposes, but are very large – which means it takes up more space on your computer.

JPG - (.jpg/.jpeg) (pronounced "jay-peg") stands for *Joint Photographic Experts Group* and is good for emailing photographs to friends, and for web page or blog use, because it's one of the smallest. But JPG uses lossy compression on every save which means that **SOME QUALITY IS LOST EACH TIME THE FILE IS SAVED**, and it cannot be recovered. This is similar to copying a cassette tape to another cassette tape, or making a copy of a copy. The quality is degraded with each copy.

BMP - (.bmp) Works with all Microsoft programs (Word, Excel, PowerPoint, Publisher, etc.), but not necessarily other non-Microsoft applications. It's effective for graphics, but **not as effective for photographs.**

GIF - (.gif) *Graphics Interchange Format* have historically been the best for use with clip art, logos, and drawings, but is **poorly suited for photographic purposes**. GIF also allows a transparent background which is important for creating logos and icons.

PNG - (.png) *Portable Network Graphics* is a bitmapped image format that employs lossless data compression. It was **created to improve upon and replace GIF** as an image-file format not requiring a patent license.

You should consider saving your images in TIF format for archiving purposes, and then you may want to re-save them as a JPG file for e-mailing, Web pages, and other uses.

Your graphics program will allow you to convert an image from a TIF format and save it as a JPG file.

and know whether a file will work on your computer and whether you will need a particular type of software to play or view it. It's helpful to know about a little bit about the most common file formats.

Audio File Formats
Storing audio data on a computer

MP3 - (.mp3) the most popular format for downloading and storing music for both Mac and PC. A 1 Mb file is equal to about one minute of music. Uses a **lossy compression** which is designed to greatly reduce the amount of data required to represent the audio recording and still sound like a faithful reproduction of the original uncompressed audio for most listeners. Compressing the data and then decompressing it retrieves data that is different from the original, but is close enough to be useful in some way.

WMA - (.wma) the popular Windows Media Audio format developed by Microsoft to compete with .mp3. Designed with digital rights for copy protection.

M4P - (.m4p) A proprietary format with digital rights for copy protection developed by Apple for use in music downloaded from their iTunes Music Store.

WAV - (.wav) standard audio file format used mainly in Windows PCs. Commonly used for storing uncompressed, CD-quality sound files, which means that they can be large in size—around 10 MB per minute.

AAC - (.aac) Advanced Audio Coding format based on the MPEG2 and MPEG4 standards.

RA - (.ra) Real Audio, a proprietary system for playing streaming audio on the Web.

Video File Formats

AVI - (.avi) The standard video format for Windows.

MPEG - (.mpg) (.mpeg) MPEG-2 is widely used as the format of digital television signals, direct broadcast satellite TV systems, and DVDs. MPEG-4 (.mp4) is a patented format for web (streaming media) and CD distribution, voice (telephone, videophone) and broadcast TV.

M4V - (.m4v) used for TV, movies, PodCasts, and music videos in the Apple iTunes Store, iPod and iPhone.

MOV/QuickTime - (.mov/.movie) (.qt) A proprietary multimedia format developed by Apple, capable of handling various formats of digital video, media clips, sound, text (for subtitles), animation, music, and interactive panoramic images for both Mac and Windows.

RAM - (.ram) A popular format from RealNetworks for streaming video.

Scanning Your Family History
Bring the past into the present...and future

Converting your family memories into a digital format is an endeavor worth doing. With your computer and a scanner you can collect, organize, and archive your memories for all generations, present and future, to enjoy.

Once you've got your family pictures on your computer, your photographs will no longer fade over time. They can be enhanced and fixed with photo editing software. You can quickly make copies or prints for framing, e-mail them around the world, and most importantly make archive copies of them that can be safely stored away.

You can also create some fun projects with these photographic memories by creating themed scrapbooks, calendars, refrigerator magnets, or slideshows set to music for viewing on your DVD player. Each of these make great gifts.

Here are some useful tips to help you get the most out of your scanning projects.

Tips for Successful Scanning

Flatbed scanners are the most popular. For high-resolution scans, you need a scanner that can capture color images at a minimum of 1200 or 2400 "dots per inch". Image resolution is usually measured in *pixels or dots per inch* (ppi or dpi). Pixels are the tiny squares of color that make up digital images. An image with a very high resolution, or a high ratio of pixels to inches, shows more detail in the photograph. An image with a low resolution will start to look jagged and distorted as you zoom in to see details. This distortion is called "*pixilated.*"

If rich and vibrant color is a must, choose a scanner with 48-bit color depth. To scan 35mm negatives or old slides, look for a scanner that comes with a "transparency adapter." The great thing about scanning pictures or family items is that you can experiment with your scan to ensure that you get the image you want. If you don't like what you've scanned, simply delete the file from your computer and start again. Using image editing software such as *Photoshop*, you can change an image's size and resolution but you can only make images smaller and less detailed. *You can't make images larger or more detailed once the high resolution original is gone.* That's why it's important to save high resolution originals rather than low resolution copies.

- Periodically clean the scanner glass and check the underside of the lid for dirt, lint, hair, or bits of paper.
- When scanning a 3-D object, such as a watch or necklace, be careful not to scratch the glass.
- Never take scissors to your precious historical documents. If you only want to scan part of the document, then do the cropping digitally, on the scanned image.

- The *.TIF* file format is the format of choice for archiving scanned images because of its high quality. If you plan to send the scanned images by e-mail, however, you'll want to convert the files to *JPG* format, which is compressed to a much smaller and more manageable size.

- Rename your scanned images to names you can easily find later.

- For color items or photos, the higher the dpi resolution (2400 dpi), the better the quality of the scan. Set your scanner to 32-bit or 48-bit color for better quality. Be aware that higher dpi and color depth make for a larger file size on your hard drive. It may be tempting to keep low resolution files because they take up less memory, but if you discard the high resolution originals you will lose the details of the photograph forever.

- Use the gray scale option in your scanning software to scan black and white documents or images.

- Before you experiment with a scanned image, such as editing, cropping, rotating, or resizing it, be sure to make a backup of the original file in case you make a mistake. It's a good idea to keep the original scan in a separate folder on your hard drive or on a archive quality DVD.

- Never force down the lid on bulky objects such as books or keepsakes as this could crack the scanner's glass. Instead, drape a black cloth on top of the object to block out light from above.

But don't limit yourself to photos. You can scan all sorts of things to immortalize precious family memories. A scanner can be used to preserve irreplaceable historical documents, such as birth certificates, marriage licenses, deeds, a child's drawings, newspaper articles, cherished letters, sentimental keepsakes, etc.

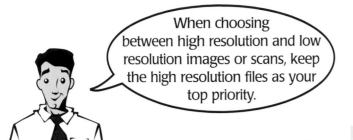

When choosing between high resolution and low resolution images or scans, keep the high resolution files as your top priority.

If you want easy-to-share photos to email, make low resolution JPG copies of your files and keep them separate from your permanent digital archive.

Here are some file-naming tips to consider.

Start the file name with the year, include a subject, but keep it short. When naming a subject with more than one word, do not insert spaces. Start each word with a capital letter. Use a hyphen or underscore to separate years, subjects and series numbers.

Organizing Your Digital Files

The task of organizing digital files can be daunting with the thought of organizing hundreds — or even thousands — of files. But once you have a system established, you'll be able to drag-and-drop files and complete the project fairly quickly. Its also important to create a caption about who is pictured, and where and when the photo was taken.

Group Your Materials into Categories & Subfolders

Once you've evaluated your digital files, you can begin a more detail-oriented organization. Sub-folders can be created to reflect specific subjects such as events, people, places, etc., as well as the types of media (e.g. videos, photos, etc.). As with any labeling or organizing project, keep it simple. If you give your folders "high level" names, you can add photos and other digital files to your folders and subfolders as time goes on.

Naming Your Files

Once your photos and documents are grouped in folders and subfolders, you should standardize the names of the photos and documents themselves. Names for your files should be short and simple. Each name should cover the basics, capturing some of the "who, what, when, where and why." Keep in mind that your photos or documents may one day become separated from the folder you're putting them in, so it's a good idea to include enough information in the file name to identify the file without the folder name.

Preserving Your Digital Files

Digital files are fragile. Computers crash, CDs and DVDs record errors and fail, and it's easy to accidently delete a file. The good news is that it can be as simple as purchasing the proper hardware and tools, and then transferring your files. After your files are organized, you can make duplicate back-up copies and store them separately from the main files housed on your computer or an external hard drive. *For more information on Web sites for caring for and organizing your photos, see pages 110-111.*

Backing-Up at Home

You have many options when it comes to making backup copies of your digital files. All storage options have their benefits and drawbacks. For example, writing and erasing a CD, DVD or external hard drive repeatedly may wear it out, making it susceptible to failure. So it's a good idea to purchase separate disks or devices for everyday use, as well as for preservation storage. You should also consider the longevity of different storage devices. Most CDs, DVDs or external drives have a shelf life ranging from 5 to 10 years, if properly formatted. Archive-quality DVDs have a reflective layer comprised of 24 karat gold which can last significantly longer than ordinary silver recordable DVD discs.

CDs and DVDs seem to offer the most flexibility, but the regular disks have a relatively short shelf life and can fail within a few years. External hard drives are a better option for the storage and preservation of your digital files because they tend to last longer.

6 Organize

If your entire digital archive will not be stored or won't fit on your home computer, it's a good idea to choose two of these options and store them separately. That way if one of your storage methods fails or is damaged, you'll have a back-up.

Remember that social sites such as *Facebook* and *FamilyLink* are a great way to share photos, but they aren't a substitute for archiving your digital photo files.

Likewise, family history Web sites, such as Ancestry.com and FamilySearch.org are a great way to share your family history, but aren't a substitute for archiving all of your research. Most social sites limit the file sizes you can upload, so if you rely on them for back-up, you may end up with only low-resolution images that don't preserve the details you'll wish you had years in the future.

Storing Your Archive

Once all of your valuable memories – documents, mementos, photos, film and video materials, and digital files – have been organized and preserved, your family archive

You will need to decide where you want to permanently store your photos and documents.

At first, you may want to simply save files to your "C" drive in assorted folders you create under *My Pictures*. Soon thereafter, back them up at home or online.

should be stored in a safe place within your home or a storage facility. The ideal archival storage location will allow for temperature and humidity control, be far enough away from pipes or major sources of water (such as a water heater or appliances) or sources of heat (such as a furnace or wood-burning stove), be easily accessible, and be protected from direct sunlight.

DO NOT store your family archive in an outdoor shed or building, on the floor (especially in a basement), within 10 inches of a brick or cinder block wall (moisture can pass through bricks or cinder blocks), in a location that can be accessed by family pets or children, or in a tightly contained space that does not allow for air circulation (such as under a plastic covering).

Backing-Up Online

A good option for backing up and archiving your files is an automatic online backup system, such as:

Carbonite.com -
www.carbonite.com

Automatically backs up your computer files, through the Internet, and then updates them routinely as you

add new files. Your files are protected in the event of fire or flood or other natural disasters that could impact files stored at home. Secure and encrypted. Easy file recovery. Unlimited capacity. 15-Day Free trial. $54.95/year.

Mozy.com -
www.mozy.com

2 GB free, maximum security. Unlimited capacity. $4.95/month.

Transporting Your Data

Flash Drives (jump drives, thumb drives, USB flash drives, flash memory) have become wildly popular in the last few years and for good reasons. A USB flash drive is a memory data storage device with a USB (universal serial bus) interface to connect directly with your PC computer or laptop. They are removable and rewritable, smaller than a tube of lipstick and easily fit into your pocket or purse. Storage capacities typically range from 64 MB (megabyte) to 64 GB (gigabyte), allow 1 million write or erase cycles, and have 10-year data retention. They are cheap, rugged, very convenient and are now the standard for transporting your data from one computer to another, or temporary storage of information that you are transporting.

Nothing actually moves in a flash drive. It consists of a small printed circuit board protected inside a plastic, metal, or rubberized case, and is robust enough for carrying in your pocket or on a key chain with no additional protection. They provide a lot of capability and allow you to find and retrieve information almost instantly. They are the convenient equivalent of thousands of floppy disks, hundreds of CDs, or even dozens of DVD disks. You can easily store your entire address book (with thousands of names, addresses, and e-mail addresses), calendar, thousands of photos, etc. You can purchase a 32 MB for as little as $3.99, or up to a 64 GB for about $60.

Home Movies

Your family's home movies add another dimension to your family history archives. You may want to consider having your home movies converted to DVD which is less fragile, more permanent, and easier to watch and share. But you will probably need a professional who has the equipment to convert them. Different types of

home movies include: Recent VHS video tapes, and movies on reels of film – 8mm, Super 8, or 16mm. No one makes film movies any longer, and the projector accessories are only available through specialty camera stores. A basic service will convert them into DVD files, but some may offer editing or restoration as well. Call your local camera stores to inquire.

VHS movies are usually priced by the minute to convert them, whereas reels of film are usually priced by the foot. Another option to consider is to refilm an old movie yourself. If you have the proper equipment, play your old home movies, and while they are playing record it with your digital video recorder. The quality is usually reasonable and you can then burn DVDs with the digital files. A DVD is not a permanent solution either, but it will last much longer than VHS or film.

8mm film ca. 1932

Keeping Up With Technology

Technology is a wonderful thing. It's essential to everything around us today, even those things

Check out this Library of Congress site for advice on the care, handling and storage of your valuable photos, videos, books, CDs, tapes, newspapers, and other historical items.

Caring for Your Photos - *FREE*
ww.loc.gov/preserv/careothr.html

that aren't considered technological. You deal with technology daily in your home, office, all forms of travel, security systems, air conditioning, computers, networks, software, phone systems, and much, much more.

Keep in mind that computer storage media changes over time. Remember the 5.25" computer diskettes we used just a few years ago, and the magnetic tape reels 20 years ago?

3 1/2" floppy disk ca. 1973-1997

Remember when CD drives cost hundreds of dollars and were slow as molasses? When media changes, we can no longer read the data. No doubt the flash drives, CD-ROMs,

Technology has enabled us to trace our own family roots and stories today that wouldn't have been possible a short time ago. And it's fun and much easier today because of technology.

DVDs, Blu-Ray (the next-generation optical disc format that is considered cutting-edge today), and flash drives we use to digitally store our data today will also become obsolete in the future. We will probably need to transfer our photographs and data to newer storage media in the future to keep pace as technology changes.

It turns out that technological innovations take a while to seep into the collective consciousness and become widely accepted, and that gives us a chance to properly digest them. Don't get frustrated about not keeping up. We're all in the same boat, so let's all paddle together. Relax, don't get discouraged, and be confident in the pursuit of slow and steady progress in your family history journey.

Portable Scanners

In computing, a scanner is a device that optically scans images of any kind – printed text, charts, maps, photographs, handwriting, an object, etc. – and converts it to a digital image. A scanner is a good alternative to using a photocopier and can help capture data for your family history research. Scanners come in portable hand-held, feed-in, and flatbed (which produces the highest quality). A portable scanner can save the digital images of up to 50 letter-size documents at once.

The scanned result is a non-compressed digital image, which can be either downloaded to a printer, transferred to a computer's memory (hard disk) for further processing and storage, or attached to an e-mail message. Pictures are normally stored in image formats such as uncompressed Bitmap, *losslessly* compressed TIFF and PNG (allows the exact original data to be reconstructed from the compressed data), and *lossily* compressed JPEG (allows an approximation of the original data to be reconstructed, in exchange for better

compression rates). Documents are best stored in TIFF or PDF format; JPEG is good for pictures, but particularly unsuitable for text. PDF (Portable Document Format) files have become a generally accepted standard for electronic document distribution and they can be viewed by anyone with free Adobe® Acrobat Reader software (go to www.adobe.com).

Digital Cameras

Due to increasing resolution and new features (such as anti-shake), digital cameras have become an attractive alternative to scanners. You can copy more information quicker than scanning or by hand, and easily manage a large number of files (rather than a large amount of paper). It's fast, portable, and you can digitize thick books without damaging the book spine. Some disadvantages may include distortion, reflections, shadows, and low contrast. Here are some tips for using your digital camera.

Move in and focus. It is important to use a macro (close-up) setting so that the page or paragraph-sized information will fill the page. You don't need to record the page margins; you want an image of the information on the page. Lay the book on the desk and stand above it, getting your camera shooting as perpendicular to the book as possible. Don't forget to physically turn the camera to a vertical view as most pages are taller than they are wide and you can get closer that way.

Always copy the title page and the publication information. Make sure that the page number can be read, even if that means you must take a separate shot of just the page number. Check your image. Always immediately review your shots. Sometimes you might find that the camera didn't focus properly or that you copied only part of the information you wanted. You can erase and immediately shoot a better image. Try to hold the camera steady, squeezing the shutter button, trying not to jerk the camera.

You may want to consider some photo editing software. Many photos will need to be taken at an angle to avoid reflections or with different camera rotations to match the subject. Pretty much any software can handle the rotation, but other software can remove the distortions caused by strange camera angles as well as apply many types of correction to bring out hard to read images. Check out side-by-side comparisons review at http://photo-editing-software-review.toptenreviews.com.

Once captured as digital images by your scanner or camera, printed documents such as wills, biographies, and obituaries can be converted from image files into text files by downloading the images to your PC. You can then copy it into your family history software program to add to your family web site, blog, or other information.

Of course, with a digital camera you can also take pictures of memorabilia and heirlooms, e.g. Grandpa's old rocking chair, grandma's treasured family photos from the wall or that special piece of china that she always used for Sunday dinners, the family Bible inscriptions that are in your Aunt's safekeeping especially if she won't let those treasured family keepsakes out of her sight. Then get the story of the memorabilia or heirloom from those that remember.

A wind-up phonograph ca. 1907 used for playing vinyl records

Handheld Computers

A handheld computer or PDA (personal digital assistant) is a small computer that can fit in your shirt pocket or purse, and is a very useful device today. It was originally used to maintain and manage personal information like To Do Lists, calendars, and contacts. However, like everything else, the computing power has increased dramatically and now PDAs can be used like portable PCs to run word processing, spreadsheets, presentations and you can also browse the web if it has wireless capabilities. *Smartphones,* such as Apple iPhone and Blackberry phones, are popular devices because they combine the functionality of PDAs and phones to handle phone calls, e-mail and mobile-office functions.

This means that now with genealogy software programs for handheld computers you can conveniently take your family history with you when you travel. You no longer have to carry a bunch of three-ring binders or even a laptop PC with you to the library or Family History Center. A large, complete family history database can be carried in your pocket or a purse, and can save you time and increase your efficiency.

Sometime in the future, even census enumerators will use handheld computers to collect data. The handhelds will replace the millions of costly paper forms and maps that enumerators must carry when going door to door to visit people who did not mail in their census forms.

Do What Works For You

No one filing system works for everyone. Your family history is a personal thing, and the options for organizing your information are endless. But by developing and using a system to organize all your information and documents, you will have the data you need, where you need it, when you need it. Establish a method for how you handle new information. Find the system that works best for you. Once you've established a system, it becomes easier to stay organized. Stay with your system, and all your records will stay organized, making them more valuable to you, and allowing you to use your limited family history time more efficiently.

Get started today to digitize and archive your precious photographs and documents to preserve them for posterity and share them with other family members. Don't wait until a disaster happens to them.

Handheld Software

Pocket Genealogist -
www.northernhillssoftware.com

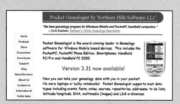

Genealogy software for Windows mobile-based devices, including the PocketPC, Smartphones, and Handheld PC. Supports most data types including events, facts, notes, sources, repositories, addresses, to do lists, latitude/longitude, DNA, multimedia (images) and LDS ordinances. Basic version $20, Advanced $35.

My Roots - www.tapperware.com/MyRoots

A full-featured shareware genealogy program for Palm OS handhelds,

can display ancestor and descendant trees for any person. It also offers searching, sorting, filtering, and many other features. It lets you take your genealogy data with you wherever you go. Since handheld computers can fit in your shirt pocket or purse, they are much more convenient than a laptop or a 3-ring binder. With My Roots, you can stay organized and work more efficiently whether you're at a courthouse, library, or family reunion. A free conversion utility, for PC or Mac, lets you import data from or export data to standard GED files. Free trial version available. $24.95

PAF (Personal Ancestral File) - **FREE**
www.familysearch.org

Works only on Palm OS handhelds and only allows you to view the data on your Palm, not enter new data.

6 Organize

CHAPTER 7

Leaving an Enduring Legacy

SHARING YOUR FAMILY'S STORY, WRITING YOUR FAMILY HISTORY, ORAL INTERVIEWS

© by Intellectual Reserve, Inc.

Everyone has a story to tell.

Some people may mistakenly believe they have nothing of importance to pass on to others...no legacy they can leave. But you need to know that you don't have to be wealthy, famous, or talented to leave a meaningful legacy for your descendants. Some of the most inspirational, enduring legacies are from people outside of history books and newspaper headlines. Everyday, plain ordinary people are creating and passing down inspirational, historical legacies. And you can be one of them.

Gawain and Gayle J. Wells

Journaling Helps Us Get Past Difficult Times

"...important in journal writing is the recording of both our failures and successes. If we can look back and see where we failed in the past and why, we are better able to chart a course for success in the future. Likewise, recounting triumphs and accomplishments can be a great source of strength in periods of discouragement and frustration and can help us get past other difficult times."

Gawain and Gayle J. Wells

Suggested Activities

1. Conduct an oral interview with a parent, grandparent, aunt, etc.
2. Make a commitment to start keeping your personal history. Record your thoughts and feelings as well as the events of your day-to-day life.
3. Begin to write your own life story. Which ancestors on your pedigree chart do you identify with the most? If you could talk to them about their lives, what questions would you ask? What would you like to know about them that you haven't been able to find through your research? With that in mind, begin to write your own life story.
4. Record some personal, biographical information about yourself, including a physical description, the places you've lived, and your professional training and experience.
5. Compile a list of other topics that you would like to include in your personal history, keeping in mind the things you wish you knew about your ancestors, and schedule a regular time for working on it. If writing it down seems difficult, talk into a tape recorder or video camera and then find someone who can do a written transcription for you.

Family History Insights - 7

Ellen Goodman

Our Most Valued Legacy

"What the next generations will value most is not what we owned, but the evidence of who we were and the tales of how we loved. In the end, it's the family stories that are worth the storage." Ellen Goodman, Pulitzer Prize winning syndicated columnist, www.BostonGlobe.com.

Dennis B. Neuenschwander
© by Intellectual Reserve, Inc.

Gathering and Sharing Family Keepsakes

"Every family has...keepsakes. ... These include genealogies, family stories, historical accounts, and traditions. These eternal keepsakes... form a bridge between past and future and bind generations together in ways that no other keepsake can. ... Bridges between generations are not built by accident. Each [individual] has the personal responsibility to be an eternal architect of this bridge for his or her own family. ...

If I want my children and grandchildren to know those who still live in my memory, then I must build the bridge between them. I alone am the link to the generations that stand on either side of them. It is my responsibility to knit their hearts together through love and respect, even though they may never have known each other personally. My grandchildren will have no knowledge of their family's history if I do nothing to preserve it for them. That which I do not in some way record will be lost at my death, and that which I do not pass on to my posterity, they will never have. The work of gathering and sharing eternal family keepsakes is a personal responsibility. It cannot be passed off or given to another.

A life that is not documented is a life that within a generation or two will largely be lost to memory. What a tragedy this can be in the history of a family. Knowledge of our ancestors shapes us and instills within us values that give direction and meaning to our lives." Dennis B. Neuenschwander

Spencer Kimball
© by Intellectual Reserve, Inc.

Your True Self

"Begin today to write and keep records of all the important things in [your] own lives and also the lives of [your] antecedents. ... Your own private journal should record the way you face up to challenges that beset you. Do not suppose life changes so much that your experiences will not be interesting to your posterity. Experiences of work, relations with people, and an awareness of the rightness and wrongness of actions will always be relevant. ...

No one is commonplace. ...Your own journal, like most others, will tell of problems as old as the world and how you dealt with them. Your journal should contain your true self rather than a picture of you when you are 'made up' for a public performance. There is a temptation to paint one's virtues in rich color and whitewash the vices, but there is also the opposite pitfall of accentuating the negative. ... The truth should be told, but we should not emphasize the negative. ...

Your journal is your autobiography, so it should be kept carefully. You are unique, and there may be incidents in your experience that are more noble and praiseworthy in their way than those recorded in any other life... Your story should be written now while it is fresh and while the true details are available...What could you do better for your children and your children's children than to record the story of your life, your triumphs over adversity, your recovery after a fall, your progress when all seemed black, your rejoicing when you had finally achieved? Some of what you write may be humdrum dates and places, but there will also be rich passages that will be quoted by your posterity.

Get a notebook...a journal that will last through all time, and maybe the angels may quote from it for eternity. Begin today and write in it your goings and comings, your deepest thoughts, your achievements and your failures, your associations and your triumphs, your impressions and your testimonies." Spencer W. Kimball

Leaving an Enduring Legacy

LEGACY: A GIFT TRANSMITTED BY OR RECEIVED FROM AN ANCESTOR

One Hundred Years from Now, Will Anyone Know Who You Are?

Knowledge you have acquired about your ancestors during your lifetime instills within you values that give direction and meaning to your life. Whether you realize it or not, you have profited in your lifetime by the experiences, achievements and heritage of your parents and fore fathers. Likewise, do not suppose otherwise that your acquired knowledge, values, achievements and life challenges that you have overcome will become of great benefit to your descendants.

What legacy will you bequeath to your heirs? A life that is not documented will largely be lost to memory within a generation or two. If you do not record your life, the memory of your life will be largely lost at your death. You have a wonderful opportunity to leave an enduring, historical legacy to your kin. The whole world is in your hands – the legacy of your life (or the life of a family member) may be determined by what you do today. Are you up to the challenge?

One hundred or two hundred years from now, your descendants can know who you are. And they may find their lives forever changed for the better because of the legacy of uplifting, faith-promoting strength you left them. You should record your life history and experiences for your children and grandchildren, and beyond. In this way, they can benefit and learn from your life. Even if they have never met you, they can come to love you and "turn their hearts" to you. Through keeping journals and writing personal and family histories, you can build the bridge between your past and future generations.

Your Journals Will be a Source of Inspiration

Spencer Kimball
© by Intellectual Reserve, Inc.

"Any...family that has searched genealogical and historical records has fervently wished their ancestors had kept better and more complete records. On the other hand, some families possess some spiritual treasures because ancestors have recorded the events surrounding their [life] and other happenings of interest. ... People often use the excuse that their lives are uneventful and nobody would be interested in what they have done. But I promise you that if you will keep your journals and records they will indeed be a source of great inspiration to your families, to your children, your grandchildren, and others, on through the generations." Spencer W. Kimball

Our Posterity is Interested in All We Do and Say

"We may think there is little of interest or importance in what we personally say or do—but it is remarkable how many of our families, as we pass on down the line, are interested in all that we do and all that we say. Each of us is important to those who are near and dear to us—and as our posterity read of our life's experiences, they, too, will come to know and love us. And in that glorious day when our families are together in the eternities, we will already be acquainted." Spencer W. Kimball

Receive Strength and Guidance

John H. Groberg
© by Intellectual Reserve, Inc.

"So often we think of our responsibility to do something for those who have gone before. We need to understand that probably one of the most important benefits of preserving our heritage is what it does for us today. If we want our problems to be solved, one of the surest ways of doing that is to search for our past, for therein we receive strength, guidance, and understanding. [You] are giving an added eternal dimension to your lives as you learn and study the past. We can receive strength and help from those who have gone on before. To raise our families today, we need to do family research and genealogy." John H. Groberg, Chairman of the Olympic Events Executive Committee, Press Conference 2002

Theodore M. Burton
© by Intellectual Reserve, Inc.

Provide Uplifting, Faith-Promoting Strength

"Much of what we now regard as scripture was not anything more or less than men writing of their own spiritual experiences for the benefit of their posterity.... we ought to write of our own lives and our own experiences to form a sacred record for our descendants. We must provide for them the same uplifting, faith-promoting strength that the ancient scriptures now give us." Theodore M. Burton

"Old Testament Prophet" by Judith Mehr
© by Intellectual Reserve, Inc.

Resources For Writing Your History

Writing our personal and family histories may sometimes seem discouraging. We may not know where to begin, or what to say or how to organize our thoughts. Here are some ideas and excellent resources to help you get started and organize your work.

Getting Started Keeping A Journal

Keeping a journal is not necessarily difficult. But does take some discipline. Here are some suggestions:

Choose a Convenient Method - Select either a book to handwrite your journal or a computer. By choosing a method that is convenient, you will be more likely to follow through. Specialized computer software is available (see below), or you can use just your word-processing software if you choose. You could consider turning the writing into a ritual. Choose the *right* book to write in, and with a pen that feels good to you and looks good on the page.

Establish a Schedule - Like any new habit, keeping a journal is something that you must work at, especially at first. You will discover more about what you are experiencing if you write in your journal at the same time in the same place every day or every time. Decide how often you will make entries: daily, weekly, monthly, etc. When will you make the entries—early in the morning, at bedtime, on Sundays? With todays busy schedules, we often find ourselves rushing from one task to the next. By scheduling a little time to record your personal history, you are allowing time for yourself to reflect on the day and on your life as a whole. This may be very therapeutic for you. When you have decided, stay with it.

Decide What to Record - A journal is a record of your day-to-day life, but it is more than just a diary. It deals with your experiences and how you handled them. It deals with the values and principles you have learned and how you applied them in your life. It should also record events in your life, such as education, employment, marriage, and children. It should be something you can reflect back on...and learn from. Allow your mind to roam freely through the present, the distant past, and the shifting future. Don't deny whatever comes up as you are writing, no matter how silly it seems. You remembered it for some reason.

Be inspired by others. Check out your local library for other people's family histories. Reading the works of others may inspire you in your own writing.

Hidden Benefits of Keeping A History

Gawain & Gayle Wells

Gawain and Gayle J. Wells provide us with excellent insight on the many hidden benefits that come from: 1) gathering and reading histories of our progenitors, 2) writing our own personal history, and 3) keeping a journal. Here are some excerpts from a wonderful magazine article they wrote:

"Many unanticipated joys and blessings come from keeping a history. The blessings come not only from *completing* the records, but also from the process of *writing* them. What are some of these unexpected blessings?"

We Are Strengthened

"It can be a great thrill to discover a diary or journal written by a grandparent or loved one. For example, the record of a great-grandmother's experiences as a bride and young mother can touch the heart of a granddaughter and cause deep love, even though the two are generations apart. ...We greatly benefit from the testimonies of our own ancestors as they recount for us their trials and sacrifices. But many of our parents and grandparents left no written account of their lives for us to read. Even so, it is possible – and important – to obtain a record about them. ... Discovering our family and our heritage can help us discover ourselves."

Reliving Each Experience

"As I began recording my earliest recollections for chapter one of my personal history," Gayle recalls. "I found myself reliving each experience. Details and images came into my mind that I hadn't remembered before. I became so absorbed that I found myself weeping–and laughing–as I recorded certain incidents. It was as if I were actually stepping back in time. ... I was experiencing my own past, but observing it now with the advantage of maturity and perspective. ... We can also gain a greater appreciation for our parents as we write about them in our personal histories. Recalling our lives' formative events from an adult point of view helps us recognize how often we depended upon our parents for emotional support as well as physical help."

Touching the Lives of Others

"Writing in a journal is the best way to keep our personal history current. But a journal can best play its important role in our lives if we use it consistently. We might consider our journal as a map of our past, present, and future. We can look back to see where we have been, and then, with greater understanding and perspective, go forward, strengthened by our own experiences. ... We are and must continue to be a history-keeping people. As we are blessed in reading records kept by ancient prophets as well as our own ancestors, we...may touch the lives of those who follow us. And...we will experience greater joy and meaning in our lives." Hidden Benefits of Keeping a History, Gawain and Gayle J. Wells

Take It Easy - Writing your personal history may seem overwhelming at first, but if you do it a little at a time, it's much less intimidating. If you focus on short periods of your life, it will seem much more manageable. And you don't have to write in chronological order. You can write about any event or period of your life as your memories are stirred.

Ideas Help Stimulate - Include news events that were happening at that time in your life which not only help set it against the circumstances of the times, but also make your story more interesting. You may also find that by remembering historical events, you will be stimulating more of your personal memories. Memorabilia can also help bring back memories, such as: music, photos, letters, talking with family or friends, even familiar smells and sounds.

Be Personable - Record your triumphs over adversity, your recovery after a fall, your progress when all seemed black, your rejoicing when you had finally achieved. Share your thoughts and feelings; give your descendants a glimpse into the real you.

Be Creative - Have fun creating your memoirs and most likely others will enjoy reading it. You can include interesting things like photos, maps, news articles, receipts, favorite quotations and jokes, cards, etc.

Let your memories be a reflection of you and your devotion to writing your family history. But do it!

Your journals and records will be a great source of inspiration to your children, your grandchildren, and others through many generations.

Helpful Software and Websites for Writing Your Story

Personal Historian.com -
www.personalhistorian.com

Software which assists you in writing personal histories about yourself and other individuals. It breaks this seemingly monumental task into small, manageable pieces and then reconstructs it into a complete, publishable document. It includes an extensive library of timelines, historical facts, cultural trivia, and memory triggers which give color and context to the history. You can publish your completed history to your printer, word processor or PDF file. $29.95

Write Your Life Story! - http://home.netcom.com/ ~genealogy/life_story.htm

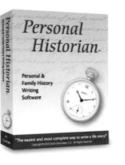

This is a software program that was created after talking to a group of writers. When asked "how do you even begin…" they all replied, "Make an outline of each year of your life." With this program you are guided through creating your basic outline right through to the finished manuscript. It can be difficult to organize the various data you have collected and generate a life story. The software can help you organize the details of an ancestor's life or your own. $19.95

Writing the Journey - *FREE*
www.writingthejourney.com

This is an online writing website that includes ideas, information about

journal-keeping software, a free newsletter, an online workshop, exercises to improve your journal-writing skills, and more. The heart of this website is their online journal writing workshop. You can explore some of the concepts important to journal writing, and complete exercises designed to teach you new journal writing techniques. They believe that journal writing is one of the great tools for listening to your heart. They developed this website to share information about how to get the most from your journal. With your heart to guide you, your life is a spiritual adventure!

Genwriters - www.genwriters.com *FREE*

Writing for Future Generations. A source to find ideas and resources to bring your family history to life.

Association of Personal Historians.org - *FREE*
www.personalhistorians.org

The Association is an organization dedicated to helping others preserve their personal histories and life stories. Here you can search out a professional to help you record your own (or a loved one's) life stories. You can also find tips on the many different ways you can capture your own memories. Discover the joys of preserving personal history. Producing life story legacies through books, oral histories or videos - with thoughts, feelings and memories - this site helps enrich lives for generations to come.

Life Story Center - *FREE*
http://usm.maine.edu/olli/national/
lifestorycenter > *Center for Life Stories*

Can you remember what's happened in your lifetime? Here's a nostalgia website which has great pages for triggering memories and historical events and dates. It has lots of entertaining and useful links.

Cyndi's List.com -
www.cyndislist.com/writing.htm *FREE*

Start with the collection of websites under the "Writing Your Family's History" section.

Librarians' Internet Index - www.lii.org *FREE*

A publicly-funded website and weekly newsletter with a searchable database for the best of the Web organized into 14 main topics and nearly 300 related topics.

Internet Public Library - www.ipl.org *FREE*

A convenient service called *Ask an IPL Librarian* in which their dedicated online volunteer staff answers reference questions. Do a search for "writing family history".

About.com Journaling - *FREE*
http://genealogy.about.com > *Journaling* –or– > *Writing & Publishing*

Learn how to get started with journaling your personal stories or writing your autobiography with these inspirational techniques and workshops. Provides articles with links to websites for journaling and personal history writing. One of the articles outlines 10 ideas for recording your personal history.

Keeping a Journal - www.wofford.edu > *FREE*
Search "Keeping a Journal"

Articles and a workshop on keeping a journal from Wofford College.

Writing Resources on the Web - *FREE*
http://web.mit.edu/uaa/www/writing/links

MIT online web link resources for general and technical writing.

Writing.org - www.writing.org *FREE*

This non-commercial site offers how-to articles for writers (and especially for new writers). The goal is to help you break into the writing business and avoid being victimized by scam artists.

Books to Consider

You may want to have some reference books at your fingertips. They'll save you lots of time in your pursuit of creating your legacy.

Producing a Quality Family History $

This is one of the best-written guide books for anyone looking to create a useful, lasting history of their family. Patricia Law Hatcher guides you through the steps required to create an attractive, functional family history report, and have made understanding the organization and creative process simple. It covers every aspect for the beginner and focuses the attention of even the advanced family historian and experienced writer on what is needed to generate a high quality publication. $19.95

Joan R. Neubauer Books $

Award winning author and acclaimed speaker has written several books about writing and journaling.

Dear Diary: The Art and Craft of Writing a Creative Journal - How to use a journal to accomplish goals, achieve spiritual growth, and keep a great family record. $5.95

From Memories to Manuscript: The Five-Step Method of Writing Your Life Story - Steps to create your autobiography and teaches you the full process of publication. $5.95

The Complete Idiot's Guide to Journaling - How to get started, the benefits of journaling, elements of a good journal, and helps you decide what to write about. $16.95

Writing Family History Made Very Easy $

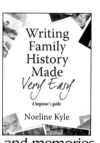

Noeline Kyle offers practical and innovative suggestions to writing family histories and beautifully preserving your legacy for centuries to come. Features varied samples and styles of writing to effectively capture family traditions and memories. All aspects of the writing and researching process are explained, from choosing a format to publishing a family history. $14.95

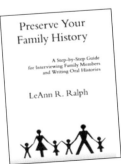

Preserve Your Family History: A Step-by-Step Guide for Interviewing Family Members and Writing Oral Histories $

To preserve your family stories, all you need is a list of people to interview, a tape recorder and a copy of this book by LeAnn Ralph which contains more than 400 questions on 30 different topics. $11.95

You Can Write Your Family History $

How to record the fascinating tales of your ancestors by Sharon Carmack. The best methods for: Conducting historical and thematic research, organizing materials, outlining and plotting a story, illustrating with pictures and charts, and making money writing the histories of other families. $19.95

George Morgan's Web Articles

George G. Morgan is the author of the "*Along Those Lines ...*" weekly genealogy column at Eastman's Genealogy Newsletter, www.eogn.com, (previously at www.Ancestry.com), president of the International Society of Family History (www.rootsweb.com/~cgc), and author of scores of books, articles for magazines, journals and newsletters across the U.S., Canada, and in the U.K. http://ahaseminars.com

> Among the scores of magazine and journal articles, George wrote articles about connecting with your ancestors. Here's a brief review and the web links to a few of his *Along Those Lines...* articles.

Picturing Your Ancestors - FREE
www.ancestry.com/library/view/columns/george/6574.asp

What family history would be complete without descriptions of your ancestors? George Morgan

> It's important to place your ancestors into the context of the times, places, and events in which they lived.

discusses photo options: when great photographs are available, when photographs cannot be reproduced, and when there are no photos. What do you do? After you develop your family history, and having

researched history, geography, social conditions, environment, personal images, etc., now weave it all together into a compelling story.

Picturing their Environment - www.ancestry.com/library/view/columns/george/6553.asp **FREE**

We all are influenced by the environment in which we live. One way to add details to your written family history is to paint a picture of the environment in which they lived. He examines the details that can be developed to add "color" to your family's history, as well as some resources that may help. Our ancestors had nothing more than quills and ink to write with,

and they traveled by horse and wagon, steamer ship, sailing ship, handcart, etc. It's hard to imagine what that must have been like. Study the places where your ancestors lived and the conditions at the time: transportation, food, medicine, agriculture, industry, home life, clothing, religion, politics, government, weather, etc. We can weave those details into the descriptions of our ancestor's environment and   better understand them.

Defining Local Context - www.ancestry.com/ library/view/columns/george/6533.asp *FREE*

In this article, George examines some of the resources which may be available to add accuracy, depth, and a greater interest to your written family history. He said that although it's useful to know details of their life, it's more important to know any stories and details of the influences in their life. Our ancestors may have lived in dramatic and historic places and times, and placing them into a global or national context is essential to understanding and writing their stories. Delve into the place they lived and gather the most concise picture you can in order to paint an accurate biographical, historical and social picture.

A Contextual Timeline - www.ancestry.com/ library/view/columns/george/6511.asp *FREE*

It's essential to build a historical and social context for your ancestors. In order to unravel mysteries and flesh out their stories, research the times and places your ancestors lived. Everyone's life is influenced by where they live and the events occurring around them. You must delve into the everyday lives of your

ancestors if you are to understand who they were and why they made the decisions they made. The ordinary day-to-day activities help define who they are and are a reflection of their lives and times. George discusses the *WHO, WHAT, WHERE, WHEN,* and *HOW* of a story. "Researching the time period is essential so that you know what historical events were transpiring and what everyday life was like: food, clothing, transportation, communication, socialization, etc."

Collecting Your Family Stories

Every person has a story to tell. Family stories are tales about people, places, and events related to your family and your ancestors. The memorable stories of our lives and of others in our family take on special importance, even if everyone tells different versions of the same event. These tales are family heirlooms held close to the heart. They are a gift to each generation that preserves them by remembering them and passing them on to future generations, and will become some of the most valuable and exciting information you can document about your family history. We call these family stories *oral history*, which is history the way our parents and grandparents remember it.

There is some urgency in collecting these precious family stories because older people will obviously not be around forever. Often, a parent, grandparent or great aunt is the last living person who knows these stories, and if

Tell your own story using your pictures.

tab and Dr. Doug Boyd, Director of the Louie B. Nunn Center for Oral History, discusses in-depth the basics of using digital audio and portable recorders. The website also contains informational videos about some of the more popular recorders, and hotlinks to other useful sites.

> You can produce better quality and longer life recordings of oral history interviews using a good digital recorder than using a regular analog cassette tape recorder.

they pass on before their story is recorded, it is lost forever and may never be known. By gathering your family stories, and learning more about the personalities and heritage of your ancestors, they become more than just names and dates. They become real people with real struggles and dreams and triumphs in their lives just like you.

It doesn't matter if your family was famous or just regular people like most of us, there is great value in getting to know them. Start with older people who you believe might not be able to wait for you to get around to gathering their story. Decide what you would like to learn about from each family member, and don't delay in interviewing them. And don't limit yourself to one person, collect several perspectives on the same subject by getting lots of stories from different family members. One thing you can count on, your family stories are guaranteed to become absolutely priceless possessions in your family for many generations to come.

Oral History Association -

www.oralhistory.org > *Oral History* **FREE**

Provides general principles and best practices for oral history. Also click on the Technology

Digital Audio Recordings

It's also much easier to preserve and share the valuable recordings with others by email and on a computer and website. The quality of digital recordings depends on the recording, processing, storing, and editing, as well as the selection of equipment. Excellent guidance and tutorials for digital audio and video recording are available online.

iTalk Recorder -

www.griffintechnology.com/products/italk **$**

Apple has several iPods on the market including the iPod Touch, iPod Classic, and even the iPhone (OS 3.0 or later) capable of decent audio recording. But you need to purchase the iTalk Recorder feature for $1.99 (download) which lets you record directly to your iPod. An intuitive user interface lets you start/stop, choose recording quality, and manage the list of your recordings, all with just one fingertip. Run iTalk to record on your iPhone or 2nd generation iPod touch. Email your recording straight from iTalk, or run iTalk Sync on your computer to transfer your recordings from your iPhone to your computer.

Library of Congress Guide -

www.digitalpreservation.gov/formats/index.shtml **FREE**

A comprehensive guide to understanding digital formats, including audio, digital images and text files.

Vermont Folklife Center - **FREE**

www.vermontfolklifecenter.org > *Archive* > *Field Research Tools* -or- www.vermontfolklifecenter.org/archive/res_audioequip.htm

Andy Kolovos provides the up-to-date information on all aspects of digital audio recording. The site includes equipment reviews and recommendations, advice on recording technique, and extensive links to further online and print sources of information.

Oral History Workshop -

www.baylor.edu/oral_history/index.php?id=61236 **FREE**

A good digital oral history workshop with Internet resources, equipment, transcribing, and editing recommendations.

Historical Voices - **FREE**

www.historicalvoices.org/oralhistory/audio-tech.html

On this Web site are detailed explanations of most aspects of digital audio recording, equipment selection, and effective recording practices, as well as digitization. The site includes online tutorials with downloadable audio samples.

Conducting an Oral Interview

Whether your interview is in person, by phone, or by mail, there are some important steps which will encourage a more open and thorough interview.

Older relatives can be very helpful in piecing together your family's history. Often there is at least one person in a family who has assumed the role of family historian – *the keeper of the flame* – and may already have accumulated and organized a great deal of genealogical information. Get reacquainted with family members through family history interviews.

Some of the things you will need to conduct an interview are: digital recorder or video camera, and a list of questions to help you remember what things you want to know about this person. You can *listen* better if you don't have to be thinking about your next question.

Usually, the *less talking* you do, the better the interview. So don't interrupt when they're telling their story. And usually limit your interview to 1½ hours so they don't get worn out. Store your recording in a safe place and make a transcription as soon as convenient.

Interview Guidelines

BYU Capturing the Past - *FREE*

www.byu.org/capturingpast

They provide four main guidelines and valuable tips for conducting an oral interview with family members: 1. Planning, 2. Preparing, 3. Conducting and 4. Preserving the Interview.

Baylor Oral History Workshop *FREE*

www.baylor.edu/oral%5Fhistory/index.php?id=23560

Carries you step-by-step through the process of creating oral history, including selecting your topic, applying the best

interviewing techniques, and sharing your oral histories. They have a good workshop on using digital equipment.

Cyndi's List.com Oral History Interviews -

www.cyndislist.com/oral.htm *FREE*

Links to many general resource web sites, plus libraries, archives and museums publications, computer software and supplies, and some associations to help with oral histories.

Here's a list of possible questions for your interview, but don't feel bound by them. Write down other ideas and questions you can ask at an appropriate time.

Interview Questions

FamilyTree Magazine.com - *FREE*

www.familytreemagazine.com/article/20-questions

20 Questions for interviewing relatives to use as a springboard for planning your oral history interviews.

BYU Capturing the Past - *FREE*

www.byub.org/capturingpast/conducting.asp

Sample Interview Questions.

Genealogy.com List - *FREE*

www.genealogy.com/00000030.
html?cj=1&o_xid=0001029688&o_lid=
0001029688&o_xt=1029688

Suggested topics and questions for oral histories.

JewishGen Questions - *FREE*

www.jewishgen.org/InfoFiles/Quest.html

A list of questions and topics that may be used when interviewing family members.

Continued next page...

About.com 50 Question - *FREE*

http://genealogy.about.com/cs/oralhistory/
a/interview.htm

Fifty questions for family history interviews. What to ask the relatives.

OralHistory.org - www.oralhistory.org *FREE*

The Oral History Association (OHA) website, newsletter, and the new www.oralhistory.org/wiki/OHA wiki, a place where you can find and share information resources about oral history. Dr. Doug Boyd has a good article on the basics of digital recording at www.oralhistory.org/technology/audio_basics.

Making Sense of Oral History -

www.historymatters.gmu.edu/mse/oral *FREE*

A guide by Linda Shopes, historian at the Pennsylvania Historical and Museum Commission, offers tips to finding and using oral history online and what questions to ask.

Get started in creating your legacy today! Do It!

Use your pedigree chart to help determine what you want to learn from your interview with a family member.

Interview Tips

- Prepare your questions in advance (see interview questions).

- Check to make sure your recording equipment is working properly and that you have enough tape, batteries, and other accessories for the interview.

- Give the person you are interviewing time to prepare for the interview, at least a week if possible.

- Ask the person you are interviewing to start gathering family photographs, documents, letters, or any other items that will help them share their memories with you.

- Bring someone with you to the interview if possible to handle the digital camera or digital recorder so that you can keep your attention focused on the person you are interviewing.

- Store the recording in a safe place and transcribe the interview to help preserve it.

- Enter the information you gather in the interview on your pedigree chart, family group record, and research log.

Suggested Activities

Identify your oldest living relatives and decide which one you would like to interview first. Schedule a time for a personal visit. Look at the information you have recorded on your pedigree chart and make a list of questions to ask your relative that will help you fill in the blank spaces on your chart. When you have completed the interview, record the new family history information on your pedigree chart, family group record and research log.

CHAPTER 8

Other Rewarding Opportunities

8 Other Rewarding Opportunities

Suggested Activities

1. Hold a family reunion.
2. Start a family newsletter or blog.
3. Create a family web site.
4. Create a list of all the descendants of your grandparents and share it with all of your cousins.
5. Protect and preserve irreplaceable family records and heirlooms.
6. Publish a family history of your ancestors.
7. Look for ways to express your family history through painting, needlework, music or other creative channels.
8. Link into your ancestral homelands through traditional foods, festivals, and customs.

There are many rewarding opportunities in family history other than building your family tree and connecting with the lives of your ancestors. Technology has made other family history activities – such as, creating your own family web site, family blog, online photo album, or just holding a family reunion – very fun, easy, and exciting. I hope you explore all of these other rewarding opportunities. You don't have to be a genius or computer guru to accomplish great things, even if you never considered them previously. Just have a little courage to jump in and start paddling and you will discover miraculous things happen to you and your family as a result.

Spencer Kimball
© by Intellectual Reserve, Inc.

Connected With Our Past

"Whether we recognize it or not, we are connected with our past... people who care nothing for the past usually have no thought for the future and are selfish in the way they use the present." Spencer W. Kimball, World Conference of Records, 1980

Family History Insights - 8

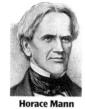
Horace Mann

Do As Our Ancestors

"It would be more honorable to our distinguished ancestors to praise them in words less, but in deeds to imitate them more." Horace Mann (1796-1859), Education reformer, politician

Mark Twain

Good in Every Heart

"God has put something noble and good into every heart His hand created." Mark Twain (Samuel Clemens) (1835-1910), Author and humorist

Marvin J. Ashton

Nobody is a Nobody

"In God's eyes, nobody is a nobody. We should never lose sight of what we may become and who we are." Marvin J. Ashton (1915-1994)

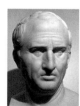
Melvin J. Ballard

You Will Find It

"The spirit and influence of your dead will guide those who are interested in finding those records. If there is anywhere on the earth anything concerning them, you will find it." Melvin J. Ballard (1873-1939)

Marcus Cicero

Knowing Our Ancestors

"To be ignorant of what occurred before you were born is to remain always a child. For what is the worth of human life, unless it is woven into the life of our ancestors by the records of history?" Marcus Cicero (106-43 BC), Roman philosopher, stateman

Backwards Progress

Only a genealogist regards a step backwards as progress. Unknown

Ralph Waldo Emerson

The Best Day

"Write it on your heart that every day is the best day in the year." Ralph Waldo Emerson (1803-1882), Philosopher and poet

Richard G. Scott
© by Intellectual Reserve, Inc.

You Will Find a Way

"I don't need to tell you the details of where to go and who to see. When you determine you are going to succeed, you will find a way. You will discover those who can help you. I promise you the Lord will bless you in your efforts...and He will guide your... efforts to [find] your ancestors." Richard G. Scott (1928-)

What Does "Third Cousin Once Removed" Mean?

Most of the time family relationships are simple. We know our father and mother, our brothers and sisters, aunts, uncles, grandparents, etc. In our society, *cousinhood* is our way of expressing how closely two people are related to each other. We do this by counting generations back to our common ancestor, and subtracting one. For example, two people who share the same grandparents count two generations to their common ancestors. Two minus one equals one, so they are "first" cousins. If their closest common ancestors were their great great grandparents, they would be "third" cousins (four generations, minus one, equals three). We say *removed* when the number of generations is unequal. If you count three generations to a common ancestor (your great grandfather), and your cousin counts four generations to that same ancestor (her great great grandfather), your *cousinhood* is expressed first in terms of the closest relationship (second cousins), with an amendment showing the difference of one generation (once removed). Determining relationships can sound complex, but if you remember that you're simply counting generations, it's easier.

Cassiodorus

Invited to Great Things

"He is invited to great things who receives small things greatly." Cassiodorus (c. 485 - c. 585), Roman statesman, writer

Sharing Your Family History

There are more really good, easy and fun ways to share your family history today than ever before.

Easy Ways to Share Your Family History

- Submit your info to large family tree databases

- Create your own family web site (either hosted by your Internet Service Provider or by a social networking site)

- Create your own family blog

- Create your own online family photo album

- Email information and documents or send simple GedCom's to other family members *(see Chapter 2 for information about how to create and send a GedCom file).*

Once you have dug up your family history records and organized them into a computer database file, you may want to share your information and stories with others. It's important to share them for many different reasons.

It's more meaningful to you personally when you share with your dear relatives, plus sharing helps preserve your history for future generations. Sharing your family tree on the Internet is a great way to connect with your extended family and collaborate on your shared family history, and it helps them get involved. It allows other relatives to view your information and add their own, thus making it more complete. It's also a great way to exchange family photos, recipes and stories. By sharing your information you can help others in their research and reduce the duplication of effort.

Publishing Your Family Tree on the Web

The Best Places to Put Your Family History Online

You can easily publish your compiled family tree online simply by uploading a GedCom to an existing family tree database. Some are free and some require a membership fee. Your GedCom can contain your entire family history or just one or more family lines. It can also exclude personal information about living people. There are several websites that allow you to deposit your information, index your family names, view the data, and download a GedCom to interested parties. *See Chapters 1 and 2 for more details on these websites.*

Free Existing Family Trees *FREE*

*See pages 43-45 for more
information on online family trees.*

Ancestry World Tree (and RootsWeb WorldConnect) -
www.ancestry.com/trees/awt 468 million, last updated
Oct 1997. Need to register (free) to search.

FamilySearch Pedigree Resource File www.FamilySearch.org
About 225 million family tree names; updated regularly.
Search the index online but the details are currently on CDs
available for free at Family History Centers.

FamilySearch Ancestral File - www.familysearch.org
About 37 million, last updated 2000.

Global Tree - http://www.gencircles.com/globaltree
Over 90 million names.

GeneaNet.org - www.Geneanet.org
Over 500 million names; Content: UK, Germany, France,
Holland Spain, and Italy. Free, but you pay for advanced
functions and no commericals.

Subscription Family Trees $

OneGreatFamily.com - www.OneGreatFamily.com
Contains over 200 million submitted pedigree-linked names in
their family tree database.

MyTrees.com - www.MyTrees.com
A pedigree-linked database with over 370 million names

GenServ.com - www.Genserv.com A collection of GEDCOM
data files; 23+ million names, free trial if you submit your info.
$12/year.

Ancestry OneWorldTree - www.ancestry.com >
Search > Search All Records > Family Trees
192 million, last updated Apr 2004. You can search for free, but
must become a member to view details.

Ancestry Millennium File - www.ancestry.com > *Search >
Search All Records > Family Trees*
880k, last updated Apr 2005. These lineages extend back to
nobility and renowned historical figures. You can search for free,
but must become a member to view details..

Ancestry Private Member Trees - www.ancestry.com > *Search
> Search All Records > Family Trees*
162 million, updated regularly. Can only be viewed by Ancestry
members to whom the owners have granted permission to see
their tree.

Ancestry Public Member Trees - www.ancestry.com >
Search > Public Member Trees
586 million, updated regularly. Can be viewed by all Ancestry
members.

How to Submit Your Family Tree Online

First, save your genealogy as a GedCom file.
See the instructions provided with your family
history software for more information on how
to do this, but most programs are simple. For
example, click on *file > export and then* indicate
where you want to export to, i.e. which folder
to save your GedCom file. When you are
ready to submit the file, go to the internet site
you want to submit your family tree to, after
logging-in (or registering) select the *Share Your
Information* or *Submit your Family Tree* button.
Then select the GedCom file you wish to
submit (or upload). It's that easy!

More Family Trees Online

Geni.com - www.geni.com

FamilyLink.com - www.familylink.com

GenealogyWise.com - www.genealogy-wise.com

MyFamily.com - www.myfamily.com

MyHeritage.com -
www.myheritage.com

GeneTree.com - www.genetree.com

Genes Reunited.com - www.genesre-united.com

Amiglia.com - www.amiglia.com

Our Story.com - www.ourstory.com

WeRelate.org - www.werelate.org

KinCafe.com - www.kincafe.com

Famiva.com - www.famiva.com

Creating Your Own Family Web Site

Social Networking Web Sites

Social
networking
refers to
web sites
and services
that allow
you to

connect with friends, family, and colleagues online, as well as meet people with similar interests or hobbies. At these web sites you can connect with your family, swap stories and recipes, share family photos, and build collaborative family trees. You and your extended family can collaborate and share information on your shared family tree.

Some of the sites use advanced technologies like wikis (a type of website that allows the visitors to add, remove, and sometimes edit the available content), RSS (subscribed to timely updates or web feeds from favored websites), mapping, and online family tree building to help you connect with your family and ancestors. All of these family history social networking sites have great appeal, wonderful capabilities, and are private and secure. Here are the most popular social networking sites to explore. *(See Chapter 2 for more information on each of these networking sites.)*

How to Create Your Own Family Web Pages

1. Use a Family History Computer Program to convert your family information
to web pages. Essentially all family history software programs today will provide for publishing your information on the Web (i.e. turn your database into HTML). When you create web pages, the program usually saves them on your hard disk in a folder specified by you. *(See Chapter 5 for more information.)*

Using Word Processors - You can also use a word processor like Corel WordPerfect or Microsoft Word to design the page layouts. Just do a "save as" an HTML (HyperText Markup Language used by web pages). You can include pictures, histories, tables, and decorate the pages with interesting clip-art if you want.

Using PDFs in Your Website - You can create beautiful pages in your website by using PDF (Portable Document File) documents using the free Adobe Acrobat Reader program at www.adobe.com. To create a PDF document from a family history program or a word processor, simply select the PDF button as your printer (or *Publish* to PDF under the file menu).

Hosting Your Own Family Site

Creating Web publishing for hosting your own family web site is simple, inexpensive, and widely available. Many family history software programs will create an attractive, well-indexed home page displaying your family tree. All you need to do is get an Internet Service Provider (ISP) to post it for you. In addition to your family tree, you can also share photos, post news, chat online, publish a family calendar, create a mailing address, preserve family history memories, email, etc. for your extended family to share and download. You can decide to allow people to update information on the website or just access it. Most sites provide this service for usually a modest subscription fee. Usually you need to let people know about the website and give them a password to access the information. These popular websites include:

http://tribalpages.com
www.KindredKonnections.com
www.Genealogy.com
www.familylobby.com
www.thefamilypost.com
http://familyinhistory.com
http://www.myevent.com
www.famster.com
http://getmyfamilysite.com

A free shareware program that creates great PDF files is called PDF995 at www.pdf995.com.

Creating Hyperlinks - You can help viewers navigate from one place to another on your website by creating hyperlinks in your document that point to other destinations.

For example, each name in an index or history can hyperlink to a family group sheet with that family name. Or you can embed website hyperlinks to other websites.

2. Select a Place to Store Your Web Pages on the Internet (a host or Internet Service Provider (ISP)). You can publish your family history in many places. Many ISPs allot some disk space on their computers for their users. Dozens of companies offer free web space up to about ten megabytes (10MB) as long as you allow them to display an ad on the visitor's screen. This may be sufficient for smaller sites, but you will not have much opportunity for growth.

Good Free Hosts Are Hard to Find

The following free web hosts have been around long enough to establish longevity, a track record of reasonable customer support, accessability to beginners, and a basic level of free hosting offerings. Some excel more in one area than another, and they are not equally adept in all areas. Bear in mind that none of the free hosts offer the same level of service and support provided by many budget hosts.

www.freeservers.com

Solid free web hosting. (Ad-free plans as low as $3.95/month.)

www.webhero.com

No monthly fee banner-less hosting is available with paid domain registration.

www.rootsweb.com

Free website space for genealogy users. No commercial use, personal photo albums, games, video or music

files, or adult-oriented material.

Great Low-cost Hosting Alternatives

You may decide to choose a paid web hosting service. Take a look at these top 4 low-cost hosts. They have solid reputations for good service at affordable prices.

www.myfamily.com

In a secure, password-protected environment, you can create online family photo albums, share family news, maintain a calendar of family events, and more. There's also a toll-free phone number to record your family stories and memories. The *basic site is free* which includes uploading 100 MB per member per month (with unlimited storage space) and complete backup protection. You can upgrade for extra features such as: Ad-free, professionally-designed and customizable themes, your custom domain, and 1 GB per member of monthly uploads (10x more than basic) for only $29.95 per year total.

www.ipowerweb.com

Integrated web hosting starting at $3.98/ month with no set up fee. They pride themselves on excellent customer support and offer a 30-day money back guarantee. Your special hosting needs are accommodated through bonus packages of your choice, at no extra cost to you.

www.globat.com

Their basic package is pretty amazing. Starting at $4.44 a month (with no setup fees) you get unlimited web space, unlimited email accounts, free domain registration, and NO pesky ad banners. It's hard to find a more competitively priced paid hosting plan.

www.netfirms.com $

Basically a solid hosting service, you can pick up 300 GB of webspace, and 5 free domain names for $9.95 per month.

3. After You Create Your Web Pages, you must upload or transfer all files, folders, and subfolder files to your chosen Internet site. They will probably suggest a *Website Upload Program* or they may already have one built into their website. In any case, they will provide instructions on how to set up the parameters and procedures that provide access to your website. The following Website Upload Programs are FREE. Once the transfer (upload) is complete your website is ready to use, but you should access it and determine that everything is working properly.

www.freedownloadscenter.com ***FREE***
www.nchsoftware.com
http://search.download3000.com/
web-site-upload-tool

Planting Your Family Tree $ **Online: How to Create Your Own Family History Web Site -** www.amazon.com $19.95

This book is written by Cyndi Howells, owner and webmaster of Cyndi's List, and it's loaded with

You may want to consider NOT using a free web host for several reasons. Read this interesting article.

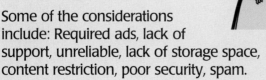

http://web-hosting-services.top choicereviews.com/why-not-free-web-hosting.htm

Some of the considerations include: Required ads, lack of support, unreliable, lack of storage space, content restriction, poor security, spam.

When sharing or submitting your family history records on the internet, *never include information on living people without their permission.* Please respect the privacy of individuals who may be living.

Privacy and Security

Some people may get upset at finding their names published online without their permission. Make sure to get permission from any living relatives to print their information. You may want to publish data only on deceased people, or publish only enough data to encourage people to write you. Do not share information that may be used to embarrass or harm people who may still be living (such as home addresses and telephone numbers, social security numbers, and mothers' maiden names).

For instance, in the PAF software program, you can mark the *Hide Details for the Living* option. When you mark this option, the program checks each individual that you select. If he or she may still be alive, it includes only a limited amount of information. If you also mark the *Include GEDCOM file* option, the GEDCOM file will contain only deceased individuals. When you need to update your web pages, just create a new set of pages and send them to your ISP, with instructions to replace your existing information with the new information.

Most host sites already have a security system. Usually, as part of the registration process you must select a password and a username. Only those with a valid username and password have access to your site. Initially, the family site administrator (creator) will invite new members and assign a temporary username and password. As family members register, they may change their passwords to ensure complete security and privacy. It is then the responsibility of site members to help keep the site secure by offering password access only to appropriate relatives and friends – those they want to have access to the site.

URLs to Web sites that will give you everything you need to create a beautiful family tree online. It's designed to take you step-by-step through the process of creating a genealogy Web site.

For instance, in the PAF software program, you can mark the Hide Details for the Living option. When you mark this option, the program checks each individual that you select. If he or she may still be alive, it includes only a limited amount of information. If you also mark the Include GEDCOM file option, the GEDCOM file will contain only deceased individuals. When you need to update your web pages, just create a new set of pages and send them to your ISP, with instructions to replace your existing information with the new information.

Most host sites already have a security system. Usually, as part of the registration process you must select a password and a username. Only those with a valid username and password have access to your site. Initially, the family site administrator (creator) will invite new members and assign a temporary username and password. As family members register, they may change their passwords to ensure complete security and privacy. It is then the responsibility of site members to help keep the site secure by offering password access only to appropriate relatives and friends – those they want to have access to the site.

Standards For Sharing Information With Others - www.ngsgenealogy.org/cs/ standards_for_sharing_information (FREE)

Offered by The National Genealogical Society.

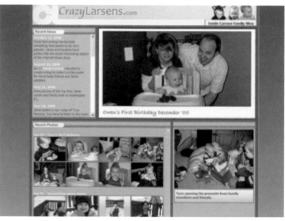

Sample Family Blog

Creating Your Own Family Blog

A blog (or web log) is a website consisting of entries appearing in reverse chronological order with the most recent entry appearing first. Blogs typically include comments, news, photos, and web links. You may want to consider creating your own family blog because it's a great way to connect with your extended family and others who may share your interests. Many people start a blog simply for fun. Blogs are easy to create and update, and rich, useful content will encourage your family to keep in touch. And you don't have to possess any special technical knowledge, or plan for months or be constrained by any deadlines – publish as much as you want, any time you want. *(See the Introduction for a list of family history blogs from noted experts and companies.)*

Blogs are very popular today as there are over 100 million blogs on the Web and growing everyday. Anyone can start a blog thanks to the simple tools readily available online. To start a blog, you have to select a blog "host" and blogging software so you can write and upload your blog to the Internet. Here are some popular blogger software and blog hosting sites to help you.

To create your own blog, you need to have both blogger software and a blog host.

Popular Blogger Software

Blogger.com - www.blogger.com *FREE*

Many novice bloggers choose to start their first blogs here because it's free and very easy to use.

WordPress.com - http://wordpress.com *FREE*

A place where you can start a blog in seconds without any technical knowledge. It provides free blogging software with a limited amount of customization with templates you can download for your blog. It is very easy to learn and provides some good features.

Wordpress.org - www.wordpress.org *FREE*

Offers free blogging software, but users have to pay to host their blogs through a third-party website host such as www.HostGator.com or www.1and1.com. For bloggers with some technical skills who need advanced customization, Wordpress.org is a great choice. The software, itself, is the same as Wordpress.com, but the customization options make it very popular among power bloggers.

TypePad.com - www.typepad.com *FREE*

Provides great features and a high level of customization without the technical knowledge of some other customizable blogging software options. Basic option $49.50/year.

Popular Blog Hosts

BlueHost - www.bluehost.com *$*

A popular blog host that consistently gets positive reviews for its up-time and support services. It offers comprehensive shared hosting packages that are suitable for most bloggers at an affordable price.

Host Gator.com - www.hostgator.com *$*

Offers blog hosting packages that suit beginner bloggers' needs as well as the needs of the most popular blogs and websites. Host Gator has a reputation for reliability and excellent support.

GoDaddy.com - www.godaddy.com *$*

A great reputation of providing blog hosting services suitable for any size blog or website. Negative reviews are typically related to domain name registration searches that yield results showing a domain name is available, but when the potential buyer returns even one day later to purchase that domain name, it displays as no longer available. Aside from that complaint, reviews are typically positive.

1and1.com - www.1and1.com *$*

A popular blog host with competitive pricing. 1&1 is both the world's biggest web host, and the fastest growing. Their global community is 7.83 million customer contracts strong.

Continued on the next page...

Continued from the previous page...

HostMonster.com -
www.hostmonster.com

A reliable blog host with competitive features and affordable pricing; rated the top choice of Top Choice Reviews at http://web-hosting-services.topchoicereviews.com.

Creating Your Own Online Photo Album

Here's some popular websites dedicated to offering image hosting services, as well as web hosting for a photo gallery of your family. Some photo hosting sites sell you prints of your photos and gifts with your photos on them. Others let you create pages to go with your photos. But they are great for creating and hosting your photo albums and videos so friends and family can share them online. It's a great way to backup your precious images off-site from your computer hard drive.

Picasa Web Albums -
http://picasa.google.com > Share **FREE**

Fast and easy photo sharing from Google; free software for organizing, editing and printing your photos.

You can upload entire albums of high quality photos, and combine your photos, videos, and music into a movie. Each account gets 1GB of free storage - that's enough to post and share around 4,000 standard resolution photos. And you and your friends can download your photos at the same high quality to print and enjoy.

DotPhoto.com - www.dotphoto.com **FREE**

A popular photo hosting site that allows you to handle all your imaging in one place for free: store, edit, share, organize, and print your photos, create gifts, tell a story, build a photo web site, sell photos, host pictures, print books, store videos and more. You can upload photos from your camera or your camera phone, and create gifts with your photos on them and have them mailed to you or your friends and family.

MyPhotoAlbum.com - **FREE**
www.myphotoalbum.com

A photo and video sharing service offering extensive features for creating highly-unique, personalized online photo albums and photo keepsakes. Easily add and safely store all your photos and videos. Upload your memories via the web, downloadable software, email, and your camera or cell phone. Unlimited online photo sharing and albums; free video storage and sharing.

Flickr.com - www.flickr.com **FREE** **$**

A popular photo storage and sharing site to store, sort, search, organize and share your photos online. You can also tell stories about them. You can make all or just some photos private or only viewable by friends and family. Basic version is free. ProAccount $24.95/year.

Shutterfly.com - www.shutterfly.com $ FREE

Offers a full range of products and services that make it easy, convenient and fun for you to upload (unlimited storage), edit, enhance, organize, find, share, create, print and preserve your digital photos. You can stay connected to your friends and family, organize your memories in a single location, tell stories, and preserve your memories. They make memory-keeping and gift-giving easy with their person-alized photo books, greeting cards, and various photo gifts suitable for any occasion. FREE

Kodak Gallery.com - www.kodakgallery.com

A free online digital photo developing service providing you with a secure and easy way to view, store and share their photos with friends and family and get prints of your pictures. The site also provides free editing and creative tools and specialty photo products.

PhotoBucket.com - http://photobucket.com FREE

Upload all your photos, videos, and images for free. Make photo slide shows to share pics with friends.

SnapFish.com - www.snapfish.com FREE

Online photo sharing, storage, and editing tools and software are free, and you can create private group rooms for event sharing with friends and family.

SmugMug.com - www.smugmug.com $

A popular, secure, easy-to-use photo hosting site with no spam or ads, and unlimited storage. Free 14-day trial. Standard (unlimited photos) $39.95, Power (+ videos) $59.95.

Organizing Your Family

A family association is an organization formed around a deceased common ancestor to accomplish specific goals. Some of the benefits of organizing your family this way include: Grow closer as a family, develop bonds of love and kindred affection, make family history work easier and faster, and avoid duplication of time and money.

Publishing a Family Newsletter -
www.absolutelyfamily.homestead.com $

A book by Jeanne Rundquist Nelson, *A Guide to Editing and Publishing A Family Newsletter,* is for family-focused people who want to keep their far-flung families in touch. $12.00

Holding a Family Reunion

Preserving Special Memories

A family reunion is one of the most special events in life, but planning it can be a little overwhelming. Whether you want to have a small get-together of your closest relatives or a huge gathering of everyone you can find in your family tree, you need to know where to start and how to keep it organized. Check out these great resources to make your reunion fun and exciting.

Your Family Reunion: How to Plan It, Organize It, and Enjoy It -
http://ahaseminars.com/ $

A complete guidebook to planning a successful reunion by George G. Morgan incorporates how-to advice, samples of helpful forms, and a wealth of great Web sites filled with invaluable reference material to help you succeed. You will learn all

Family Association Goals

Some of the goals to consider for a family association might include:

Determine and prioritize association goals, such as:

- Create a list of all the descendants of the ancestral couple

- Organize a family records center, and preserve irreplaceable family records and heirlooms.

- Guide, encourage and assist in doing systematic family history research for your common ancestors. Set up a research fund to continue research on the family lines and hold family reunions.

- Publish a family history of your ancestors, and a history of descendants which would be kept current throughout all succeeding generations.

- Create an extended family web site or blog.

Decide how to implement goals

Decide on the organizational requirements necessary to meet the goals; choose officers and committee members, and make assignments.

Identify all living descendants and get them involved in some way

Start an address / telephone / email file.

Create a periodic blog, newsletter, or website to establish communication, maintain interest, report family history research results, account for money received and spent, relate human interest stories about ancestors and living descendants, share family photos, promote and publicize family reunions, etc.

Hold family reunions

about compiling the family address book, developing a realistic budget, choosing a great venue, working with hotels, caterers and other vendors, keeping records, and sending invitations to planning activities to get people communicating, ideas for sharing and gathering genealogical information, setting up the site, managing details on-site, and evaluating the event. $24.95

Family Reunion Organizer - FREE $
www.family-reunion.com

A free family reunion planning site with organizing tips, activities, finances, food, places to hold family reunions, links to resources, and lots of ideas to make it successful. They also offer software – *Family Reunion Organizer* – that helps you plan the perfect family reunion or a family or neighborhood event as well. A checklist leads users through the steps involved in family reunion planning, including tracking a budget and expenses, creating a schedule, managing assignments, and even keeping a family address book. The program includes tools to create a family Web page. It also allows users to print most of its forms for planning purposes. Users receive a free newsletter and access to a message board to post improvement suggestions related to the product. Free demo. $29.95

FamilyReunion.com - FREE $
www.familyreunion.com

A website that provides relevant ideas, resources, information, products and services in a safe and friendly online social network environment all designed to help millions of repeat visitors and members make their next gathering of family the best ever.

Basic membership is free. Platinum membership gives you full access to all the services. $15/3 months, $39/year.

EasyFamilyReunion.com - *FREE*
www.easyfamilyreunion.com

A free checklist for putting together a family reunion. Some of the items on the checklist are basic; you need to do them for every reunion. The others are optional but can make the reunion more memorable and enjoyable. Print out the checklist and use it to guide your efforts to bring your family together.

Planning the Perfect Family Reunion - *FREE*
http://genealogy.about.com/od/family_reunions

Kimberly Powell at About.com provides free, really helpful things to consider, such as: Steps to a successful family reunion, choosing a location, fun activities, tips, ideas, etc.

Better Homes Magazine -
www.bhg.com/health-family/reunions *FREE*

The magazines free website provides aids for holding a successful reunion: planning tips, checklists, menu ideas, ice breakers and entertaining activities.

Disney's Family Fun Reunion Center -
http://familyfun.go.com > (search "family reunion") -or- <http://familyfun.go.com/parenting/learn/ activities/specialfeature/famreunion_sf/> *FREE*

Disney's Family Fun Magazine offers great helps with an ultimate, step-by-step family reunion guide, and more.

Family Reunion - www.amazon.com $

A recommended book by Jennifer Crichton. Everything you need to know to plan unforgettable get-togethers. A comprehensive, step-by-step guide to planning and staging a gathering to remember. Topics include record keeping, choosing a site, entertaining kids of all ages, and etiquette, as well as the dynamics and logistics necessary when herding a large group of people. $13.95

Family Reunion Handbook - $
www.amazon.com

This handbook by Tom Ninkovich covers how to organize a reunion including selecting a date, getting the word out, creating a budget, and delegating responsibilities. A Complete Guide for Reunion Planners. $14.99

Reunions Magazine -
www.reunionsmag.com $

The only publication written for all types of reunion planners – family, class, military and others. This is a comprehensive source of tips, ideas, advice and resources to help you plan your reunion. You'll find articles about resources like facilities, suppliers, tools, equipment, games, activities and services to enhance your reunion. Some of the best reunion solutions are in the stories reunion planners share; published 5x per year. $9.99/year

Family Reunion - www.famware.com $

An easy to use system that helps you organize and document your family's history. $79.95

To comment, or communicate with the author: paul@easyfamilyhistory.com

8 Other Rewarding Opportunities

Here's a nice glossary for you.

Family History Glossary

Ahnentafel chart - An ancestor table that lists the name, date, and place of birth, marriage, and death for an individual and specified number of his or her ancestors; an alternative to a pedigree chart. The first individual on the list is number one, the father is number two, the mother is number three, the paternal grandfather is number four, and so forth. Ahnentafel is a German word that means ancestor chart or ancestor table.

Ancestral File - A computer database file located at www.familysearch.org containing names and often other vital information (such as date and place of birth, marriage, or death) of millions of individuals who have lived throughout the world. Names are organized into family groups and pedigrees. To allow you to coordinate research, the file also lists names and addresses of those who contributed to the file.

Ancestral File Number (AFN) - A number used to identify each record in Ancestral File on FamilySearch.

Ancestry chart - A pedigree chart that contains only names and limited information about the people on it.

Archive - A place in which public records or historical documents are preserved and researched. Unlike a Library, archived records cannot be checked out but can be used in the building.

Blog (or web log) - A website consisting of entries appearing in reverse chronological order with the most recent entry appearing first. They typically are free-style, interactive web sites containing news, commentary, photos, web links, etc.

Bookmark - A saved link to a Web site that has been added to a list of saved links so that you can simply click on it rather than having to retype the address when visiting the site again.

Browser - An Internet tool for viewing the World Wide Web. Some of the Web browsers currently available for personal computers include Internet Explorer, Opera, Mozilla Firefox, Safari, Google Chrome, and AOL Explorer.

Bulletin Board - Refers to online message systems to read and post messages.

Call number - The number used to identify a book, microfilm, microfiche, or other source in a library or archive. Library materials are stored and retrieved by call number.

Cascading family group record - An option that allows you to print family group records for a specified number of generations in a family. If you printed a cascading pedigree you could select the same starting person and number of generations to print a family group record for each couple in the pedigree charts.

Cascading pedigree - An option that allows you to print pedigree charts for a specified number of generations. Each page is numbered, which allows you to keep the pages in order.

Census - Official enumeration, listing or counting of citizens.

CD-ROM (Compact Disk Read Only Memory) - A computer disk that can store large amounts of information and is generally used on computers with CD-ROM drives.

Chat Room - A location on an online service that allows users to communicate with each other about an agreed-upon topic in "real time" (or "live"), as opposed to delayed time as with email.

Chat - When people type live messages to each other using a network.

Collateral line - A family that is not in your direct ancestral line but in the same genealogical line.

Compiled Record - A record (usually in book form) consisting of information that has been gathered from original records, other compiled records and verbal testimony.

Database - Information for computer search, storage, and retrieval.

Date calculator - A feature in family history programs that allows you to determine the days, months, and years elapsed between two dates or to determine a date based on the amount of time elapsed before or after a date. For example, this is useful to approximate a birth date for a person who appears in a census.

Default - A computer term for "normal" settings of a program.

Descendency chart - A report that lists an individual and his or her children and their spouses and children.

Domain name - The Internet's way to find unique addresses on the World Wide Web.

Download - The process of retrieving information from another computer to yours.

E-mail - Short for electronic mail messages that are sent from one person to another.

End of line - The last known person in a line of ancestry. An end-of-line person has no parents listed in the database file.

Export - A feature in many family history programs that allows you to save or send information to use in another genealogical program. Information is usually saved in GEDCOM format.

Facebook.com - Connect and share with the people in your life. A free social networking website where you can add friends and send them messages. Anyone can join.

Family group record - A printed form that lists a family—parents and children—and gives information about dates and places of birth, marriage, and death. This is also called a family group sheet.

Family History Center (FHC) - Local branches of the Family History Library in Salt Lake City, Utah. There are currently more than 4,500 around the world.

Family History Computer Software Program - A computer family history program for home use. Users enter family history information electronically, thus allowing information to be printed as a pedigree chart, family group record, descendency chart, or many other formats. Information can also be given to others as a GEDCOM file for instant transfer of family history data.

Family History Library - The main family history library in Salt Lake City, Utah used by genealogical researchers worldwide. It has the world's largest collection of genealogical holdings and has both printed sources and microfilmed records.

FamilySearch - A web site and a term that refers to computer products that help people learn about their ancestors.

Freenet - A community network that provides free online access, usually to local residents, and often includes its own forums and news.

Forum - A set of messages on a subject, usually with a corresponding set of files.

FTP (File Transfer Protocol) - Enables an Internet user to transfer files electronically between computers.

GEDCOM - The acronym for "GEnealogical Data COMmunications." GEDCOM is a computer data format for storing genealogical information so that many computer programs can use it. It is the standard file format worldwide for exchanging family information between genealogical databases. If you choose, your family history software program can save your family information as a GEDCOM file.

Genealogy - The study of how individuals and their families are descended from their ancestors. It often includes learning about family histories and traditions.

Given name - A person's first name(s).

Gregorian calendar - The calendar commonly used in Western and Westernized countries. It corrected the Julian calendar, which, because of miscalculated leap years, fell behind the solar year by several days.

Hardware - A term for the nuts, bolts, and wires of computer equipment and the actual computer and related machines.

Home page - A web page that serves as the table of contents or title page of a web site.

Home person - A feature in family history programs that allows you to return to the individual record that is designated to be the home person. The term "home" can also refer to the first person in a file.

HTML - Acronym for HyperText Markup Language, the coding language of the World Wide Web.

Hyperlink Link - Highlighted text that allows you to jump to other information in a file or to another web page or web site.

Hypertext Transfer Protocol - A standard used by World Wide Web servers to provide rules for moving text, images, sound, video, and other multimedia files across the Internet.

ICON - A small picture on a Web page that represents the topic or information category of another Web page. Frequently, the icon is a hypertext link to that page.

IGI (The International Genealogical Index) - A database of names located at www.FamilySearch.org.

IM (Instant Message) - A type of chat program that allows users to send and receive text messages instantly and requires users to register with a server. Users build "buddy lists" of others using the same program and are notified when people on their list are available for messages.

Import - A feature on the menu in family history programs that allows you to add information that is stored in a GEDCOM file into your database.

Immigrant - One moving into a country from another.

Internet - A system of computers joined together by high-speed data lines. It is a repository for vast amounts of data, including family history data, that is accessed by computer through an Internet Service Provider and Web Browser. It includes data in various formats (or protocols) such as HTML, e-mail (SMTP), File Transfer Protocol (FTP), and Telnet.

ISP (Internet Service Provider) - A company that has a continuous, fast and reliable connection to the Internet and sells subscriptions to use that connection.

Julian calendar - A calendar introduced in Rome in 46 B.C. This calendar was the basis for the Gregorian calendar, which is in common use today. The Julian calendar specified that the year began on 25 March (Lady's Day) and had 365 days. Each fourth year had a leap day, so it had 366 days. The year was divided into months. Each month had 30 or 31 days, except February, which had 28 days in normal years and 29 days in leap years. This calendar was used for several centuries (until the mid 1500s) but was eventually replaced by the Gregorian calendar because leap years had been miscalculated.

LDS - An abbreviation for The Church of Jesus Christ of Latter-day Saints, also known as the Mormons.

Legacy Contributor - A person who originally submitted information to Ancestral File or the Pedigree Resource File in FamilySearch.

Link - To define family relationships between individual records or to attach a source or multimedia file to an individual or marriage record.

Living - A person who is still alive. Some family history programs define a living person as someone who was born within the last 110 years whose individual record contains no death or burial information.

Lossless Compression - A digital file where the original and the decompressed data are identical.

Lossy Compression - Digital file formats that suffer from *generation loss*: repeatedly compressing and decompressing the file causes it to progressively lose quality. It produces a much smaller compressed file which in some cases still meets the requirements of the application. For example, a JPG image file, and MP3 or WMA (music) audio files.

Maiden name - A female's surname at birth.

Match/Merge - A feature on the Tools menu in some family history programs that allows you to find duplicate records in a file and combine them into one record.

Maternal Line - The line of descent on a mother's side.

Modem - A device that allows computers to communicate with each other over telephone lines or other delivery systems by changing digital signals to telephone signals for transmission and then back to digital signals. Modems come in different speeds: the higher the speed, the faster the data is transmitted.

Modified register - A report that lists an individual and his or her descendants in a narrative form. The first paragraph identifies the individual and explains birth and other event information in complete sentences. The next paragraph describes the person's first spouse. Children and spouses are listed next. If the person had more than one spouse, those spouses and any children appear after that.

Mouse - A small device attached to the computer by a cord which lets you give commands to the computer. The mouse controls an arrow on the computer screen and allows you to point and click to make selections.

MRIN - An abbreviation that stands for "Marriage Record Identification Number." PAF software assigns each marriage record a unique MRIN and uses it to distinguish one marriage record from another.

Multimedia - A term used to refer to electronic pictures, sound clips, and video clips for use in your family history program or website. To create video and sound clips, you must already have the required computer hardware and software. Multimedia features may include: *Video Clips* - portions of digitized video images that can be displayed through various programs via the Internet. *Sound Clips* - portions of digitized sound clips that can be heard through various programs via the Internet. *Digital Images* - picture (images) that can be displayed on computers or via the Internet. These images can be displayed using various image formats, such as JPEG, GIFF, BITMAP, etc.

Multiple parent indicator - A symbol used on reports that indicate that a person is linked to more than one set of parents.

Navigation bar - Words or images on website pages with links to other sections or pages of the same website

Netiquette - Rules or manners for interacting courteously with others online (such as not typing a message in all capital letters, which is equivalent to shouting).

NGS - National Genealogical Society.

Notes - Information about an individual, marriage, or set of parents that does not fit in the individual record, the marriage record, or sources. Notes can contain additional information, research notes, or other narrative information. Also a feature on the Edit menu that allows you to add or edit the notes

associated with the selected individual or marriage.

Offline - Not being connected to an Internet host or service provider.

Online - Refers to computer connection to the Internet. Made possible through the use of an internet service provider and web browser.

Original Record - A record created at or close to the time of an event by an eyewitness to the event. (e.g., a birth record by the doctor who delivered the baby.)

PAF (Personal Ancestral File) - A free family history program available from www.familysearch.org.

Parent Link - The type of relationship selected for an individual and his or her parents. The options are biological, adopted, guardian, sealing, challenged, and disproved. If a person is linked to only one set of parents, the relationship is assumed to be biological unless you change it. On the Family screen, the parent link appears only if it is something other than biological.

Password - A set of characters that you can use to prevent another individual from inadvertently changing information.

Paternal Line - The line of descent on a father's side.

PDF (Portable Document Format) - A file format that allows a document to be saved in a certain way, no matter what kind of computer is used to display it. The machine must have Adobe's Acrobat Reader (a free program available at www.adobe.com) to display the file.

Pedigree - An ancestral line or line of descent.

Pedigree chart - A chart that shows an individual's direct ancestors—parents, grandparents, great-grandparents, and so forth. This is the traditional way to display a genealogy or 'family tree'. A pedigree chart may contain birth, marriage, and death information.

Pedigree Resource File (PRF) - A computer file containing names and often other vital information (such as date and place of birth, marriage, or death) of individuals who have lived throughout the world. Names are organized into family groups and pedigrees. The information will appear as it was originally submitted and will not be merged with information submitted by others. Available at www.familysearch.org.

Person Identifier (PID) - A number that identifies people in FamilySearch. An individual's person identifier does not change over the life and death of the individual.

Query - An online request for family history information which usually includes a name, date, location and your contact information.

RAM (Random Access Memory) - The working memory of a computer used for storing data temporarily while working on it, or running application programs, etc.

Relationship calculator - A feature on menu in family history programs that allows you to determine how two individuals are related.

Repository - The place where records are stored, such as an archive or library.

Restore - A feature on the menu of some family history programs that allows you to use a backup copy to return a certain file to its state when the backup copy was made.

RIN - An abbreviation that stands for "Record Identification Number" in the PAF program. PAF assigns a unique RIN to each individual record. This number is used to distinguish that individual record from others in a .paf file.

RSS (Really Simple Syndication) - A Web feed format used to publish frequently updated works—such as blog entries, news headlines, audio, and video—in a standardized format. They benefit readers who want to subscribe to timely updates from favored websites or to aggregate feeds from many sites into one place.

Search Engine - A tool designed to search for information on the World Wide Web. The search results are usually presented in a list and are commonly called *hits*. The information may consist of web pages, images, information and other types of files. Some search engines also mine data available in newsbooks, databases, or open directories. Unlike Web directories, which are maintained by human editors, search engines operate algorithmically or are a mixture of algorithmic and human input. Some of the major search engines are Google, Yahoo, Dogpile, Live, Ask, etc. (Note that Yahoo is a directory, not a search engine.) A web directory does not display lists of web pages based on keywords; instead, it lists web sites by category and subcategory.

Server - A computer that allows other computers to log on and use its resources.

Shareware - The try-before-you-buy concept in computer software where the author expects to receive compensation after a trial period. For example, *Brother's Keeper* is shareware.

Slide Show - A presentation that displays all of the multimedia that is attached to an individual. It displays each item for a specific amount of time, in a sequential fashion.

Software - A computer program or set of instructions. System software operates on the machine itself and is invisible to you. Application software allows you to carry out certain activities, such as word processing, family history, spreadsheets, etc.

Soundex - A type of index that groups surnames that sound similar but are spelled differently. Each surname is assigned a code that consists of the first letter of the name. The next three consonants are assigned a number. Vowels are ignored. Soundex has been used to index the 1880, 1900, 1910, and 1920 United States censuses and some other types of records, such as naturalization records and passenger lists.

Sources & Notes - This is a feature in a family history program that displays: The sources used to obtain genealogical data for a specific individual and the notes of those who entered the information to give additional helpful information. This will increase your ability to collaborate and verify your genealogical information with others doing work on your same line.

Surname - A person's last name or family name.

Sync / Synchronize - Ensuring that data is the same in two or more databases or locations. To sync two computers means to copy the data from one computer to the other.

Tag - A word or phrase used to classify the information in a note. Tags should be typed in all uppercase letters at the beginning of the note and be followed by a colon.

Tagged notes - A type of note that uses a keyword to identify the type of information contained in a note in PAF. The keyword is typed in all uppercase letters at the beginning of a paragraph and followed by a colon. For example, in the following note, "NAME:" is the tag: "NAME: This person changed her name."

Twitter - A social networking and micro-blogging service for friends, family, and co-workers to stay connected through the exchange of quick, frequent answers (known as tweets) to one simple question: What are you doing? Answers must be under 140 characters in length and can be sent via mobile texting, instant message, or the web. Located at www.twitter.com.

Upload - The process of sending a file or message from your computer to another.

URL (Uniform Resource Locator) - The World Wide Web address of a site on the Internet. For example, the URL for the White House is http://www.whitehouse.gov.

Usenet Newsgroups - A system of thousands of special interest groups to which readers can send or "post" messages; these messages are then distributed to other computers on the network. Usenet registers newsgroups, which are available through Internet Service Providers.

Virus - A program that installs itself secretly on your computer by attaching itself to another program or e-mail. It duplicates itself when the e-mail is opened and is usually intended to erase important files in your system

Vital Records - The official records of birth, death, marriage, and other events of a persons life.

Web browser - A software program that lets you find, see, and hear material on the World Wide Web, including text, graphics, sound, and video. Popular browsers are Explorer, Netscape, and AltaVista. Most online services have their own browsers.

Web page - A multimedia document that is created and viewable on the internet with the use of a world wide web browser.

Web site - Refers to one or more World Wide Web pages on the internet.

Worm - A computer program that makes copies of itself and spreads through connected systems, using up resources or causing other damage.

www (World Wide Web) - The portion of the Internet that is written in HTML. A hypertext-based system that allows you to browse through a variety of linked Internet resources organized by colorful, graphics-oriented home pages.

Family History Glossary

Index

DNA GENEALOGY

Discover your deep ancestral roots, find out where your ancestors came from, and discover their ethnic background using genetic genealogy.

Who Are Your Ancestors?

About Genetic or DNA Genealogy

How did you end up where you are today? Genetic genealogy is the newest and an exciting addition to genealogy research, and allows you to trace the path of your ancestors and find out who they were, where they lived and how they migrated throughout the world.

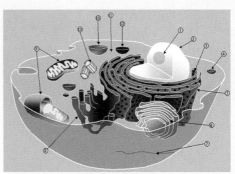

A Human Cell

What is DNA?

All living things, including humans, are made up of many different kind of cells.

Most of the cells in your body have a nucleus. The nucleus of all of your cells contains *chromosomes* which are responsible for storing your hereditary information. Chromosomes are made up of DNA (deoxyribonucleic acid). DNA is like a blueprint because it holds the informational code for all of the genetic information for you, and is unique to you. With the exception of the egg and sperm cell, all of the cells in your body contain 23 pairs of chromosomes, 46 in total.

DNA research is based on the 46 chromosomes that every human being has (with few exceptions). Each of the 23 pairs consists of one chromosome inherited from your mother and one from your father. In females, the 23rd chromosome pair consists of two X-chromosomes. Males, however, have an X-chromosome and a Y-chromosome. It is the Y-chromosome that determines male gender. The Y-chromosome can be traced from father-to-son-to-son and so on. Y-chromosome is only carried by men and is only inherited from your fathers. Men who share a common paternal ancestor will have virtually the same Y-DNA, even if that male ancestor lived my generations ago.

The male Y-chromosome is one of the most useful chromosomes in genealogical studies, because it has the unique property of being passed virtually unchanged from generation to generation. This means that a man and all his sons will have the same (or similar) Y-chromosome, and that males with a common paternal ancestor have similar Y-DNA. Unrelated males from a different family line will have a different Y-Chromosome code.

The mother has a Mitrochrondial DNA (mtDNA) which is something of an energy source for the cells. All children of one mother have the same mtDNA as do all children of that mother's daughters. MtDNA is only inherited from your mother. Mothers inherit their DNA from their Mothers, and so on back in time along one's maternal line. mtDNA can't be passed by men. The study of the *Y-chromosome* or the *mtDNA* trail forms the basis of the DNA genealogy. No